Reading Research in Action

Reading Research in Action

A Teacher's Guide for Student Success

by

Peggy McCardle, Ph.D., M.P.H.

Vinita Chhabra, Ph.D.

and

Barbara Kapinus, Ph.D.

·P·A·U·L·H·
BROOKES
PUBLISHING CO. ®

Baltimore • London • Sydney

Paul H. Brookes Publishing Co.
Post Office Box 10624
Baltimore, Maryland 21285-0624

www.brookespublishing.com

Typeset by Spearhead Global, Inc., Bear, Delaware.

Manufactured in the United States of America by
Versa Press, Inc., East Peoria, Illinois.

The individuals described in this book are composites or real people whose situations
have been masked and are based on the authors' experiences. Names and identifying
details have been changed to protect confidentiality.

Library of Congress Cataloging-in-Publication Data

McCardle, Peggy D.
Reading research in action: A teacher's guide for student success / by Peggy McCardle,
Vinita Chhabra, and Barbara Kapinus.
     p.   cm.
Includes index.
ISBN-13: 978-1-55766-964-3
ISBN-10: 1-55766-964-3
     1. Reading—Research. 2. Reading—Direct instruction approach. I. Chhabra, Vinita.
II. Kapinus, Barbara A. III. Title.

LB1050.6.M33 2008
372.41′6–dc22   2008011645

British Library Cataloguing in Publication data are available from the British Library.

2012   2011   2010   2009   2008

10   9   8   7   6   5   4   3   2   1

Contents

About the Authors

Peggy McCardle, Ph.D., M.P.H., holds a Ph.D. in linguistics from The Pennsylvania State University, a master's degree of public health from the Uniformed Services University of the Health Sciences (USUHS), and has been a nationally certified speech-language pathologist. She has held academic positions at South Carolina State College and The University of Mississippi, and she has taught at USUHS and at the University of Maryland. She has held clinical positions at both Womack Army Community Hospital and Walter Reed Army Medical Center. Since 1992, she has worked at the National Institutes of Health in various positions; she currently works as Branch Chief and Research Program Director at the National Institute of Child Health and Human Development, where she has built and managed research programs in various areas of reading, reading disabilities, language development, and bilingualism. Dr. McCardle is the lead editor of the volumes *The Voice of Evidence in Reading Research* (Paul H. Brookes Publishing Co., 2004); *Childhood Bilingualism* (Multilingual Matters, 2006); and *Infant Pathways to Language: Methods, Models, and Research Directions* (Taylor & Francis, in press); and has served as a guest editor of thematic journal issues on reading, bilingualism, and English language learner research.

Vinita Chhabra, Ph.D., holds a Ph.D. in educational psychology from the University of Virginia and has specialized in reading motivation and special education with an emphasis in reading disabilities. She has served as Research Scientist for the Child Development and Behavior Branch at National Institute of Child Health and Human Development (NICHD), where she worked as an NICHD liaison to the National Institute for Literacy and the U.S. Department of Education and assisted the branch with adolescent, bilingual, and family literacy initiatives. She has worked as a research scientist with the National Reading Panel (NRP) from its inception and managed the dissemination activities for the completed NRP report. She has also worked in the public school system and at the Yale Center for the Study of Learning and Attention, conducting educational and cognitive assessments for children being considered for special education programs and for research studies. She was recently an adjunct professor at the

University of Alaska, Fairbanks, where she taught reading and writing courses to Alaska Native teachers. Dr. Chhabra has co-authored articles and chapters on learning disabilities and reading research and is a co-editor of the volume *The Voice of Evidence in Reading Research* (Paul H. Brookes Publishing Co., 2004).

Barbara Kapinus, Ph.D., is currently a senior policy analyst at the National Education Association, where she works on issues related to literacy, curriculum, and standards. She has held positions at the Council of Chief State Schools Officers, the Maryland State Department of Education, and Prince George's County Public Schools. She has been a classroom teacher, a reading teacher, and a researcher. Her research includes studies of comprehension and vocabulary development. She has worked on several state literacy assessments, standards projects, and analyses of assessments and standards alignments. She has been involved in many aspects of the National Assessment of Educational Progress in Reading, including the development of the design, items, scoring guides, and reports. She has also worked on international assessments. In addition to several articles and chapters in books on reading, she has also served on the editorial boards of the three major journals of the International Reading Association. Dr. Kapinus received her Ph.D. in education from the University of Maryland.

Foreword

We are at an important time in the history of reading research in the United States: The research base in reading is sufficiently strong. National consensus reports have been issued in the last decade that have driven policy in reading instruction. We are 10 years from the *Preventing Reading Difficulties in Young Children* report (Snows, Burns, & Griffin, 1998), which emphasized that learning to read is an interaction of explicit instruction in the alphabetic principle, reading for meaning, and opportunities to learn. We are nearly a decade from the National Reading Panel (NRP) report (National Institute of Child Health and Human Development [NICHD], 2000), which played a crucial role in defining policy for the Reading First component of the No Child Left Behind (NCLB) Act of 2001 (PL 107-110). Working in concert with NCLB's emphasis on reducing the majority–minority achievement gap was another influential policy report in 2002 that emphasized a response to intervention (RTI) approach rather than an IQ–achievement discrepancy approach to identifying children for learning disabilities. This report by the President's Commission on Excellence in Special Education (2002) was instrumental in the reauthorization of the Individuals with Disabilities Education Improvement Act (IDEA) of 2004 (PL 108-446). During this same time, the RAND Reading Study Group (Snow, 2002) released its report, which defined *reading comprehension* as the interaction of reader, text, and activity in a sociocultural context. Following these reports was the National Literacy Panel on Language-Minority Children and Youth (August & Shanahan, 2006), which reviewed the limited research base on English language learners (ELLs) and concluded that the instructional strategies endorsed by the NRP were also relevant for ELLs. Finally, the National Early Literacy Panel (NELP, n.d.) found that the strongest predictors in preschool of later performance in word reading, spelling, and comprehension are alphabetic knowledge; phonological awareness; rapid naming of letters/digits, objects, and colors; and phonological short-term memory.

In this book, *Reading Research in Action: A Teacher's Guide for Student Success*, McCardle, Chhabra, and Kapinus celebrate the riches afforded by decades of reading research followed by the current decade of policy reports. They not only translate this research to classroom teachers, but they also provide an update of research conducted since the NRP report was published (NICHD, 2000), which includes areas comprising the language arts—vocabulary, spelling, and writing. These language arts skills, when added to systematic instruction in phonics and tutoring for struggling readers, are found to add value to reading outcomes in the Stuebing, Barth, Cirino, Francis, and Fletcher (2008) reanalysis of the reassessment of the NRP meta-analysis on phonics instruction by Camilli, Vargas, and Yurecko (2003) and Camilli, Wolfe, and Smith (2006).

Vocabulary instruction is essential if students are to understand the meaning of the words they read. Spelling instruction is necessary to grasp the depth of English orthography, so students can become fluent decoders (Foorman & Ciancio, 2005) and writers (Moats, Foorman, & Taylor, 2006). Another critical skill to writing fluency is handwriting (Berninger, 2007). The connection between writing and reading has been assumed but not tested until recently. The unidimensionality of literacy was tested and found to be valid in a sample of students in Grades 1–4 in high-poverty schools (Mehta, Foorman, Branum-Martin, & Taylor, 2005). Interestingly, language and literacy skills were found to be unidimensional at the classroom level but separable at the student level. Moreover, the weighting of these skills in the literacy construct varied over the grades with the influence of phonological awareness fading by second grade and the effect of writing becoming increasingly strong by the middle of second grade. In a secondary analysis (Mehta et al., 2005), time spent in writing instruction related significantly to literacy outcomes in Grades 2–4. In a separate study analyzing writing instruction in third and fourth grades with this same sample, Moats et al. (2006) found that *quality* of instruction, in addition to *quantity* of instruction, predicted writing outcomes.

The role of teaching quality to reading outcomes is the white elephant in the room. Whereas there is no definitive agreement on the effects of qualifications and teaching techniques to gains in achievement, there is substantial research suggesting that teachers with more content knowledge and more experience tend to affect gains in achievement (Desimone, Smith, & Frisvold, 2007; Foorman & Moats, 2004). Increase in time spent teaching reading does not by itself lead to gains in reading achievement, as the interim report of Reading First shows (National Center for Education Evaluation and Regional Assistance, 2008). Yet, the differentiated patterns of instructional activities based on student skill do relate to gains in achievement (Foorman et al., 2006), and such differentiation can be taught (Connor, Morrison, Fishman, Schatschneider, & Underwood, 2007). Both writing and reading comprehension are complex cognitive and linguistic activities that challenge teachers to go beyond foundational and literal levels of understanding to tap inferential and discourse-level processing (Taylor, Pearson, & Rodriguez, 2003).

In this book, McCardle, Chhabra, and Kapinus provide examples of quality teaching that stem from the research reviewed. They make a distinction between research-based programs and empirically based programs. *Research-based programs* are those that are consistent with research findings in general; *empirically based programs* are those that have been proven effective in particular research studies. The authors remind us that the keys to good research are the design and the questions asked. Also, the methods must fit the questions. Consequently, a mixture of qualitative and quantitative methods is often required to address the questions asked. In sections in the book called "How Might This Play Out in the Classroom?" McCardle, Chhabra, and Kapinus do not provide the reader with a tutorial on research methods but rather provide illustrations of types of research findings that can be used to answer classroom pedagogical questions. In doing so, they model the teacher–researcher stance at the core of the learning communities found to be effective vehicles for professional development (Anders, Hoffman, & Duffy, 2000). In addition, they discuss the "backmapping" of assessment to instruction required to ensure that teachers meet the needs of all students with empirically based practices. Finally, they point out the systemic issues surrounding effective implementations of RTI models. Educators need to work together to implement tiered instruction with student progress monitored to determine when more intensive and differentiated instruction is needed.

In conclusion, McCardle, Chhabra, and Kapinus have given us a timely book to help teachers carry forth into the classroom decades of reading research recently summarized in national consensus reports. This takes us one step closer to the quality teaching based on empirically proven practices that our students deserve.

Barbara R. Foorman, Ph.D.
Florida Center for Reading Research
Florida State University
Tallahassee

REFERENCES

Anders, P.L., Hoffman, J.V., & Duffy, G.G. (2000). Teaching teachers to teach reading: Paradigm shifts, persistent problems, and challenges. In M.L. Kamil, P.B. Mosenthal, P.D. Pearson, & R. Barr (Eds.), *Handbook of reading research* (Vol. III, pp. 719–742). Mahwah, NJ: Lawrence Erlbaum Associates.

August, D., & Shanahan, T. (Eds.). (2006). *Developing literacy in second-language learners: Report of the National Literacy Panel on language-minority children and youth.* Mahwah, NJ: Lawrence Erlbaum Associates.

Berninger, V. (2007). Evidence-based written language instruction during early and middle childhood. In R. Morris & N. Mather (Eds.), *Evidence-based intervention for students with learning and behavioral challenges.* Mahwah, NJ: Lawrence Erlbaum Associates.

Camilli, G., Vargas, S., & Yurecko, M. (2003). Teaching children to read: The fragile link between science and federal education policy. *Education Policy Analysis Archive, 11*(15). Retrieved May 26, 2008, from http://epaa.asu.edu/epaa/v11n15/

Camilli, G., Wolfe, P.M., & Smith, M.L. (2006). Meta-analysis and reading policy: Perspectives on teaching children to read. *The Elementary School Journal, 107,* 27–36.

Connor, C.M., Morrison, F.J., Fishman, B.J., Schatschneider, C., & Underwood, P. (2007). The early years: Algorithm-guided individualized reading instruction. *Science, 315*(5811), 464–465.

Desimone, L.M., Smith, T.M., & Frisvold, D. (2007). Has No Child Left Behind improved teacher and teaching quality for disadvantaged students? In A. Gamoran (Ed.), *Standards-based reform and the poverty: Lessons for No Child Left Behind* (pp. 89–119). Washington, DC: Brookings Institution Press.

Foorman, B.R., & Ciancio, D.J. (2005). Screening for secondary intervention: Concept and context. *Journal of Learning Disabilities, 38*(6), 494–499.

Foorman, B.R., & Moats, L.C. (2004). Conditions for sustaining research-based practices in early reading instruction. *Remedial and Special Education, 25*(1), 51–60.

Foorman, B.R., Schatschneider, C., Eakin, M.N., Fletcher, J.M., Moats, L.C., & Francis, D.J. (2006). The impact of instructional practices in Grades 1 and 2 on reading and spelling achievement in high-poverty schools. *Contemporary Educational Psychology, 31,* 1–29.

Individuals with Disabilities Education Improvement Act of 2004, PL 108-446, 20 U.S.C. §§ 1400 *et seq.*

Mehta, P., Foorman, B.R., Branum-Martin, L., & Taylor, W.P. (2005). Literacy as a unidimensional multilevel construct: Validation, sources of influence, and implications in a longitudinal study in Grades 1–4. *Scientific Studies of Reading, 9*(2), 85–116.

Moats, L.C., Foorman, B.R., & Taylor, W.P. (2006). How quality of writing instruction impacts high-risk fourth graders' writing. *Reading and Writing: An Interdisciplinary Journal, 19,* 363–391.

National Center for Education Evaluation and Regional Assistance. (2008). *Reading First impact study: Interim report.* Washington, DC: U.S. Department of Education. Retrieved May 26, 2008, from http://ies.ed.gov/ncee/pdf/20084016.pdf

National Early Literacy Panel (NELP). (n.d.). *Synthesizing the scientific research on development of early literacy in young children.* Retrieved May 26, 2008, from http://www.nifl.gov/partnershipforreading/family/ncfl/NELP2006Conference.pdf

National Institute of Child Health and Human Development. (NICHD). (2000). *Report of the National Reading Panel. Teaching children to read: An evidence-based assessment of the scientific research literature on reading and its implications for reading instruction: Reports of the subgroups* (NIH Publication No. 00-4754). Washington, DC: U.S. Government Printing Office.

No Child Left Behind Act of 2001, PL 107-110, 115 Stat.1425, 20 U.S.C. §§ 6301.

President's Commission on Excellence in Special Education. (2002). *A new era: Revitalizing special education for children and their families.* Washington, DC: U.S. Department of Education, Office of Special Education and Rehabilitative Services. Retrieved May 26, 2008, from http://www.ed.gov/inits/commissionsboards/whspecialeducation/reports.html

Snow, C.E. (2002). *Reading for understanding: Toward an R&D program in reading comprehension.* Santa Monica, CA: RAND Corporation.

Snow, C.E., Burns, M.S., & Griffin, P. (Eds.). (1998). *Preventing reading difficulties in young children.* Washington, DC: National Academies Press.

Stuebing, K.K., Barth, A.E., Cirino, P.T., Francis, D.J., & Fletcher, J.M. (2008). A response to recent re-analyses of the national reading panel report: Effects of systematic phonics instruction are practically significant. *Journal of Education Psychology, 100*(1), 123–134.

Taylor, B.M., Pearson, P.D., & Rodriguez, M.C. (2003). Reading growth in high-poverty classrooms: The influences of teacher practices that encourage cognitive engagement in literacy learning. *Elementary School Journal, 104,* 3–28.

Foreword

This book is about improving the professional practice of teachers. McCardle, Chhabra, and Kapinus combine their years of experience and considerable knowledge to link research and practice in ways that are both accessible and convincing. The authors are clear about their respect for the complex nature of effective teaching. Effective teachers bring many qualities to the classroom, including the beliefs and values that motivate them to inspire students to learn and cause them to treat students fairly. They bring a strong sense of commitment and integrity about the content they teach. They are skillful about the instructional decisions they make and the way they use time and materials. As a teacher educator, I am convinced that research can and should help to inform the multifaceted teacher qualities and behaviors that ultimately influence learning and teaching in the classroom. *Reading Research in Action: A Teacher's Guide for Student Success* provides a rich resource for this purpose.

Those of us who have had the privilege of working with highly effective teachers know that the seemingly amazing skill they demonstrate did not emerge in a vacuum. Often they are characterized as "born teachers." Indeed, some individuals do seem to be better suited to teaching than others. However, what may appear to the naïve observer as the result of good instincts or divine inspiration on the part of gifted teachers is more likely to be the accumulation of a constant search for knowledge to improve their craft. It is the wisdom of informed practice that guides them. *Reading Research in Action: A Teacher's Guide for Student Success* is crafted not only to inform teachers of the results of carefully constructed research but also to help them understand the research process and suggest concrete ways that they can make use of the results in their own instructional settings with the students they teach.

The book is organized around a set of key questions that teachers and other educators are apt to ask about reading research and its practical applications to the classroom. Throughout the book, the authors highlight the importance of the teacher as the critical force in making "research to practice" a dynamic force in the classroom. The authors lay the groundwork for understanding the fundamentals of how researchers move from theory to research questions and how they shape the design they will use to collect, analyze, and interpret the data they gather. This understanding provides a framework for helping the reader to understand what constitutes scientific research and fosters a critical stance to what may be offered as the evidence base that informs reading instruction. This is done by way of a brief introductory chapter that includes information about the scientific process and research design. To their credit, the authors present a balanced view of what constitutes credible research. A key concept, such as that *the nature of the questions or problems addressed determines the research methodology used*, is an important and sometimes difficult idea for teachers to grasp. Indeed, the authors explain that mixed or combinations of methods (qualitative and quantitative) may be used to address a question when needed. Rigor, rather than the superiority of one method over another, is stressed. Classroom inquiry is also discussed, and it is encouraged with explanations about how this differs from more formal research.

The authors rely heavily on the findings of the National Reading Panel (National Institute of Child Health and Human Development, 2000). However, they cite a wide array of rigorous studies that use a variety of research designs and methodologies. While reading is the primary focus, attention is also given to other key components of literacy education, including motivation and writing.

The fact that this book centers on reading research is of critical importance. Perhaps no other area of education has benefited more from a rich source of research than that of literacy education. A strong body of evidence exists regarding the underlying skills and abilities that support the development of reading in young children. A great deal is also known about the instructional opportunities required to support the ongoing development of successful readers. There is no doubt that there is much more to be learned. New knowledge tends to foster more questions and opportunities for further learning. Nevertheless, there is a need to help teachers become better acquainted with the existing knowledge base about how children learn to read and how they are best taught. As one who works with preservice and in-service teachers, as well as other educators, I believe this information is essential for administrators, literacy coaches, teacher educators, and classroom teachers. This book has many possible uses outside of the usual teacher education classroom. I can certainly envision it being used in study groups consisting of educators with various responsibilities. Each might read, reflect, and share the implications for their own work. Through listening and sharing, each educator would gain a sense of perspective for the work of others. Indeed, *Reading Research in Action: A Teacher's Guide for Student Success* has the potential to be a powerful

tool for establishing a shared vision of literacy education within a
school or district.

Dorothy S. Strickland, Ph.D.
Samuel DeWitt Proctor Professor of Education
Rutgers, The State University of New Jersey

REFERENCE

National Institute of Child Health and Human Development. (NICHD). (2000).
*Report of the National Reading Panel. Teaching children to read: An evidence-based
assessment of the scientific research literature on reading and its implications for
reading instruction: Reports of the subgroups* (NIH Publication No. 00-4754).
Washington, DC: U.S. Government Printing Office.

Acknowledgments

As with any authored volume, the responsibility for what is in this book, and any errors that are made in what we have said, rest with the authors. However, the support, guidance, and advice of many people have contributed to what is good about this book. Specifically, we want to thank the following individuals:

To Barbara R. Foorman and David Tilly, for their permission to use information about their work related to response to intervention (RTI) and their comments made at a conference on RTI, and to the International Dyslexia Association, for both leading the convening of that meeting and for allowing us to use information from the transcript of the meeting, we offer strong gratitude. To Virginia Berninger, Joanne Carlisle, Hugh Catts, Don Deshler, Barbara R. Foorman, Steve Graham, Patricia Graner, Elizabeth Moje, and David Tilly, for their willingness to share information about their research, on very short notice, we also offer thanks. Thanks, too, to Don, Patty, Steve, and Elizabeth, for helpful discussions. Brett Miller deserves special thanks for his candid and helpful comments on certain chapters. To all of those who listened and responded as we brainstormed the ideas that became the foundation for this book, we thank them for their patient listening and thoughtful suggestions—there were too many to name! And finally, thanks to Vinita's father, Dr. Krishan Chhabra, for the idea that became the title of this book; after much deliberation among the authors and the publisher, it was his ingenuity that helped capture the essence of this book!

To our outstanding editors at Paul H. Brookes Publishing Co., who helped us in the conceiving of and the putting together of this book, we will always be grateful. There are many folks at Brookes who have contributed, but to Jessica Allan (no longer with Brookes), for getting us started, and to Sarah Shepke and Marie Abate, for patiently and supportively seeing us through to completion, a big hurrah!

And finally, to our immediate families, who patiently suffered neglect during the many evenings, late nights, and weekends while we worked on this book, a special note of loving appreciation.

To our children,
Sonny and Sabina Chhabra Rhodes,
and our grandchildren,
Jonah LeBlanc, Grayson Carter, and Christian Kapinus,
and to children everywhere who are learning to read
and whose lives will be changed
by the teachers who offer them high-quality,
evidence-based instruction.
We hope that in some way this book will help teachers
in their daily efforts
to help all children learn to read.

How Does Research Inform Teaching?

● ● ● ● ● ● ● ● ● ● ● ● ● ● ● ● ● ● ● ●

> *"Perhaps the greatest tragedy in innovation today is that we are not adequately exploiting what is known about how effective instruction could reduce the incidence of reading failure."*
>
> (C.A. Denton & J.M. Fletcher, 2004, p. 445)

The two chapters in this section introduce the book, explain our goals in writing it, and discuss briefly how research and instruction can and should work together in the classroom. In Chapter 1, we provide a preview of the book's organization and explain how the individual sections and chapters can be useful to teachers in the classroom or in other settings. Chapter 2 focuses on the basic factors that inform teaching and how these factors relate to one another in research and ultimately in instructional practice. In that chapter, we discuss how research begins with observations about which theories are formulated. We describe the cycle of theory, research design, data gathering, analysis, and interpretation, which gives rise to new or modified theories.

REFERENCE

Denton, C.A., & Fletcher, J.M. (2004). Scaling reading interventions. In B. Foorman (Ed.), *Preventing and remediating reading difficulties: Bringing science to scale* (pp. 445–464). Timonium, MD: York Press.

CHAPTER 1

Introduction

KEY CONCEPTS

- The purpose of this book is to review research evidence on reading instruction and how that evidence is obtained.

- This book is written for teachers and educators, but it may also be useful to parents and others concerned about how reading is taught to elementary school children.

- The focus of the book is on evidence-based practice in reading instruction, guided by the belief that children are our most important asset, and that we should do all that we can to assist teachers, since we entrust the education of our nation's children to them.

Teachers want their efforts to get results. One of the best ways to do that is to use evidence-proven methods. In the past decade, the research evidence on effective instruction has been accumulating rapidly, and legislation now pushes educators to use it. In this volume we review the importance and relevance of research evidence on literacy instruction in reading for daily classroom practice. We discuss the role of theory in research, the difference between theory and philosophy, and the relevant theories for instructional practices as well as how they are tested through research and then recommended for implementation. Finally, we describe how research evidence can be used effectively by teachers in delivering classroom reading instruction. We believe that the use of theory and research in classroom instruction is a very important issue for teachers. Our goal is to make clear why it is important to begin with a theory and why researchers use the methods and approaches they do, and to review recent research findings on reading research that offer evidence for daily practice. We offer examples of implementation in the classroom as illustrations of how this might happen. This information is intended to assist teachers, and those who support and consult with teachers, in understanding the research evidence currently available as a basis for practice, thereby helping them incorporate that research evidence into their own instructional practices.

How Is This Book Organized?

The chapters in this book provide information based on research in reading that has practical implications for classroom instruction. The chapters are organized around questions that we ourselves wanted answered and thought most teachers would find interesting. Most chapters contain illustrative real-life scenarios of how the techniques discussed would play out in the classroom. Sections I and II include chapters that provide foundational information about research in reading. Research methods are discussed, and examples of high-quality research summaries are highlighted. Section III presents research findings on the major components of reading and how these findings can be incorporated into classroom instruction. Section IV offers information about how evidence in the classroom can be used. For example, we address what different types of assessment and monitoring can indicate about student learning, where the teacher's training and personal ideas fit into the implementation of evidence-based instruction, and new approaches that are being studied now, such as response to intervention. The last part of each chapter discusses other resources that are available to help teachers find evidence and implement evidence-based instruction.

There are many theories and research terms being used in education circles that can seem abstract or convoluted. Our goal is to provide teachers, tutors, and others involved in education with the tools necessary to clearly understand these theories and sort through them, to understand research findings, and to be able to consider and evaluate the evidence on instructional programs that they may wish to use in their classrooms. We hope to assist teachers in applying their own experience and skills in conjunction with new findings to provide the best education for all children. One goal of research must be to help teachers do even better what most of them already do well—teach children to read.

What Is the Purpose of This Book?

This book is first and foremost for teachers, who are the ultimate users of research evidence on reading instruction. We hope that this book will serve as a resource for teachers in their daily classroom practice and in their continuing professional development.

All too often, teachers are the last to know about new research, since researchers first focus on publishing their findings in scientific journal articles, written in relatively technical research jargon, to share their work with fellow researchers. But the value of research on reading is that it can help teachers be more effective in their reading instruction, can help them reach more children, including those who have difficulty learning, and can help them understand what underlies how the children in their classes learn. While many researchers do present their findings at national and regional meetings that teachers attend, we wanted to put this information together in one handy reference that teachers could read, use, and come back to for additional information or review.

While this volume is intended first for teachers, in support of the crucially important role they play in teaching our nation's children to read, we hope that it will also be informative to others. It may be of use to parents who want to know how their children are being taught and what evidence is available for teachers to use certain strategies in classroom practice. This should enable parents to better understand what teachers' methods are and why they use some of the materials and techniques they do. This should encourage parents to reinforce reading at home, to practice reading at home with their children, and to support what the teacher is working to accomplish in the classroom. It also may help parents understand and more fully appreciate the complex tasks that face teachers in teaching children to read. In addition, this book offers valuable information for school administrators and other educators who work with classroom teachers and students, and it may give entry-level researchers a sense of the perspective of teachers. Finally, this book might serve as a text for instructional methods courses for preservice teacher training. It is our hope that, at least in some small measure, this book may help to build a bridge we see as already under construction, between researchers and those who deliver education to children in classrooms, by demonstrating in clear language the commonalities among both communities and the usefulness of them to all. "Research to practice" must become more than just a phrase; we refer to a bridge *between* research and practice since each should and frequently does inform the other. Researchers often get great research ideas by observing talented teachers getting results with a child who has been having problems, so the two-way street is already one that is well traveled, although it could be more so. We hope this book will help make the bridge between research and practice a functional term.

How Can This Book Help Educators Actually Deliver Instruction?

When we discuss reading development and instruction, it is important to acknowledge the complexity of reading, not only as a set of individual components but also as instruction that involves teaching all reading components collectively. The integration of those components of reading—phonemic awareness, phonics, fluency, vocabulary, and reading comprehension—is crucial. Yet, teaching all these components in an integrated fashion requires far more than being able to follow a scripted program; it requires that teachers have sufficiently in-depth knowledge of all those components and how each can be taught to children at various grade levels in order to call on that total knowledge, even as they may be focusing on instruction in a single component. In each chapter of Section III, we explore these separate instructional components, with information about what each is and what we know about teaching it effectively. But we also weave these components together in instructional scenarios that illustrate the various facets of reading instruction that integrate or co-occur during the course of particular lessons. We acknowledge throughout the book the importance of engagement and motivation. Children must connect to instruction in all of these component skills and abilities if they are to achieve the goal of reading—comprehension. We offer this book humbly, with respect for all that teachers do on a daily basis, and hope that in reaching them and any of the other groups mentioned above, we in some way help to make the daily work of teachers easier and even more successful.

CHAPTER 2

The Cycle of Research and Instruction

"Research is formalized curiosity. It is poking and prying with a purpose. It is a seeking that he who wishes may know the cosmic secrets of the world and that they dwell therein."

—(Zora Neale Hurston, 1942/2006, p. 143)

KEY CONCEPTS

- Research is a scientific process with the goal of reliable findings that can be incorporated into effective instruction.

- Scientific research is made up of five cyclic factors: theory, research design, data gathering, analysis, and interpretation.

- Scientific research factors play a role in planning and evaluating the effectiveness of classroom instruction.

Mr. Wilson wanted his fifth-grade students to learn the process for writing a research paper on a science topic. He knew they would need help in all stages of the process, especially in determining what information was important in their reading and in organizing the information to present it. He conducted his own research on how to develop these skills by checking research findings related to reading comprehension, content reading, and writing. He found some helpful articles and ideas. As he began the unit, he decided to gather data on students' abilities to pick out important information and organize ideas gathered from and based on their reading.

Mr. Wilson was involved with several types of research. His students were conducting the type of research that everyday people do as they search the web, reference books, or other information sources. Mr. Wilson conducted similar research when he sought information and ideas to guide his instructional planning. In planning, he used findings from scientific research related to reading and writing, especially in the content areas. He conducted his own classroom research to track his students' growth and the effectiveness of his instruction related to the skills he wanted students to be able to apply to their assignments.

This chapter focuses on a specific type of research, *scientific research*—as opposed to library research for term papers or the gathering of information from literature. Scientific research is the type of research used by scientists in developing an understanding of the universe and practical tools for living. Scientific research is a cycle, from theories, through data collection, to findings that inform the modification of theories, which generate new hypotheses, which result in more research and more findings, which support or refute theories, which then are enhanced or modified. In order to look into that cycle of research, important questions need to be posed. What are the steps between theory and findings? How do researchers actually pursue their formalized curiosity, and what form does that poking and prying take in education research?

What Is Scientific Research, and What Are the Five Basic Factors that Make Up the Cycle of Scientific Research?

Scientific research is an effort to answer a question through planned data collection, analysis, and interpretation. It is important to also note what it is not. Scientific research is not the gathering and reorganizing of factual information, as in the research papers being developed by Mr. Wilson's class. Scientific research is fundamental to the development of new knowledge. Proposed theories and hypotheses, discussed in the following example, define what scientific research will be conducted.

Scientific research is an integral part of every field, including medicine and teaching, or essentially anything that touches our lives. If we are sick, we rely on doctors to give us a recommended treatment or medication that has been shown to be effective with other patients with the same symptoms (Morris, 2004; Stanovich & Stanovich, 2003). In the classroom, research findings can serve as a guide or tool in making instructional decisions, such as information about what we know generally about effective instruction, and how to use existing materials while employing practices and approaches that have been shown to be effective with most students in classrooms.

There are five basic factors that interact, not always sequentially, in developing research from a question to a finding that can inform practice. These are theory, research design, data gathering, analysis, and interpretation. Table 2.1 offers a brief definition of each of these factors, and some related examples are provided in the sections that follow.

Mrs. Jones knew that research has shown that phonemic awareness (PA) instruction can help a student develop decoding ability, which in turn can help with word reading and spelling. She assessed a new student who had just entered her first-grade classroom at midyear and noted that he did not seem to have developed good PA. Based on that assessment, and based on her knowledge of research on PA training, she did not just expect him to catch up, as the class was now learning more complex PA skills. Instead, she worked with this student individually to teach him the easiest PA skills and brought him up to the level of the rest of the class.

Theory

At its simplest and most basic, a *theory* is an idea. But it is also more than that. A theory is an idea that is based on known information, but takes that information and logically extends it to what might be expected, based on that known information. Theories can be grounded in ideas about certain beliefs, like how children learn. But a theory is more than just a belief—it explains why that belief or philosophy could be true, and why researchers have enough confidence in a belief to

Table 2.1.   The cycle of scientific research

Term	Definition
Theory	A theory is an idea based on logic about what is already known. Sometimes it describes a phenomenon, such as building understanding based on words in a text. It also can include what might logically happen as a result of certain activities, such as instructional techniques, new programs, and so forth. A hypothesis is a type of theory, a guess about the relationship of factors based on logic, previous knowledge, and observation.
Research design	Research is an effort to learn about something using a rule-governed set of steps to answer specific questions through the collection, analysis, and consideration of empirical information. It is most productive when the question is clearly articulated and the collection and analysis of information is carried out according to a carefully formulated plan.
Data gathering	At its most basic, data gathering or data collection is simply the collection of information about an idea or phenomenon, and is the basic material of all research. Frequently, initial data gathering consists of noting patterns in observations and gathering information about what others have learned about a question. Data collection can also be done within a carefully designed experiment, during a planned activity, or with a specific data collection instrument, such as a test or other measure.
Analysis	Researchers who have collected their data analyze or quantify it in some way, often by applying statistical treatments to the data. They examine the statistical means and probabilities to learn what the data can tell us. What they learn from these statistical manipulations are the results or findings of the study.
Interpretation	Interpretation is the section of a research report in which the researchers indicate what they think the findings mean. This may include translation to practice; that is, researchers or others may write about how they think these findings could influence practice. In the case of education-related research, this would be the instructional implications, how the technique might be implemented in classrooms, or how it applies to student learning in everyday classroom situations.

invest the time, effort, and money to conduct research to attempt to confirm or deny it, to understand it more fully. Both theories and hypotheses can be defined in this way—as ideas about what might happen given certain facts. But a theory is a bigger idea or set of ideas, built on connected research findings that enable researchers and educators to logically predict, based on what is known, what might happen next, or to explain how something came to be. For example, theories can offer explanations about how the earth came into existence, and scientists then develop hypotheses that would support such a theory and do research to explore these hypotheses. Or a theory might be developed about the role of memory in learning foreign languages; scientists would then design experiments based on specific hypotheses, and test individuals in various learning situations to gain evidence to support or refute that theory.

Theories guide research through the types of questions or hypotheses they generate, and theories provide the research study with structure and direction. A theory also lays out for other researchers the basic logic behind something like an instructional program and provides predictions about what researchers should find if the theory is valid. Morris pointed out that it is just as important to refute a theory as it is to support it and that "a theory can never be proven in any one study because evidence from multiple studies to validate the theory's correctness has to accumulate over time" (2004, p. 137). Validation of a theory also depends heavily on how well designed the studies are that support or refute it. This process can generate a considerable amount of discussion among researchers as they critique one another's designs and methods.

Theories are rarely right or wrong. They are more often shown to be partially correct and partially incorrect; then they are modified in ways that make sense, given the information and evidence gathered to that point, and more assumptions are made and more questions posed that could confirm or rebut that new version of the theory. Theory building is an iterative process.

Sometimes the information gathered in disproving a theory may give rise to a whole new theory. Some of the most important findings have been accidents or a result of serendipity; that is, scientists have stumbled on some new event, technique, or fact of nature when they were actually looking for something else. But theories are necessary to give purpose to research. Even serendipity does not have a chance unless researchers are looking for something to begin with! An often-cited example of serendipity is vaccination, which was discovered by Edward Jenner, an English physician. Jenner noticed that milkmaids who had caught cowpox, a benign condition in humans, did not catch smallpox. He then formed a theory that somehow cowpox could confer immunity and experimented to explore this idea. In fact, he demonstrated that cowpox was protective, confirming his theory.

In addition, even scientific research can seem contradictory, as in various studies of the beneficial and harmful effects of drinking coffee. Finally, scientific research about human beings usually indicates what happens to most people given a certain situation, but it is seldom the case that everyone in a study has the same positive or negative response to a situation, substance, or action. Summaries of several studies, such as the report of the National Reading Panel (National Institute of Child Health and Human Development, 2000) can help by indicating those findings supported by several different studies.

One example of a reading theory based on research is the idea that students use their own background knowledge to understand what they read. This theory has been expanded by scientific research that studied whether some students do not use their background knowledge at all, whether some use the wrong background knowledge, and whether some students have so much background knowledge that they do not pay attention to new ideas in what they read. Researchers can examine all of these possibilities and, based on the findings, modify the theory to include the circumstances under which background information helps or hinders students in the reading comprehension process.

For example, in one study of how to get students to use their background knowledge in understanding text, students were asked to write what they knew about spiders on strips of colored paper before reading a text about spiders. Then, after reading about spiders, they wrote the new information they gathered on different colored paper strips. The students then wove the two paper strips together to indicate how they used both their own background knowledge and the information from the reading to understand the text. Their scores on remembering new information from the passage were higher than those of students who did not actively engage their background knowledge (Pearson, Hansen, & Gordon, 1979). This led to the development of widely used, research-supported instructional practices, such as Know, Want to Know, Learned (KWL; Ogle, 1986) and Reciprocal Teaching (Palincsar & Brown, 1984), both of which involve students calling to mind what they already know about the subject of their reading.

How Can Educators Determine Whether Research Theories They Read Are Dependable and Applicable to Their Students?

Not all scientific research is equal. It is important to ask good questions when reading about research findings. How many students were in the study, and were they similar to students in the teacher's classroom in gender, culture, economic status, and achievement? How large was the *effect* of the research intervention? Effect size is a statistical measure of the strength of the relationship between two variables. An effect of about .20 is small, one of about .50 is medium, and .80 is large (Cohen, 1988, 1992). If a study shows something to have only a small effect, then the results are not as dependable as with a large effect. That does not mean that the strategy studied is not a promising practice, but it does mean that more research is needed on how it works in a variety of contexts, and with a variety of students, before educators can have real confidence that it is worth changing practice.

What were the conditions of the research? Are the findings the result of the factors identified, or could other factors also have influenced the findings? Were the instructional activities done one-on-one, with small groups of students, or with entire classes? It is important to consider all of these factors because a program or technique that is shown to work with a specific type of student or under very specific conditions may not work under other conditions or with students who are different from those in the study. For example, an instructional program that is effective with students who are native speakers of English may not work well with English language learners because of both linguistic and cultural differences and may need significant adaptations to be effective with that group of students.

Research Design

There are many ways to test a theory. The questions being posed based on that theory will determine the type of research design used. Data gathering and analysis are guided by the study design, and depend on a well-designed study in order for researchers to be able to answer the questions posed, so design is extremely important. See Chapter 4 for information on different types of research designs.

Data Gathering

Gathering data is an important contributor to decision making. After a theory or hypothesis is proposed, then data, or bits of information, must be collected to test a theory. Data can take many forms, and data collection happens at many levels. Researchers may gather data to attempt to understand what might be going on in order to develop ideas (hypotheses), to capture what is actually happening in a situation (observation), or to get information on baseline performance and changes in performance over time (assessment) in order to quantify behaviors. In education, data is gathered through testing, observing, recording (e.g., written note taking, audio recording, videotaping), interviewing, conducting surveys, conducting experiments, or collecting information in other ways. All of this information can then be used to help make decisions once it has been analyzed. Usually data collection is carefully planned when the research study is designed.

Analysis

Once the research problem has been identified, the study designed, and the data gathered and analyzed, the main purpose behind research comes to light. What does all of this mean? How can educators use the information that has been revealed by this research process? At this point in a research study, and in the paper that the researcher writes to share the fruits of the team's labors (most research is done by teams of researchers working together), the findings should answer the question that was posed in the beginning. What does the analysis tell us about that question? Does the theory still hold, or has it been countered or refuted? Did the researchers find what they expected? If not, what might be the reasons? And what does all of this mean for everyday life? In the case of education research, what does this mean for practice in the classroom? The ultimate goal of all research is to identify how the findings can be used for practical purposes—how they will affect people's lives and surroundings.

How Can Educators Use This Information in Making Decisions for Students?

The cycle of research generates a database for decision making. Research seeks to confirm, refute, extend, or refine theories that predict what educators might expect to find and why. Thus theory is a driving force that not only supports and guides the best research but also explores why some instructional approaches work better than others. Therefore, theory and research are cyclic. This cycle can inform classroom practice. While researchers are developing and modifying a research theory, and seeking, for example, to figure out why a particular instructional technique worked better than another, educators can begin implementing the instructional techniques that work well in the classroom. Ideally, researchers will be working with these teachers as they implement the techniques, and will study what is happening in those classrooms (i.e., looking for the "why"), while teachers are getting results by using the effective instructional techniques.

Interpretation

Interpretation of the findings from the analysis of data is a very important step in the research cycle. This is the point at which researchers explain what their results mean, how they support or refute the theory, and why. Researchers may also indicate how the results have led them to modify their theory and what remaining or new questions need to be investigated in the future. Thus the cycle begins again, with a modified theory driving research questions, for which a design will be developed, data will be gathered, analysis will be conducted, and findings will be reported and interpreted.

Inquiry Using Classroom Data

The use of inquiry in gathering and using data at the classroom level parallels what researchers do. For example, teachers have an idea of what instructional technique might work in the classroom, and that idea is based on prior experience, prior successes or failures, and what they have read and learned. Teachers formulate an instructional technique, try it out, and then both observe and measure student responses to have some indication of whether the technique worked, how well it worked, and for which students. For this technique to work, assessment and instruction are necessarily integrated (see Chapter 13 for much more on assessment and the various roles it plays in the classroom).

The difference between inquiry in the classroom and full-scale research is that researchers take theory-generated ideas and "pilot" work in classrooms and test those ideas with research designs that control, as much as possible, the factors that might present alternative explanations for why something appears to work. Researchers follow a set of rules in designing their studies and analyzing the findings. While the use of inquiry in the classroom can be used to develop clever approaches and creative ideas that may appear to work for many students in a class, teachers have neither the time nor the resources to mount well-controlled, full-scale research studies of an approach's effectiveness. These approaches still need to be tested more rigorously before being considered reliable and effective for classroom application. Researchers need to be sure that the reason a technique was effective was not because of the interesting books a teacher chose to implement as part of a new teaching method, or because the teacher happened to have an exceptional group of students that year, or even because the teacher's personal charisma and jaunty style might have motivated students to perform better. Once researchers have examined all of these possibly confounding factors, researchers can have greater confidence that a new approach will work with other children, even when delivered by other teachers. Both the use of inquiry and more formal research are important for a teacher to do the best job possible. Table 2.2 explains the differences between using formal research and classroom data to plan or differentiate instruction for students. Note, too, that progress monitoring is a form of data collection that teachers conduct in the classroom, and it guides instructional planning for individual students (see Chapter 13, on assessment, and Chapter 15, on

Table 2.2. Formal scientific research versus classroom data used to plan or differentiate instruction

Research factors	Scientific/formal research	Data-driven classroom planning
Hypothesis	A guess or idea based on past research findings, observations, or theories	A guess about a student's needs or a potential instructional strategy based on observations in the classroom, scientific research, experience, and theories
Research intervention or activities	A series of activities, specified by the rules of research and statistics, to test the hypothesis through an experiment or to gather information that clarifies the hypothesis with descriptive information, in order to inform the field	A series of activities integrated with classroom activities and curricula to determine what will improve student learning and achievement
Data gathering	Information collected in order to isolate variables and yield findings that are acceptable in the research community	Information collected, usually from activities related to current curriculum, instruction, and education goals in order to determine whether instruction is effective and how it can be modified to meet the needs of students
Analysis and results	Careful application of statistical or qualitative procedures for analysis	Careful analysis of data, usually looking for patterns or indicators of improvement
Interpretation	Inferences and generalizations applied to the entire field or a large segment of the field. Usually there are indications of a need for further information	Inferences applied to planning for instruction. Usually there is a continuing need to form new hypotheses and test them, especially since students vary in their individual responses to instructional interventions

response to intervention techniques, for more information on progress monitoring).

HOW CAN TEACHERS USE ALL
• • • OF THESE TECHNIQUES IN THE CLASSROOM? • • •

Ms. Wells had a third-grade student, Jean, who had low scores on the state reading test (assessment). The teacher observed Jean's reading in class and noticed that she was usually reading word by word and had little expression in her reading. Her responses to questions indicated she had some comprehension of what a story was generally about but had gaps in her understanding (inquiry). The teacher knew that reading theory indicated students needed to read fluently enough to pay attention to meaning (theory). She checked a summary of some recent research on reading fluency and comprehension and found that fluency training can help students improve their comprehension and overall reading achievement (research). Through the summary, she learned about some instructional strategies that might work with Jean and two other students who had similar problems. She planned some lessons that incorporated those strategies. For example, she found several stories that feature animal characters—Jean's favorite type of story. She had Jean practice reading the stories aloud and then had Jean record reading the stories and listen to herself. When Jean was satisfied with her recording, she took it home to share with her parents. Ms. Wells also paired Jean with another student and had them take turns reading aloud. Paired reading of this type is a highly researched instructional approach to building reading fluency (interpretation/translation) (Topping, 2006). She gathered evidence of Jean's progress in both fluency and comprehension (data gathering/ assessment). Ms. Wells continued to observe Jean to determine what type of instruction she should plan next in order to continue to improve Jean's reading achievement.

REFERENCES

Cohen, J. (1988). *Statistical power analysis for the behavioral sciences* (2nd ed.). Mahwah, NJ: Lawrence Erlbaum Associates.

Cohen, J. (1992). A power primer. *Psychological Bulletin, 112*(1), 155–159.

Hurston, Z.N. (2006). *Dust tracks on a road*. New York: HarperCollins Publishers, Inc. (Original work published 1942)

Morris, R.D. (2004). Clinical trials as a model for intervention research studies in education. In P. McCardle & V. Chhabra (Eds.), *The voice of evidence in reading research* (pp. 127–150). Baltimore: Paul H. Brookes Publishing Co.

National Institute of Child Health and Human Development. (2000). *Report of the National Reading Panel. Teaching children to read: An evidence-based assessment of the scientific research literature on reading and its implications for reading instruction: Reports of the subgroups* (NIH Publication No. 00-4754). Washington, DC: U.S. Government Printing Office.

Ogle, D. (1986). KWL: A teaching model that develops active reading of expository text. *The Reading Teacher, 39*, 564–570.

Palincsar, A.S., & Brown, A.L. (1984). Reciprocal teaching of comprehension fostering and monitoring activities. *Cognition and Instruction, 1*, 117–175.

Pearson, P.D., Hansen, J., & Gordon, C. (1979). The effect of background knowledge on young children's comprehension of explicit and implicit information. *Journal of Reading Behavior, 11*, 201–209.

What Is This Evidence Base, and Where Did It Come From?

● ●

> *"Those who are enamoured of practice without science are like a pilot who goes into a ship without a rudder or compass and never has any certainty where he is going."*
>
> (Leonardo da Vinci, *The Notebooks of Leonardo da Vinci*, 1939, p. 910)

Today, nearly everything claims to be *research based*. But what does that really mean? And is that term the same as *evidence based*? No, it is not. These two terms do not represent the same thing. The term *research based* means that the program or instructional approach is based on what research has demonstrated works. For example, the National Reading Panel (NRP) indicated that direct, explicit instruction in phonemic awareness (PA) and phonics is effective in teaching children to read (National Institute of Child Health and Human Development, 2000). That does not mean that every PA instructional program will be effective. If a program to teach phonics is developed based on the findings in the NRP report or other research that has demonstrated the effectiveness of this type of instruction, then it truly can be called *research-based instruction*. And that is a good start to developing a program, a much better approach than just developing something on a hunch and hoping it might work. However, whether that particular program is actually effective depends on the evidence (if any) that has been gathered using that specific program. When evidence is available to show that a program or approach is effective, then we can call that practice *evidence based*. Those are programs and practices we can have the greatest confidence in.

It makes sense to have two stages when choosing a program or instructional approach. First, it is important to see if the developers used what is known from research studies to build it. That gives some assurance that it should be useful and worthwhile to use with students. Second, educators should check to find out if there have been any studies actually using this program, comparing it to other programs or using a pre- and posttest design, in which students were tested before and after they were taught using this program to measure their progress. There might have also been experiments done comparing the use of that program to other programs under similar conditions. It is important that the measures or tests used in this research be aimed at the specific skills or abilities that are targeted by the program. In addition, there should be a control or comparison group, in order to confirm that the instructional program is what truly made the difference, and that the progress seen is not just growth over time that the children would have experienced regardless of which program was used. There are other factors to consider, too, and we will discuss those in Chapter 4.

In this section of the book, we cover theory, research methods, and some summaries of research studies. Chapter 3 explains what a theory is and discusses some research-based theories that are widely accepted based on the reading research. Chapter 4 explains how studies are designed, why they are designed the way they are, and what to look for in reading research studies. Different types of research are outlined, along with the type of information found when reviewing or evaluating various research methods. The information presented can serve as a guide to reading and evaluating research literature and developing an understanding of various research methods. For example, teachers will know how much confidence to put in a given study and what things to look for in the classroom when trying out some new technique that research has shown to be effective.

Chapter 5 involves a discussion of summaries of educational research, including national reports that discuss findings from research on various aspects of reading. In addition, we discuss how you can use the summary information to guide how you can plan classroom instruction and make decisions for your students. For example, under research methods, if educators want to know if an instructional approach is effective, then it should be compared with something else (e.g., the usual curriculum or program that the school has been using), then outcomes in the targeted ability should be measured in both the experimental and the comparison group, and the students should be comparable (hence the term *comparison*) in both groups.

Another thing to look for when choosing a program is whether the students for which the evidence is provided are similar to the students in the educator's classroom. Was the program tested on students who were all middle class? Or was the program tested in inner-city schools? This is the kind of information worth searching for when choosing a program. This information should be provided in summaries, syntheses, and in reports of single studies. It is also the kind of information that educators will want to look for in the research. If there are no programs available that have good, solid evidence regarding their specific effectiveness, then educators may want to choose a program that is at least research based. If the effectiveness has been demonstrated in children very different from the students in the teacher's classroom, the instructor may want to use it but monitor and adapt it to better fit his or her students. Sometimes teachers have to use the materials that are available or that are provided—they do not always have the luxury of buying the newest materials every year. However, even the adaptation of materials can often be based on research findings.

REFERENCES

da Vinci, L. (1939). *The notebooks of Leonardo da Vinci.* (E. MacCurdy, Trans.) New York: Reynal & Hitchcock.
National Institute of Child Health and Human Development. (2000). *Report of the National Reading Panel. Teaching children to read: an evidence-based assessment of the scientific research literature on reading and its implications for reading instruction: Reports of the subgroups* (NIH Publication No. 00-4754). Washington, DC: U.S. Government Printing Office.

CHAPTER 3

The Role of Theory and Research in Reading

"It is the theory that decides what can be observed."

— (Albert Einstein, 1926)

KEY CONCEPTS

- A theory is a logical explanation for something that has been observed and links together known facts.

- Many education theories can be confirmed or disconfirmed through research.

- Researchers use theories to predict future outcomes of observation.

- Convergence of evidence is important in confirming or disconfirming theories.

- Reliance on theory is key to developing evidence about reading instruction.

Ms. Able noticed several of her fourth-grade students were struggling with comprehending their social studies book. All of the students could read aloud fluently. Ms. Able's theory of what happens when a student comprehends text included the need to connect the words with background knowledge. Based on that theory and what she observed, she theorized that building a better conceptual understanding of the vocabulary in the chapter would help her students comprehend it. She also knew that readers needed to activate or be aware of their background knowledge related to what they are reading. She tested her hypothesis by adapting her instruction to include more time building understanding of key terms and using the Know, Want to Know, Learned (KWL; Ogle, 1986) approach to reading the social studies text. KWL has four steps:

1. Students take a look at the selection and discuss what they already know about the topic. They list their ideas on a chart.

2. Students add to the chart a list of what they want to learn about the topic that might be in the chapter.

3. Students read the chapter, looking for new information and confirming what they believe they already know.

4. Students confirm what they listed before reading and list what they learned.

Eventually, Ms. Able had students doing the charts in small groups. She kept records of their comprehension and learning and found that her theory of students needing to connect words with background knowledge was correct.

People can mean a lot of different things when they use the word *theory*. You might hear someone say, with a wry grin, "Well, theoretically, that's true, but" and then you know they are actually telling you that what they are discussing is a nice idea with no functional or actual reality. But researchers are told by their colleagues and peers who review grant applications and journal submissions that their work *must* be based on coherent theories. So what *is* a theory, anyway? And what impact should this have on what educators do in the classroom?

What Is a Theory, and How Do Researchers and Educators Know Which Theories Are Right?

When the word *theory* comes to mind, people often think about academics—perhaps research, medical, or even mathematical theories that they learned in school. In reality, theories are part of people's everyday lives, guiding the decisions they make, how they raise their children, the way they view the world, what doctors they choose, and how they interact with people. The term *theory* can be defined in various ways, but here we regard it as a foundational part of the scientific method.

The scientific method has four steps: 1) observation or description, 2) development of a hypothesis to explain that observation or description, 3) use of that hypothesis to predict new events that would happen under certain conditions, and 4) experimental testing to see if the hypothesis can be proven. A *hypothesis* is a statement of what researchers think will happen before they have conducted experiments to test whether that is the case, and usually that hypothesis deals with cause and effect. The hypothesis reflects what researchers think caused that event, or how events or characteristics are related and contribute to causing events.

A *scientific theory* represents a group of related hypotheses that have been shown to be true repeatedly through experimental testing and observation. In simple terms, a scientific theory is a logical explanation of something that has been observed, that links together known facts, that can be confirmed or refuted through experimental testing, and that is capable of predicting the outcomes of future observations of the type it claims to explain. It is built on hypotheses, some of which can be empirically tested. So for scientists, theories and fact do not oppose one another, as they would seem to in the expression "theoretically, that's true," which we mentioned at the beginning of the chapter. Rather, a scientific theory is an explanation of a set of facts, some of which can be confirmed by careful observations and experiments constructed to test them, and which, although they may not be decisively proven, are facts that are at least generally accepted by the scientific community studying that phenomenon. Theories, even theories about the universe or chemistry, use inferences that link those components that have been proven with those that attempt to explain what has not yet been tested or observed. As new tools and ways of observing phenomena arise, even the parts of theories once thought to be proven can be reconsidered or revised. This has happened frequently in the recent history of nuclear physics. Scientists can even develop new or different theories about phenomena, depending on the inferences they draw from the data.

One example of a theory currently in the news and beginning to affect the behavior of many people in the United States and worldwide is the theory that human behavior influences climate change. Although it is not definitively proven (as many theories never are), this theory has enough evidence that people are at least beginning to change their practices to some degree, whether they accept the entire theory or not.

Whether people believe that global warming is a real phenomenon, there is certainly a great deal of evidence that human energy consumption and the waste products of that consumption affect the environment. People can actually observe the haze over cities, the impact of waste on the waterways, and other scientific indicators of environmental change. Environmental scientists are continuing to gather data, but even as they do, they are inferring that many human behaviors have an impact on the climate. As a result, people are encouraged to reduce fossil fuel emissions, be more conscious and responsible in the consumption of energy and natural resources, and recycle as many waste products as possible. People are asked to do this not just based on their own beliefs, or the beliefs of others, or even based simply on their own observations; they are asked to do this based on a theory of climate change and environmental impact on which science has brought considerable, if not absolutely conclusive or definitive, evidence to bear.

Scientific research in all areas is guided by theories that seek to explain what is observed. Researchers in reading, just as in other areas of science, use a conceptual framework based on observations and facts that have been learned to that point to generate research questions and predict potential answers. The nature of those questions, their value and potential significance as well as what kinds of information it will take to answer them, are what determines the research design and methods that will be used. The value or potential significance of the answers is important in identifying how the research will progress and what methods will be used (Fletcher & Francis, 2004). (Research designs and methods are explained more thoroughly in Chapter 4.)

It is important to realize that research itself would not be possible without theories and questions defined by curiosity, observations, and the need to find answers to questions. These answers will perhaps improve instruction for students or empower various groups, including teachers, education specialists, and indeed educators at all levels, to more effectively address the issues of reading and writing, reading failure, and remediation and prevention of reading disabilities. There is a kind of dance between research and theory as each process influences the other; this is illustrated in a quotation from *Scientific Research in Education,* a report on research in education by the National Research Council:

> Knowledge is generated through a sequence of interrelated descriptive and causal studies, through a constant process of refining theory and knowledge. These lines of inquiry typically require a range of methods and approaches to subject theories and conjectures to scrutiny from several perspectives. (Shavelson & Towne, 2002, p. 123)

How Are Theories Confirmed or Refuted?

Theories are built based on a set of observations and inferences and are an attempt to explain phenomena in our world. Given a theory, a researcher or a team (research tends to be done by groups of researchers working together) predicts what would happen in certain situations and considers what sorts of information it would take to confirm or disprove that particular theory. It may be that additional observational data can help confirm or strengthen the case for this theory, but usually the researchers try to develop experiments that will challenge or extend the theory.

Researchers will argue that theories can never (or rarely) be definitively proven; it is easier to disprove a theory than to prove one because there always is another possible case that could disprove it. The best researchers can do is continue to add evidence that helps to confirm, extend, or modify a theory. As researchers find information indicating that a particular aspect of the data is not accounted for by their theory, they may modify the theory to better fit the data. This should offer a closer approximation of the truth, or an explanation that better fits all the available data. Sometimes theories are disproven and new theories are developed, but more often theories are modified based on new information and results of observation and studies. Research is, in that sense, incremental, where researchers seek increasingly clear and accurate explanations for the phenomenon under study.

In theory confirmation, the concept of *convergent evidence,* or using multiple methods with multiple samples, is crucial. Researchers challenge theories by investigating them in various ways, using various research methods. If different sets of researchers studying the same basic question in different ways all find the same or similar answers, then their findings might be considered convergent—they all seem to point to the same theory, confirming the same or similar explanations for the phenomena or events that were observed and tested. Sometimes the same team of researchers will use different approaches to study the same questions, and then use the data from the various approaches or methods to verify the accuracy of what they have already found. Thus, they bring various data sources to bear on the same question; this approach is referred to as *triangulation* (Fletcher & Francis, 2004). For example, a study addressing a question about the impact of comprehension strategies on third graders might incorporate various assessments like reading scales, observations of students, and teacher surveys. In other instances, research done by different researchers is pulled together and analyzed to develop or extend a theory. Meta-analyses, or systematic syntheses of research studies, represent efforts to bring together findings of various studies (for more explanation of meta-analysis, see Chapter 4). Researchers focus on specific research questions, and generally begin with a theoretical framework within which they develop their questions and to which they then apply the convergent evidence from their analyses.

It seems only fair that researchers should be relatively confident of the trustworthiness of research findings before they advocate that these findings should be used in practice. If someone were sick and the doctor were to prescribe an antibiotic, that person would trust that the doctor had confidence that that particular antibiotic had helped to cure other people who presented with similar symptoms. The doctor would have to have confidence in the medication itself and the fact that it had been tested for this specific illness, with different populations using different assessments over a long period of time. While theory may have guided the original inquiries in that particular area of medicine, to treat that particular medical problem, most people would not want the physician to treat them based on a theory that had not been proven by a large body of experimental evidence. However, research is not infallible. Even given the best knowledge of the research, the doctor might not know how a particular individual will react to an antibiotic. That is why doctors (and other professionals, including teachers) must be continually gathering information about the individuals with whom they work.

In education, for so-called experts to advise teachers to change what they are doing in classrooms, without basing that advice on a theory supported by evidence, does not make sense and is potentially harmful to students. There should be enough research on a topic to give confidence that the new approaches will work before teachers are asked to adopt them. That is, researchers must have enough evidence to be convinced that the theory is relatively sound, and that it is worth the time, effort, and expense required to change educational practice. That is why the development of theories and hypotheses needs to be substantiated with adequate and reliable evidence; researchers and educators must be confident that such changes will ultimately benefit children's learning.

How Do Theories Affect What Teachers Do in the Classroom?

The ultimate goal of theories is to provide a framework for understanding the world and making decisions to best serve certain goals. Since the focus of this book is on education, the theories in which we are most interested involve how to promote learning.

The work of the National Reading Panel (NRP) is a good example of how research theories can converge to change practice (National Institute of Child Health and Human Development [NICHD], 2000). First, researchers wanted to know if there was sufficient confirmation of the theory that phonemic awareness (PA) and phonics were essential to learning to read, so that they could base practice recommendations on this theory. The researchers hypothesized that if students were explicitly taught PA, letter–sound correspondences, and phonics, they would learn to read English more readily than students who were not taught these skills or who were taught these skills only incidentally. Researchers designed experimental and quasi-experimental studies to test theories about PA and phonics instruction and then reported their findings in peer-reviewed journals. The NRP searched the literature in peer-reviewed journals to find these studies and then compiled and examined all of the findings. They conducted meta-analyses, whereby they were able to examine the outcomes of multiple studies and find whether they converged on specific findings or not.

Once the NRP report was published (NICHD, 2000), there was a widespread effort by various groups to take these findings and move them to practice in the classroom. (For more information on the NRP, see Chapter 5 and the chapters on the components of reading in Section III.) That effort to implement the NRP findings resulted in a call for change. Organizations and individuals called for using reading programs whose instructional practices were based on evidence that they work for most children in most classes. While no single approach will work for every child under every situation, enough evidence does exist to show that explicit instructional approaches for many aspects of reading work well for the majority of students, allowing educators to implement them with confidence.

Clearly the field of education does not know everything it needs to know about how best to teach reading, to prevent reading difficulties, or to remediate reading difficulties. Therefore, it will be important for researchers to continue to develop theories and test existing theories of how children learn to read and how best to instruct them. And it will be important for educators to continue to adapt their instruction and interventions as more is learned. As mentioned earlier, theories are guided by questions or hypotheses, and it is those questions that determine how a research study is designed and implemented. Theories essentially define areas of research, and the research findings can provide new opportunities for teachers to add and change components of their instruction to ensure success for every student. If the research questions match the design and method, then the study is starting on a strong and clear foundation. The research findings, especially if they can be replicated, can be used to accept, reject, or modify the theory being investigated, and the cycle begins again.

What Are Some Other Research-Based Theories that Have Been Widely Accepted?

Understanding theories is fundamental to understanding research. However, theories themselves are most useful to the majority of people when they are supported by evidence that can ultimately be used in practice. Since we have been focusing on reading, some research-based theories that are widely used and successful are discussed in the following paragraphs. Specifically, we look at the role of peer interaction in reading comprehension.

The term *comprehension* refers to the goal of reading, the opportunity and ability to use all reading skills to understand what is read, and to enjoy reading. In order for students to develop and employ reading comprehension, there are several classroom strategies that can be used as part of comprehension development.

One such approach is *cooperative learning*, in which students work in small groups to apply reading skills to defined tasks (Kamil, 2004). This approach has been studied and found to be an effective way for students to develop comprehension skills. Various applications of this approach have been studied extensively using different research methods, such as observations and interviews, and across various school and small-group populations. Cooperative learning was identified by the NRP as an important part of a multiple comprehension strategy method, based on extensive review and analysis of reading comprehension studies (NICHD, 2000).

Peer-assisted learning is another specific example of using peer interaction. The hypothesis that peer-assisted learning is an effective means to develop and employ students' reading comprehension grew out of a broader theory that was developed during the 1980s (Bloom & Green, 1984). This theory described the reading process as the construction of meaning through a dynamic interaction of the text, the reader, and the context. Reading researchers, influenced by studies and theories of the social factors in learning and child development, studied how student interaction with peers affected reading and learning. The early research on peer-assisted activities in reading comprehension was based on observations that having students work together and help one another on assignments seemed to result in gains in learning on those topics. Based on these observations, hypotheses were formulated and experiments developed to test whether structured tasks that involved peer-assisted learning were more effective in teaching students than other methods of instruction, such as independent classwork. Several researchers explored the effects of students collaborating on learning tasks. For example, researchers Ellice Forman and Courtney Cazden explored theories connecting social aspects of a type of peer-assisted learning and development (Forman & Cazden, 2004). Forman and Cazden's research on a type of peer-assisted learning indicated that tutors, along with the students being tutored, benefited from engagement in peer-tutoring activities. Further research comparing students' problem solving and learning on individual and cooperative tasks indicated some advantages for peer assistance on the problem-solving tasks. These studies also indicated that the cognitive and social processes of the peer-assistance situation were complex and varied across dyads of students.

Subsequent research has supported the use of cooperative learning activities to develop reading skills and improve learning (NICHD, 2000). This research has merged with research on how to develop students' capacities to be strategic active readers. Research has shown that *reciprocal teaching*, or teaching comprehension strategies in the context of a reading group (Palincsar & Brown, 1984), is an effective means of promoting students' comprehension. This approach was later modified to include students working together on the reciprocal reading tasks and is known as collaborative strategic reading (Klingner & Vaughn, 1999; Vaughn & Klingner, 1999). Research indicated the effectiveness of this structured approach when implemented in a context of peer assistance. The weaving together of different theories and research has led to a better understanding of how the learning environment or context can be adapted to promote comprehension, thinking, and learning.

Is All of This Reliance on Theories Something New?

There is a long and rich history of how educational theories influenced research. For an excellent review, see Alexander and Fox (2004). It is important for teachers to have their own theories of reading and learning that guide their decision making. While it is difficult for teachers to find the time to read research, it is important that they do so from time to time in order to continue to grow in their capacity to teach. Sometimes progress in understanding what works in reading instruction comes from teachers and researchers developing approaches based on theory and then eventually testing them in research studies.

Teachers need to be cognizant of how theories are implemented. The lists of studies that have resulted in changes in practice also indicate that some in the educational field have not been particularly careful about matching the nature of a study to the changes teachers adopt. The use of questions in comprehension, story maps, instructional techniques that highlight prior knowledge, and the whole language approach each gained important impetus from research, but none of these instructional practices had undergone studies that showed that such approaches actually worked with students. These instructional practices all came from studies that were either trying to reveal potential problems or that were designed to figure out how something worked. None of these practices were adopted based on research that showed the approach improved the teaching of reading, although in some cases, later studies did support these widely adopted instructional practices (Shanahan, 2002, p. 21). This issue highlights the need for ongoing research, and why we advocate having convergent evidence before teachers are asked to put their intellectual as well as material resources into major changes in daily classroom practice.

HOW MIGHT THIS APPROACH TO
• • • RESEARCH PLAY OUT IN THE CLASSROOM? • • •

Mr. Wells had a research-based theory of what good readers do that guided his reading instruction in his third-grade classroom. He also knew about research that supported specific strategies for improving comprehension. He used a variety of questioning strategies with his students, including having them develop their own questions using a question classification system of *right there, you and the author,* and *on your own* (Raphael, 1982). In the teacher inquiry group at Mr. Wells's school, the group decided to read and discuss *Questioning the Author* (Beck, McKeown, Hamilton, & Kucan, 1997) This book gave Mr. Wells a new perspective on how to have students develop more purposeful, engaging, and thought-provoking questions. He realized that students not only needed to develop their own questions but also needed to do so with a purpose and in a way that encouraged broad, critical thinking. He revised his theory of good readers to include the ability to consider the author's stance and purposes and to engage deeply and critically with the meaning of the text.

REFERENCES

Alexander, P.A., & Fox, E. (2004). A historical perspective on reading research and practice. In R.B. Ruddell & N.J. Unrau (Eds.), *Theoretical models and processes of reading* (5th ed., pp. 33–68). Newark, DE: International Reading Association.

Beck, I.L., McKeown, M.G., Hamilton, R.I., & Kucan, L. (1997). *Questioning the author: An approach for enhancing student engagement with text.* Newark, DE: International Reading Association.

Bloom, D., & Green, J. (1984). Directions in the sociolinguistic study of reading. In P.D. Pearson (Ed.), *Handbook of reading research* (pp. 395–421). New York: Longman.

Einstein, A. (1926). *Quotes on theory.* Retrieved August 15, 2007, from http://thinkexist.com/quotes/with/keyword/theory/

Fletcher, J.M., & Francis, D.J. (2004). Scientifically based educational research: Questions, designs, and methods. In P. McCardle & V. Chhabra (Eds.), *The voice of evidence in reading research* (pp. 59–80). Baltimore: Paul H. Brookes Publishing Co.

Forman, E.A., & Cazden, C.B. (2004). Exploring Vygotskian perspectives in education: The cognitive value of peer interaction. In R.B. Ruddell & N.J. Unrau (Eds.), *Theoretical models and processes of reading* (5th ed., pp. 163–186). Newark, DE: International Reading Association.

Kamil, M.L. (2004). Vocabulary and comprehension instruction: Summary and implications of the National Reading Panel findings. In P. McCardle & V. Chhabra (Eds.), *The voice of evidence in reading research* (pp. 213–234). Baltimore: Paul H. Brookes Publishing Co.

Klingner, J.K., & Vaughn, S. (1999). Promoting reading comprehension, content learning, and English acquisition through collaborative strategic reading (CSR). *Reading Teacher, 52,* 738–747.

National Institute of Child Health and Human Development. (2000). *Report of the National Reading Panel. Teaching children to read: An evidence-based assessment of the scientific research literature on reading and its implications for reading instruction: Reports of the subgroups* (NIH Publication No. 00-4754). Washington, DC: U.S. Government Printing Office.

Ogle, D. (1986). KWL: A teaching model that develops active reading of expository text. *The Reading Teacher, 39,* 564–571.

Palincsar, A.S., & Brown, A.L. (1984). Reciprocal teaching of comprehension fostering and monitoring activities. *Cognition and Instruction, 1,* 117–175.

Raphael, T.E. (1982). Question–answer strategies for children. *Reading Teacher, 36,* 186–190.

Shanahan, T. (2002). What research says: The promises and limitations of applying research to reading education. In A.E. Farstrup & S.J. Samuels, *What research has to say about reading instruction* (pp. 8–24). Newark, DE: International Reading Association.

Shavelson, R.J., & Towne, L. (Eds.). (2002). *Scientific research in education.* Washington, DC: National Academies Press.

Vaughn, S., & Klingner, J.K. (1999). Teaching reading comprehension through collaborative strategic reading. *Intervention in School and Clinic, 34*(5), 284–292.

CHAPTER 4

Research Methods

"The design of a study does not make it scientific. A variety of legitimate scientific approaches exist in education research. Designs and methods must be carefully selected and implemented to best address the questions at hand."

(R.J. Shavelson & L. Towne, 2002, pp. 97–98)

KEY CONCEPTS

- The design and methods used in research studies are determined by the nature of the questions being asked.

- Descriptive research describes what is happening and can use a variety of methods.

- Questions about change over time, such as studies of growth or development, require longitudinal methods with measurement at multiple time points.

- A combination of both experimental and qualitative methods is often the optimal approach to fully addressing complex research questions.

"Ms. Belfield, why does the moon change its shape?" Martin was an inquisitive young boy with lots of questions for his teacher, and this was a question that his teacher had heard many times before. But Martin was at an age where simple answers were not sufficient. He wanted the full, detailed explanation, and Ms. Belfield was ready with an answer. She began by discussing how the moon reflects the light of the sun and how the position of the earth and the moon in their orbits can cause the shadow and light pattern to make the moon seem as if it is a different shape at different times of the month. She also described how scientists learned about the phases of the moon from observation and research. She knew that supplying an answer was not nearly as powerful as helping students find the origin of the answer. Therefore, she planned two kinds of lessons. One lesson focused on how to use the library resources to find information on specific topics to help her students find answers to their questions. The other lesson addressed the scientific method, to help her students understand how scientists develop theories and then do research to find out if their theories are right or not. She helped them draw some inferences from observations of the moon with basic information about the sun, the moon, and the earth, and then acted these out with a light, moving the "moon" and "earth" (balls of relative sizes) through space to block the light.

Teachers deal with this type of question frequently from students who are thirsting for knowledge and information. When students ask questions, teachers give them the best, most comprehensive answers they can. But by helping students learn how and where to find answers, teachers give their students lifelong skills necessary along the road of learning. When teachers ask questions about curricula or programs, they, too, deserve a comprehensive, thorough answer and some guidance in how to figure out for themselves what the answers are, including whether those curricula or programs can deliver what the teacher wants to accomplish with students and how effective they might be. In order to provide, find, and fully understand those answers, teachers need to know how to identify reliable information that is supported by data and scientific evidence, and they should have the knowledge base to evaluate that evidence so that they can independently evaluate what they are told and what they have read about research evidence. They know that their students deserve the most accurate information available, and it is the teacher's responsibility to give that information. It is equally important for the research community to do the same for teachers.

This chapter will not reveal all that you need to know about research methods. What it will do is help you understand how research is designed and why certain designs and methods are chosen over others. Our goal is to offer an overview of the wide variety of methods that are used to answer different types of questions about education, as well as how research designs and methods are chosen to answer those questions. Comprehensive coverage of research methods would take several books on its own, rather than a single chapter, and many such books have been written. In the Recommended Reading section at the end of this chapter, we provide some key references for further in-depth information about any of the types of research methods we touch on in this chapter. But, as indicated in the quote that opens this chapter, the most important thing about research methods is that they fit the questions being asked. Research designs and methods can be regarded as tools—many tools look alike, but the right tool enables a person to do a job right!

This chapter provides some of the tools necessary for teachers to make solid decisions about new practices they are considering implementing in the classroom or to enhance practices already in place by better implementing them. Clearly these decisions will require energy and dedication on the part of each teacher, resource allocation within the school, and will impact students for years to come.

How Is Research on Reading and Reading Disabilities Designed and Conducted, and Why?

In evaluating information used in education, particularly in classrooms, even researchers may dispute what is considered to be good research. As Fletcher and Francis (2004) noted in *The Voice of Evidence in Reading Research,* there has been a false dichotomy drawn in discussions of education research, with quantitative research being touted as real science and qualitative studies as nonscientific. Fletcher and Francis made it clear that while it is important to understand the various types of research methods and approaches, no one design, method, or approach is more scientific than any other. In their words,

The principles of scientific inquiry are universal and can be found in all areas of human inquiry. The single most important part of scientific research is the question that leads to the investigation. Methods alone do not make a particular study scientific....The key to strong inference in any research is the design, not the method of observation. Depending on the nature of the underlying question, one approach to inquiry may lend itself to stronger inferences than another….It all starts with the question to be investigated, which leads to the methods of observation and design and a set of reasoned inferences. (Fletcher & Francis, 2004, p. 60)

The major principle for all research is that the design and methods are selected based on the types of questions posed. That is, research methods follow purpose, and the purpose of research is indicated by the type of question that is being addressed. Shavelson and Towne (2002) also noted that "a great number of education research questions fall into three [interrelated] types: Description—what is happening? Cause—is there a systematic effect? And process or mechanism—why or how is it happening?" (p. 99). We use these three major categories of questions to organize our discussion. The next section presents examples of the types of questions that a teacher might be interested in, and then discusses what methods could be used to answer each question.

Description—What Is Happening?

Studies that answer the question of what is happening are descriptive—they literally seek to describe what is happening. Such studies can document trends and issues, provide rich descriptions, and reveal relationships between variables. Here are some examples of the types of questions that represent this type of educational research and some types of research that are used to address those questions.

What Is the National Status of Reading in Grades 4, 8, and 12 in Any Given Year?

To answer this question, a national study is done periodically. That study is one most teachers recognize—the National Assessment of Educational Progress (NAEP). The NAEP is a large, cross-sectional study conducted to obtain a snapshot in time of how U.S. students are functioning. It is the only nationally representative and continuing assessment of what America's students know and can do in various subject areas. Assessments are conducted periodically in mathematics, reading, science, writing, the arts, civics, geography, and U.S. history. There are actually three different NAEPs: the main NAEP, the long-term trend NAEP, and the high school transcript study. We are speaking here of the main NAEP, which provides national and state data on groups of students at one point in time.

The NAEP is an example of descriptive research. The data collected are meant to describe the nation's students' overall performance in the areas assessed. The data can report information about students by state as well as nationally, but the main NAEP cannot indicate whether specific students have made progress from year to year or from Grade 4 to Grade 8. Rather, it reveals whether a higher percentage of fourth-grade students in a state are reading at the proficient or advanced level over time. That is, a study like NAEP cannot be used to study student growth over time.

What the NAEP can do, and was designed to do, is offer a good picture of how students in schools are performing nationally in the subject areas that are studied. It serves as an indicator of the nation's educational well-being, just as a major sampling of blood pressure of adults age 30 to 60 would provide an indicator of the overall cardio-vascular health of the nation's adults without revealing anything about an individual's health status. Not every student takes part in the NAEP assessment, since the goal is a national picture rather than individual data about specific children. The large number of students who take the NAEP are selected to be nationally representative, so that the results can be taken to represent a general picture. If only a few students were assessed, and those students were selected from only one school or state, it would not be possible to generalize and say they represented the entire country because they might all be from one racial or ethnic group, or from one socioeconomic level, or from the best or poorest performing school in a district. One thing to look for in research studies, therefore, is how the sample of students studied is selected; the NAEP uses a randomly selected sample, so each student has an equal likelihood of being assessed. While few studies are as large as the NAEP, it is important with any study to know whether the students who were studied are similar to the students in the classroom where the teacher will be working.

The NAEP also studies teachers, using a survey of their training, their professional experience, and the instructional methods they use. This allows an analysis of the relationship between teacher characteristics and student performance. The National Center for Education Statistics (NCES), the group responsible for the NAEP and its data, reported that eighth graders whose teachers had majored in mathematics or math education in college scored higher than students whose teachers had not majored in these areas (NCES, 2000). This does not mean that the teachers' training in math necessarily caused the students' higher math scores. It simply means the two facts are associated and that they co-occur. There could be other explanations.

Shavelson and Towne (2002) discussed the example of a comparison of Catholic and public schools in mathematics. For example, in 1993, Bryk, Lee, and Holland studied Catholic and public schools and found that students in Catholic schools had higher average math achievement than those in public schools. They did not jump to the conclusion that Catholic schools were better at teaching math, since again the research only showed an association or relation between the two facts—better math scores and attendance in Catholic schools. Other hypotheses that could also explain how these two things coincided had to be explored in order to learn why these two facts co-occurred.

What Is Qualitative Research and How Can It Improve Instruction?

Qualitative research can also address what is happening. It is a method of research in the behavioral and social sciences that involves seeking an in-depth understanding of human behavior and the reasons underlying it. Generally, qualitative research uses smaller, more focused samples than does quantitative research and involves collecting, analyzing, and interpreting data based on observations of what people do and say. This type of research is context based (i.e., it takes into consideration unique aspects of the environment and individuals rather than trying to control them as in experimental research). Case studies and ethnographies are examples of specific types of qualitative research. Ethnographies are useful for documenting contexts within which behavior occurs or events happen, and case studies provide careful descriptions of behaviors and changes in behavior to help researchers understand why they may be occurring. In addition, these and other types of qualitative studies can generate hypotheses about what is causing changes, and these hypotheses can then be tested by more quantitative methods

Qualitative researchers use various methods to directly gather information about subjects, including observations and interviews. Probably the most familiar methods are ethnographies and case studies, but other types of descriptive research also come under the category of qualitative research. Qualitative research is an important and necessary part of the cycle of developing theories, testing them, understanding their context, and evaluating the results that will influence reading instruction.

The research design of qualitative studies, like all research, involves a focus and a purpose of the study. Methods of collection include interviewing, observing, conducting focus groups, and reviewing artifacts (e.g., student work, teacher logs), documents (e.g., policy statements, classroom guidelines), and records (e.g., grades, teacher notes). A qualitative research design places researchers in the empirical world and connects them to specific people, groups, and/or relevant documents (Denzin & Lincoln, 2000). The most important feature of the design is that the setting itself is not altered; the researcher adapts to the situation. Data is gathered in natural settings without manipulating the research context. Researchers will often gather data from multiple sources, using multiple approaches or methods of data collection, in order to establish the validity of their findings. As mentioned in Chapter 3, this approach is called *triangulation*. While any type of research can use triangulation, it is common in qualitative studies. Triangulation must be planned for, that is, it must be part of the research design, since the design lays out the plan for data collection and analysis.

In some studies, the data gathered by observations is quantified (organized and reported in some numeric fashion) by looking for patterns or using a checklist for observations, developed based on patterns noted in previous observations. The data from other types of data-gathering activities, such as surveys, interviews, and questionnaires, is also quantified, and that numerical data is analyzed along with other data on student achievement, to indicate the degree to which certain factors are linked to reading achievement.

The research on schoolwide reading improvement provides an example. Taylor, Pearson, Peterson, and Rodriquez (2005) studied the effectiveness of an overall school change program and the specific classroom factors that contributed to improving student achievement in schools with high poverty student populations. They used interviews, observations, and artifacts of school improvement efforts, and analyzed their relation to scores on assessments of reading fluency, comprehension, and writing. Studies like this consume considerable time and resources but offer useful insights into a complex phenomenon—changing a school's way of operating at multiple levels to improve student achievement.

Teachers can often find useful instructional ideas in case study and descriptive research. For example, a teacher might read the description of students' work and responses in using learning logs in a social studies class and decide to try out the strategy in her own class. The descriptive research could provide information on how students might be expected to respond, how to introduce the strategy, and how to support students. This descriptive research is frequently absent in experimental studies that describe a treatment but often do not have enough information to allow teachers to actually replicate it in their classrooms.

There is a great deal of qualitative research on using portfolios in classrooms. Again, that research can be very useful to a teacher looking for what to include, how to conference with students, what tools can be used by both teachers and students to evaluate the portfolios, and ways to communicate portfolio assessment information to parents.

What Skills in the Early Grades Predict Reading Abilities in Later Elementary Grades?

To answer this question of how what is happening at one point in a student's education relates to what is happening at an earlier or later point in time, researchers use longitudinal research. The answer to this question actually changes with time and growth, which demonstrates two points: 1) the value of following children over time as they grow, and 2) the fact that an answer to a question for children at one stage of development, which may well be a valid answer, may not be the same answer researchers find for older children. While longitudinal data can indicate a great many things about growth and change over time, in this example we are focused only on using the data to predict from one point to another.

Wagner and colleagues (Wagner et al., 1997) conducted a longitudinal study in which they measured several indicators of early reading and investigated what measures could be used to predict later reading performance. They found that phonemic awareness (PA) in kindergarten contributed to word reading in second grade, but that this same measure in first and second grade contributed far less to being able to predict how well students could read words in third and fourth grades, respectively. They concluded that PA measures in the primary grades do contribute to predicting later word reading. This conclusion was later refined by Torgesen (1999) to indicate that the limited amount of information gained from the assessment of PA beyond second grade may not warrant the use of a PA assessment as a useful predictive measure. (Note that this does not rule out using such a measure for individual students when it may be clinically indicated.)

Following up on this study, Catts, Fey, Zhang, and Tomblin (2001) found that a kindergarten measure of PA was one of five factors that predicted the presence of a reading disability in second grade. Hogan, Catts, and Little (2005) reported a subsequent investigation to determine whether an assessment of phonemic awareness was useful in addition to a measure of letter identification in the early grades (i.e., kindergarten and second grade) in predicting subsequent word reading ability (i.e., in second and fourth grades). Hogan and colleagues used information on a subsample of a larger longitudinal study of language impairment in over 7,000 elementary school children (Tomblin, 1995). (Note other recent publications resulting from the parent longitudinal study: Tomblin et al., 1997; Tomblin, Zhang, Buckwalter, & O'Brien, 2003.) Hogan et al. studied 507 of these children, who were followed through the fourth grade. (They statistically controlled for the fact that this sample included larger percentages of students with language and nonverbal impairments than found in the original epidemiological sample of more than 7,000 students from which the longitudinal sample had been drawn.)

Hogan et al. (2005) found that the kindergarten PA measure, in addition to letter identification, was helpful for predicting second-grade word reading ability, but that this was not true in attempting to predict from second to fourth grade since it added nothing to what could be predicted from second-grade measures of word reading and phonetic decoding. They found that for second to fourth grade the relationship was reversed; that is, second-grade word reading actually predicted fourth-grade PA. Based on their own findings and that of earlier work indicating the value of kindergarten measures of PA (e.g., Ehri et al., 2001), Hogan and colleagues recommended that PA measures be included by speech-language pathologists and others when assessing kindergarten reading or prereading skills.

However, given their results for making predictions from second to fourth grade, specifically that the measure of PA in second grade adds little to the ability to predict reading ability in fourth grade, Hogan et al. (2005) recommended that a measure of word reading should instead be used in predicting future reading outcomes for second graders. They did find that a measure of phonetic decoding added unique information for second graders, and therefore also recommended its use in assessing second graders. They also clearly indicated that while it is not useful in predicting later reading outcomes for all second-grade students, PA information may provide useful information in determining intervention goals and assessment progress for students receiving intervention in second grade or even later.

Another example of predicting reading abilities is a longitudinal study of Spanish-speaking English language learners (ELLs) conducted by Lindsey and Manis (Lindsey & Manis, 2005; Lindsey, Manis, & Bailey, 2003). They followed a group of over 300 children, who began kindergarten with little or no knowledge of English, in an early-exit bilingual program in a Texas border town. These students were initially taught to read in Spanish; gradual transition to English began in the middle of first grade. Reporting on 6 years of data collection, Lindsey and Manis (2005) explained the multiple measures in both Spanish and English that were administered at the beginning and end of each school year to these students. They used this longitudinal data and sophisticated statistical analyses to determine which measures at early ages (beginning or end of kindergarten or first grade) could help predict how well students would perform on various measures of reading by third or fifth grade. They felt that knowing this could help predict which students are at risk for possible reading difficulties. Studies to develop and test preventive interventions for ELLs could then build on this information.

What Lindsey and Manis (2005) found was that the predictions varied depending on the outcome measures used and the language of assessment, Spanish or English. Using Spanish measures at the end of kindergarten, they were able to predict with over 95% accuracy how well a student would be able to read words in third grade, but prediction of passage comprehension was not as good. These same measures were less useful (although still better than 50%) in predicting reading skills in fifth grade. Since what they were seeking to predict was ability in reading English, they began to also measure early skills in English at the end of first grade, when students had exposure to English. They found that they could predict third grade English letter–word identification well at 91% and passage comprehension at over 80%; for fifth grade, the overall prediction rate was over 80% for both word reading and passage comprehension. Overall, they found that the best predictors in Spanish at the beginning of kindergarten were Spanish letter–word identification and Spanish memory for sentences. The English measures at the end of first grade that were most useful for predicting third and fifth grade English reading ability for Spanish-speaking ELLs were letter–word identification, word attack, rapid automatized naming (RAN), and memory for sentences.

As seen from these examples, one use of longitudinal research can be to determine what skills at one age might be useful in predicting ability at a later age. Identifying this information can help researchers predict which students might benefit from early prevention efforts, possibly avoiding later reading problems. This sampling of studies also illustrates the ability to compare changes with time and the growth that naturally occurs over time with the growth that results from instruction. This highlights the value of following children over time as they grow, and the need to study many different groups of children, including monolingual English students, ELLs with and without learning and/or language difficulties, and students from different socioeconomic and cultural backgrounds. It also underscores the importance for teachers to have research on students representative of the students in their classroom to best guide instruction for those students.

Cause—Is There a Systematic Effect?

Research examining cause and effect builds from those hypotheses that are generated by theories and descriptive research. Research that seeks to demonstrate one event or factor (A) caused something else (event or factor B) is usually built on previous research that has shown that there is a relationship (e.g., correlational studies) and that event or factor

A occurs or usually occurs before or in the same situation as event or factor B and thus could plausibly cause event or factor B. Hypotheses will have thus been built from the prior descriptive research (whether large, correlational studies or perhaps a cluster of case studies or ethnographies) and usually require experimental or quasi-experimental design. Experimental and quasi-experimental studies seek to test a hypothesis and are used to show cause and effect, to answer questions, such as "Does it work?" or "Is this method/approach effective?" Using multiple qualitative methods can be very helpful in eliminating possible explanations of why something has happened and thus narrowing down the focus of what may be causing a certain event or relationship to occur. As Shavelson and Towne said, "In education, research that explores students' and teachers' in-depth experiences, observes their actions, and documents the constraints that affect their day-to-day activities provides a key source of generating plausible hypotheses" (2002, p. 109). The section that follows presents some typical questions that might be or have been posed by researchers, with a discussion of research that can be used to address these questions.

What's the Difference Between the Behaviors of Good and Poor Readers?

As researchers sought to improve reading achievement, they wanted to know what the differences were between what good readers did and what poor readers did. They designed studies to explore this using read-alouds (Paris & Myers, 1981), think-alouds, interviews, and analyses of summaries of reading (Brown & Day, 1983). They found that one of several ways that more accomplished readers differ from less accomplished readers is that the better readers monitor their comprehension, noticing when what they are reading does not make sense, and applying strategies (e.g., rereading) to fix their understanding (Duke & Pearson, 2002). Researchers built on this descriptive research to develop ways to teach and improve comprehension monitoring and conducted experimental or quasi-experimental studies to test the efficacy of the instructional strategies. The strategy of *reciprocal teaching* (see Chapter 9 on reading comprehension for more information) was developed and studied as a result of this line of inquiry.

What Is the Effectiveness of Multiple Tiers of Intervention on Reading and Behavior Outcomes?

Several research projects began in 2002 to study the implementation of a *tiered approach* to prevention of and intervention for reading problems.

(A tiered approach is explained in more detail in Chapter 15.) It is essentially an approach in which there are tiers, or levels, of increased intensity of instruction or intervention. One of these projects at the University of Texas, Austin, used a longitudinal design with treatment and control groups at each of the three tiers (Vaughn & Chard, 2006). For the primary tier, there was a treatment and a historical control condition; for the second and third tiers, an experimental design was used with random assignment of students to treatment or comparison conditions. Students were assessed at multiple time points and were followed from grade to grade. Teachers were given professional development appropriate for key reading instruction at the grade level they were teaching. While this study is still in progress, initial findings are that the primary intervention (prevention) is effective; students demonstrated greater reading growth than the historical control group students. The secondary intervention for at-risk students was also effective, in that all but 5% improved their reading abilities sufficiently to exit the secondary intervention and return to the primary instruction.

This study (Vaughn & Chard, 2006) combines longitudinal and experimental designs and addresses whether a tiered reading intervention approach is effective in preventing reading difficulties. Because it uses randomization, it is considered a *true experiment*. While there are various ways to demonstrate effectiveness, it is best and most clearly demonstrated through true experiments, generally considered to be the gold standard of research for this purpose.

As illustrated previously, experimental studies are designed to compare two or more groups, one of whom undergoes some experimental manipulation or treatment while the other serves as a control or comparison group that does not receive the manipulation or treatment. The units under study are randomly assigned to either the treatment group or the control group. Randomized, controlled trials are common in medical research, but whether there is a no-treatment control or a "treatment as usual" comparison group depends on whether it would be ethical and safe to allow one group to have no treatment. For instance, if a cancer patient is to receive a new experimental drug, the comparison would be the most effective drug commonly used to treat such patients; it would be unethical not to treat a patient if there is a standard treatment that works at least in part even for some individuals, yet researchers definitely need to test new drugs that might work better. Similarly, for reading instruction, there would not be a no-treatment control as this would mean not delivering reading instruction at all, a ridiculous idea that no one would even suggest. In addition, in such an imaginary study, if there were a difference between the groups, researchers would not know whether it was simply the fact of receiving any instruction at all that made the difference or whether there were some elements of the new instructional approach or program that made the difference. In such cases, where it is not possible to have a true control group, comparison groups are used instead, as they are in the study described previously.

When randomization is not used to assign students to treatment or control groups, the study is considered to be quasi-experimental rather than a true experiment. It is not always feasible to randomly assign individuals to groups, especially in schools, even when treatments are ostensibly equal. Parents may not consent to having their students randomly assigned to a classroom, for example, or schools may have other factors guiding their class assignments and find randomization disruptive. Therefore, sometimes quasi-experimental methods are used to compare groups that exist naturally. The researchers must then find other ways of ensuring fair comparisons, such as statistical techniques. The major weakness of quasi-experimental studies is the potential selectivity bias, that is, the possibility that something inherent in the groups is responsible for the changes observed rather than the treatment being studied. However, with careful design and implementation, quasi-experimental studies can provide valuable information. The causal inferences are not as strong as true experiments, but they do offer some evidence, and when multiple quasi-experimental studies result in similar findings, confidence grows that the findings are credible.

In some of the studies reported in the NRP report (NICHD, 2000), students were not randomly assigned to instructional groups. Instead, when (quasi-) experiments were done to test the effectiveness of explicit phonics instruction, they were compared to reading instruction that did not include phonics instruction and to programs that taught some phonics but did so only incidentally, rather than explicitly and in a systematic way. That way, the outcomes would tell them not only whether having phonics instruction was helpful but also whether it was the explicitness of the delivery of instruction that made the difference. The compilation of multiple studies in the meta-analysis that was done and reported by the NRP showed a convergence of evidence across studies.

How Is Reading Prosody Related to Decoding and Reading Comprehension Skills?

Schwanenflugel, Hamilton, Kuhn, Wisenbaker, and Stahl (2004) conducted a study of the role of prosody in fluency to determine what role it plays in decoding and reading comprehension. *Prosody* is the intonation and stress patterns of language or the "music" of speech. It is what makes reading sound natural and conversational when people read aloud. Schwanenflugel and her colleagues statistically compared two versions of how general decoding speed, comprehension, and prosody might relate using structural equation modeling. One model was a much better fit; that is, it explained the data better. Model 1 showed that children with faster decoding are more likely to read prosodically but suggests that prosody plays only a minor role in skilled reading comprehension. They concluded from this that decoding speed is the major factor in both prosodic reading and improved reading comprehension. The authors of this study stated that their findings

> Could be used productively…to suggest that, when children are reading prosodically, one can probably infer that they are well on their way to having automatic and fluent word decoding skills, and our instructional efforts can be placed elsewhere. (p. 128)

Correlational research like that of Schwanenflugel and colleagues (2004) can help researchers and educators understand patterns of how different aspects of a complex skill are related, as noted earlier in the section that discusses the "What's Happening" questions. Yet, it can be used to at least approach issues of what causes what, in some circumstances. Shavelson and Towne indicated that "when correlational methods use what are called 'model-fitting' techniques based on a theoretically generated system of variables, they permit stronger, albeit still tentative, causal inferences" (Shavelson & Towne, 2002, pp. 114–115). As researchers are able to empirically reject competing theoretical models, they gain increased confidence in the explanatory power of the remaining models. As we discussed previously, theories are never really proven to be true; rather they are confirmed or disconfirmed. So it is with model fitting; researchers can refine models to be better and better fits, but there is rarely, if ever, one right model.

What Impact Does Teachers' Use of Time Have on Students' Learning?

As part of a large research project studying 1,400 ELLs, Foorman and colleagues needed to be able to measure how instructional time was spent in the classroom (Foorman, Goldenberg, Carlson, Saunders, & Pollard-Durodola, 2004). They indicated that their examination of the literature revealed that typical reading instruction does not provide sufficient periods of instructional engagement for many students to really progress in reading (Gelzheizer & Meyers, 1991; O'Sullivan, Ysseldyke, Christensen, & Thurlow, 1990; Simmons, Fuchs, Fuchs, Mathes, & Hodges, 1995; Vaughn, Hughes, Schumm, & Klingner, 1998). Two studies (Allington & McGill-Frantzen, 1989; Simmons et al., 1995) they reviewed indicated that approximately two thirds of students' time was spent in teacher-independent reading activities, nonreading activities, or indirect reading activities, and that they were passively listening and watching during 70% of the time the teacher was providing instruction. O'Sullivan et al. (1990) found that the students most at risk were the ones with the least engaged reading opportunities. Similarly, Arreaga-Mayer and Perdomo-Rivera (1996) reported observations of 24 ELLs in six schools during a school year; the most frequently coded student behavior was no talking (in over 90% of instances in both general education classrooms and classrooms with English as a second language) and no use of oral or written language (nearly 80% in both situations). Thus, Foorman and colleagues developed a means of measuring the language and literacy content of instruction. They described the development of their time-sampling system. They were able to document which languages (Spanish or English) were used and to what extent, by both students and teachers, in different instructional programs in the schools under study. They then used this system to investigate whether students would benefit from having English language development (ELD) as a separate block of instruction or integrated with reading and language arts instruction (Saunders, Foorman, & Carlson, 2006). They studied 1,237 kindergarten students in 85 classrooms in 35 schools, assessing them in both Spanish and English in reading outcomes. Using the teacher classroom observation instrument, they documented the extent to which teachers used a separate ELD block, the language, and the instructional content during that block. Their design therefore was a cross-sectional, 2×2 comparison: bilingual or immersion kindergarten program crossed with ELD instruction block or no ELD block. They found no differences between the bilingual and the English immersion classes. However, what they did find was that students in classrooms where teachers used separate ELD blocks outperformed those whose teachers did not use ELD blocks; ELD block students scored higher in English oral language, word identification, and letter–sound correspondences. The teachers using ELD blocks spent more time on actual instruction, using their time more effectively.

In addition, Saunders et al. (2006) found that there was little variation in the instruction, regardless of type of program, whether or not ELD blocks were used, and regardless of language of instruction. Most of the time (over 90%) was spent in discussion or on listening comprehension. Only 6% of instructional time was spent on target vocabulary, language structure, or strategies. These authors concluded that if teachers are to help ELL students improve their academic language abilities, then teachers must focus on teaching targeted vocabulary and the structure of language (syntax, semantics, and phonology).

How Can Studies of This Type
Help Teachers in the Classroom?

Teachers can use information about these types of studies to make decisions about how to spend instructional time, choosing strategies and activities that research has connected to improving students' reading. They can also decide what strategies might work best for which students. For example, if a teacher notices that some students are not really paying attention to whether they understand what they read, then he or she can plan instruction to help students monitor their understanding and apply strategies to fix comprehension when it fails. In addition, teachers may want to consider their own time use during reading and language arts instructional periods, and they may want to think about how much time students spend actively engaged in the class activities.

Process or Mechanism—
Why or How Is It Happening?

Knowing what causes an outcome is not always enough. Once researchers know what causes an outcome, they also want to know how this causation happens, for which students, and under what circumstances. This is how teachers can know whether it will work for them and their students in their classrooms.

Do Family, Friendship, Community,
and Cultural Connections Motivate
Adolescent Students to Develop Reading
and Writing Skills, and How Does This Happen?

This is a complex set of questions. Thus, as might be expected, the research addressing these questions will require a complex approach. Eccles, Wigfield, and Schiefele (1997) used longitudinal data on students and the choices they made in school and out of school. They wanted to test the hypothesis that participation in a specific activity is influenced by values and expectations associated both with that activity and other activities, and that students will choose the activity with greater value to them. Thus, if activities not associated with school have higher value to a student than school activities, those more highly valued outside activities can divert student energy and attention away from academic activities. Eccles and colleagues (Eccles, Roeser, Vida, Fredricks, & Wigfield, 2006; Eccles & Roeser, 2005) examined adolescent motivation, expectancy value, and development in and across different social and cultural contexts and were able to confirm their theory. Moje and colleagues (McCarthy & Moje, 2002; Moje, 2000; Moje, Willes, & Fassio, 2001) have extended this work to adolescent Latino students' learning and literacy practices both in and out of school. They noted that students who seemed indifferent to literacy activities in school were able to rapidly learn and use complicated gang writing styles, rules, spellings, and dress codes. This contradiction led them to pose questions about why this occurred.

While Eccles and colleagues (2005, 2006) conducted longitudinal studies to examine the correlations among variables and test the relationships among them with sophisticated modeling statistics, Moje et al. (2004) chose both to use the longitudinal data and to examine in depth the activities of individual students using ethnographic methods. In her ethnographic work, Moje learned about the in- and out-of-school activities and choices of activity that these students engaged in. She and her colleagues (Moje et al., 2004) learned what kinds of texts motivated their small sample of 35 Latino students. To better understand the linguistic and structural complexity of the types of texts these students were reading as well as to determine whether the behavior of these students was seen more broadly, she launched a new study. In this next phase of her research, building on her earlier findings, she wanted to understand adolescent literacy development in depth across all levels, from basic processing to higher level, critical reading and writing, and the social, cognitive, and cultural mediation of those skills, and to examine whether the expectancy value model applied to what she had observed ethnographically.

Thus, Moje et al. (2004) proposed what is often called *mixed methods*; the question with which we began this discussion is being examined by Moje and colleagues using analyses of survey and interview data (both from existing data sets and new data collected by her research team), longitudinal data, and experimental examination of how well skills transferred from out-of-school literacy activities to in-school academic literacy tasks. They also collected structured and in-depth qualitative interviews and descriptive observations of students. With these data, Moje and her colleagues are answering both "What's Happening" and "How and Why" questions, using a combination of research methods (Moje, 2004; Moje, Overby, Tysvaer, & Morris, 2007; Moje & Speyer, 2008). One conclusion from this project is that many students often characterized as having weak literacy skills are capable readers and writers in contexts other than school:

> [Many students] are capable readers and writers in contexts that value their skills and allow them to draw on other text forms to mediate their

reading and writing with print. However,…even as researchers seek ways to reshape the contexts and make texts more approachable, we must also develop interventions … that can support teachers in scaffolding adolescent students' reading of the demanding texts of the content areas. (Moje, 2006, p. 14)

As a final note on mixed methods research, it is not without its challenges. Moje (personal communication, September 23, 2007) stated that it is important to acknowledge the problem and potential of coming up with divergent representations via the different data sources or methods. For example, Moje found youth reporting one practice on the surveys but then doing something different when the researchers observed them (e.g., saying that race doesn't matter in what they choose to read but then consistently selecting texts that reflect their own racial identities across several dimensions). This is a powerful aspect of mixed methods, because it demonstrates that what those who are being studied think about a particular construct and their practice of it are not necessarily aligned (which can be explained by cognitive development, social desirability, lack of awareness of what race means, and a lack of understanding of the questions). Mixed methods design can allow for an analysis of method, which can contribute to greater confidence in the findings, although they may need to be presented with more caveats or qualifications at times.

How Can Studies of This Type Help Teachers in the Classroom?

Studies that address the how and why of learning can help teachers build an understanding and a personal, professional theory of what readers need to be able to do, what helps them acquire the requisite skills and attitudes, what causes them to have problems, and how to fix those problems. For example, if a teacher notices students having difficulties understanding a particular chapter in a history text, the teacher might consider whether the students have enough background knowledge and conceptual development related to the ideas in the text to fully understand the material. He can consult research on how students learn conceptual information and choose some strategies that will help students build the knowledge base they need to understand their textbooks. In addition, he might want to teach targeted vocabulary prior to each chapter to help students become more familiar with concepts they will encounter in the text, and then have them write summaries of the information using those vocabulary words to be sure they fully understand both the concepts and how to use the words.

• • • **HOW MIGHT THIS PLAY OUT IN THE CLASSROOM?** • • •

Ms. Reese was reading a case study of two students whose main language was not English. She was very interested in the description of how their teacher worked with them to develop both language and literacy skills. Ms. Reese had three such students in her own class. First, the study gave her insights into some of the possible causes of her students' problems. It also gave her ideas about how she might adapt her instruction. Some of the ideas worked well. This spurred her to look for more research about students like hers with similar problems, including related experimental research findings and instructional strategies to help her support her students' learning.

What Additional Resources Are There If I Want to Learn More About Research Methods?

As noted at the beginning of this chapter, we did not set out to give a comprehensive tutorial on research methods, but rather to illustrate the many types of research methods than can be used to address research questions, and to link them to the types of questions they can be used to address. There are volumes on research methods. Some volumes cover all types of research, and some volumes are specific to certain aspects of research. For example, we have cited Shavelson and Towne (2002) extensively and used their conceptualization of three types of research questions as a framework for this chapter. Some references by researchers who are often cited as leaders in research methods are cited in the Recommended Reading section that follows this chapter. For someone just beginning to delve into research methods, these may be difficult reading, and it may be more helpful to start with some introductory textbooks on research methods.

We end this chapter as we began it, with a quote from Shavelson and Towne (2002). The field of education research has long been caught in a sometimes heated debate about the relative value of different types of research, of what is scientific and what is not, and this debate often reduces itself to a seemingly simple quantitative–qualitative dichotomy. We have chosen not to invoke that dichotomy, but to embrace what the best methodologists and researchers we know will tell anyone who asks them—that what drives the choice of research method is the question being posed. There are many types of research methods, and these enable us to address many different questions and to investigate many sides of the same issues: "What is happening?"

"What causes it to happen?" and "How and why does it happen?" There is an ongoing need for more knowledge about the process of education. Shavelson and Towne said the following:

> Knowledge is generated through a sequence of interrelated descriptive and causal studies, through a constant process of refining theory and knowledge. These lines of inquiry typically require a range of methods and approaches to subject theories and conjectures to scrutiny from several perspectives. (Shavelson & Towne, 2002, p. 123)

RECOMMENDED READING

Cohen, L., Manion, L., & Morrison, K. (2007). *Research methods in education* (6th ed.). London: Routledge.

Cook, T.D., & Campbell, D.T. (1979). *Quasi-experimentation: Design and analysis issues for field settings.* Boston: Houghton Mifflin.

Cook, T., Cooper, H.M., Cordray, D., Hedges, L.V., Light, R.J., Louis, T., & Mosteller, F. (1991). *Meta-analysis for explanation.* New York: Russell Sage Foundation.

Cook, T.D., & Reichardt, C.S. (Eds.). (1979). *Qualitative and quantitative methods in evaluation.* Thousand Oaks, CA: Sage.

Cooper, H.M., & Hedges, L.V. (Eds.). (1994). *The handbook of research synthesis.* New York: Russell Sage Foundation.

Denzin, N.K., & Lincoln, Y.S. (Eds.). (2000). *Handbook of qualitative research* (2nd ed.). Thousand Oaks, CA: Sage.

Hedges, L.V., & Olkin, I. (1985). *Statistical methods for meta-analysis.* New York: Academic Press.

Hedges, L.V., Shymansky, J.A., & Woodworth, G. (1989). *A practical guide to modern methods of meta-analysis.* Washington, DC: National Science Teachers Association.

Raudenbush, S.W. (in press). Designing field trials of educational innovations. Proceedings from *Conceptualizing Scale-Up: Multidisciplinary Perspectives Conference.* Washington, DC: Data Research and Development Center.

Raudenbush, S.W., & Bryk, A.S. (2002). Hierarchical linear models (2nd ed.).Thousand Oaks, CA: Sage Publications.

Shadish, W.J., Cook, T.D., & Campbell, D.T. (2002). *Experimental and quasi-experimental designs for generalized causal inference.* Boston: Houghton Mifflin.

REFERENCES

Allington, R.L, & McGill-Frantzen, A. (1989). School response to reading failure: Instruction for Chapter One and special education students in Grades 2, 4, and 8. *Elementary School Journal, 89,* 529–542.

Arreaga-Mayer, C, & Perdomo-Rivera, C. (1996). Ecobehavioral analysis of instruction for at-risk language-minority students. *Elementary School Journal, 96,* 245–258.

Brown, A.L., & Day, J.D. (1983). Macrorules for summarizing text: The development of expertise. *Journal of Verbal Learning and Verbal Behavior, 22,* 1–14.

Bryk, A.S., Lee, V., & Holland, P. (1993). *Catholic schools and the common good.* Cambridge, MA: Harvard University Press.

Catts, H.W., Fey, M.E., Zhang, X., & Tomblin, J.B. (2001). Estimating the risk of future reading difficulties in kindergarten children: A research-based model and its clinical implementation. *Language, Speech, and Hearing Services in Schools, 32,* 38–50.

Cook, T.D., & Reichardt, C.S. (Eds.). (1979). *Qualitative and quantitative methods in evaluation.* Thousand Oaks, CA: Sage Publications.

Denzin, N.K., & Lincoln, Y.S. (Eds.). (2000). *Handbook of qualitative research* (2nd ed.). Thousand Oaks, CA: Sage Publications.

Duke, N.K., & Pearson, P.D. (2002). Effective practices for developing reading comprehension. In A.E. Farstrup & S.J. Samuels (Eds.), *What research has to say about reading instruction* (3rd ed., pp. 205–242). Newark, DE: International Reading Association.

Eccles, J., & Roeser, R. (2005). School and community influences on human development. In M.H. Bornstein & M.E. Lamb (Eds.), *Developmental science: An advanced textbook* (5th ed.). Mahwah, NJ: Lawrence Erlbaum Associates.

Eccles, J.S., Roeser, R., Vida, M., Fredricks, J., & Wigfield, A. (2006). Motivational and achievement pathways through middle childhood. In L. Balter & C.S. Tamis-LeMonda (Eds.), *Child psychology: A handbook of contemporary issues* (2nd ed., pp. 325–356). New York: Psychology Press.

Eccles, J.S., Wigfield, A., & Schiefele, U. (1997). Motivation. In N. Eisenberg (Ed.), *Handbook of child psychology* (5th ed., Vol. 3, pp. 1017–1095). New York: John Wiley & Sons.

Ehri, L.C., Nunes, S.R., Willows, D.M., Schuster, B.V., Yaghoub-Zadeh, Z., & Shanahan, T. (2001). Phonemic awareness instruction helps children learn to read: Evidence from the National Reading Panel's meta-analysis. *Reading Research Quarterly, 36,* 250–287.

Fletcher, J.M., & Francis, D.J. (2004). Scientifically based educational research: Questions, designs, and methods. In P. McCardle & V. Chhabra (Eds.), *The voice of evidence in reading research* (pp. 59–80). Baltimore: Paul H. Brookes Publishing Co.

Foorman, B.R., Goldenberg, C., Carlson, C.D., Saunders, W.M., & Pollard-Durodola, S.D. (2004). How teachers allocate time during literacy instruction in primary-grade English language learner classrooms. In P. McCardle & V. Chhabra (Eds.), *The voice of evidence in reading research* (pp. 289–328). Baltimore: Paul H. Brookes Publishing Co.

Gelzheizer, L.M., & Meyers, J. (1991). Reading instruction by classroom, remedial, and resource room teachers. *Journal of Special Education, 24,* 512–526.

Hedges, L.V., & Olkin, I. (1985). *Statistical methods for meta-analysis.* San Diego: Academic Press.

Hedges, L.V., Shymansky, J.A., & Woodworth, G. (1989). *A practical guide to modern methods of meta-analysis.* Washington, DC: National Science Teachers Association.

Hogan, T.P., Catts, H.W., & Little, T.D. (2005). The relationship between phonological awareness and reading: Implications for the assessment of phonological awareness. *Language, Speech, and Hearing Services in Schools, 36,* 285–293.

Lindsey, K.A., & Manis, F.R. (2005). Development of reading skills in Spanish speaking English language learners: A 6-year longitudinal study. *Perspectives in Language and Literacy, 31,* 22–26.

Lindsey, K.A., Manis, F.R., & Bailey, C. (2003). Prediction of first-grade readings in Spanish speaking English language learners. *Journal of Educational Psychology, 95,* 482–494.

McCarthey, S.J., & Moje, E.B. (2002). Identity matters. *Reading Research Quarterly, 37*(2), 228–237.

Moje, E.B. (2000). To be part of the story: The literacy practices of gangsta adolescents. *Teachers College Record, 102,* 652–690.

Moje, E.B. (2004). Powerful spaces: Tracing the out-of-school literacy spaces of Latino/a youth. In K. Leander & M. Sheehy (Eds.), *Space matters: Assertions of space in literacy practice and research* (pp. 15–38). New York: Peter Lang.

Moje, E.B. (2006). Motivating texts, motivating contexts, motivating adolescents: An examination of the role of motivation in adolescent literacy practices and development. *Perspectives, 32*(3), 10–14.

Moje, E.B., Overby, M., Tysvaer, N., & Morris, K. (2007). *The complex world of adolescent literacy: Myths, motivations, and mysteries.* Manuscript submitted for publication.

Moje, E.B., & Martinez, M. (2007). The role of peers, families, and ethnic-identity enactments in educational persistence and achievement of Latino and Latina youths. In A.J. Fuligni (Ed.), *Contesting stereotypes and creating identities* (pp. 209–238). New York: Russell Sage Foundation.

Moje, E.B., McIntosh-Ciechanowski, K., Kramer, K., Ellis, L., Carrillo, R., & Collazo, T. (2004). Working toward third space in content area literacy: An examination of everyday funds of knowledge and discourse. *Reading Research Quarterly, 39*(1), 38–71.

Moje, E.B., & Speyer, J. (2008). The reality of challenging texts in high school science and social studies: How teachers can mediate comprehension. In K. Hinchman & H. Thomas (Eds.), *Best practices in adolescent literacy instruction* (pp. 185–211). New York: Guilford Press.

Moje, E.B., Willes, D.J., & Fassio, K. (2001). Constructing and negotiating literacy in the writer's workshop: Literacy teaching and learning in seventh grade. In E.B. Moje & D.G. O'Brien (Eds.), *Constructions of literacy: Studies of teaching and learning literacy in and out of secondary classrooms* (pp. 193–212). Mahwah, NJ: Lawrence Erlbaum Associates.

National Center for Education Statistics. (2000). *National Assessment of Educational Progress*. Retrieved September 22, 2007, from http://nces.ed.gov/nationsreportcard/

O'Sullivan, P.J., Ysseldyke, J.E., Christensen, S.I., & Thurlow, M.L. (1990). Mildly handicapped elementary students' opportunity to learn during reading instruction in mainstream and special education settings. *Reading Research Quarterly, 25*, 131–146.

Paris, S.G., & Myers, M. (1981). Comprehension monitoring, memory, and study strategies of good and poor readers. *Journal of Reading Behavior, 13*, 5–22.

Raudenbush, S.W., & Bryk, A.S. (2002). *Hierarchical linear models* (2nd ed.). Thousand Oaks: Sage Publications.

Raudenbush, S.W. (in press). Designing field trials of educational innovations. Proceedings from *Conceptualizing scale-up: Multidisiciplinary perspectives conference*. Washington, DC: Data Research and Development Center.

Saunders, W.M., Foorman, B.R., & Carlson, C.D. (2006). Is a separate block of time for oral English language development in programs for English learners needed? *Elementary School Journal, 107*(2), 181–198.

Schwanenflugel, P., Hamilton, A.M., Kuhn, M.R., Wisenbaker, J.M., & Stahl, S.A. (2004). Becoming a fluent reader: Reading skill and prosodic features in the oral reading of young readers. *Journal of Educational Psychology, 96*(1), 119–129.

Shavelson, R.J., & Towne, L. (Eds.) (2002). *Scientific research in education*. Washington, DC: National Academies Press.

Simmons, D.C., Fuchs, L.S., Fuchs, D., Mathes, P.G., & Hodges, J.P. (1995). Effects of explicit teaching and peer mediated instruction on the reading achievement of learning disabled and low performing students. *Elementary School Journal, 95*, 387–408.

Taylor, B.M., Pearson, P.D., Peterson, D.S., & Rodriquez, M.C. (2005, January/February/March) The CIERA school change framework: An evidence-based approach to professional development and school reading improvement. *Reading Research Quarterly, 40*, 40–69.

Tomblin, J.B. (1995). *Midwest collaboration on specific language impairment*. Washington, DC: National Institute of Deafness and Other Communication Disorders.

Tomblin, J.B., Records, N., Buckwalter, P., Zhang, X., Smith, E., & O'Brien, M. (1997). Prevalence of specific language impairment in kindergarten children. *Journal of Speech, Language, and Hearing Research, 40*, 1245–1260.

Tomblin, J.B., Zhang, X., Buckwalter, P., & O'Brien, M. (2003). The stability of primary language disorder: Four years after kindergarten diagnosis. *Journal of Speech, Language, and Hearing Research, 46*, 1283–1296.

Torgesen, J.K. (1999). Assessment and instruction for phonemic awareness and word recognition skills. In H.W. Catts & A.G. Kamhi (Eds.), *Language and reading disabilities* (pp. 128–153). Needham Heights, MA: Allyn & Bacon.

Vaughn, S., & Chard, D. (2006). Three-tier intervention research studies: Descriptions of two related projects. *Perspectives, 33*, 29–34.

Vaughn, S., Hughes, M.T., Schumm, J.S., & Klingner, J. (1998). A collaborative effort to enhance reading and writing instruction in inclusive classrooms. *Learning Disability Quarterly, 21*, 57–74.

Wagner, R.K., Torgesen, J.K., Rashotte, C.A., Hecht, S.A., Barker, T.A., Burgess, S.R., et al. (1997). Changing relations between phonological processing abilities and word-level reading as children develop from beginning to skilled readers: A 5-year longitudinal study. *Developmental Psychology, 33*, 468–479.

CHAPTER 5

Summaries of Key Educational Research

KEY CONCEPTS

- There are several major reports on reading research that affect how reading is taught.

- Based on the findings of several major reports, the five major components of reading—phonemic awareness (PA), phonics, fluency, vocabulary, and reading comprehension—are effectively taught through explicit instruction.

- Several reports on educational research call for increased rigor and quality of research in order to provide information that can guide the most effective educational practices.

This chapter contains a listing of the key reports at a national level that have affected the move toward evidence-based practice in reading. A brief overview of the key information from these reports, including suggestions for how to access companion documents is provided (see Table 5.1 for key information about four major reports discussed in this chapter). The later chapters of this book rely heavily on some of these reports. The reports were developed by panels of experts, often at the request and direction of governments, in an effort to summarize what could be gleaned from the research literature to inform public policy on education. Those who wish to have more in-depth information about the specific findings and recommendations found in these reports, and how the panels arrived at their findings and recommendations, may want to read portions of the original reports. But the brief overviews that follow are offered for those with insufficient time to read the original reports.

These reports are available free as downloads on the Internet, or they can be read on the web, and links for the web sites are given for each report in the Online Resources section at the end of the chapter. We selected the panel reports for specific reasons. First, as reports of groups of individuals that brought to bear a variety of perspectives from within the research and practice communities, they clearly represent the views of multiple people and various organizations or associations by virtue of the multiple professional affiliations of the members of the group. In addition, they used specific criteria for selecting the research they included in these reports; thus, the reports were systematically done, which provides an important element of objectivity.

What Are Some of the Major National Reports that Deal with Reading Research?

From 1997 to 2007, there have been several major reports that have summarized, analyzed, and synthesized research in reading or education issues that included reading. These reports can be very informative and helpful in understanding the research that can and should guide practice in the classroom. These major reports include the *Preventing Reading Difficulties* in Young Children (PRD) report (Snow, Burns, & Griffin, 1998); the National Reading Panel (NRP) report (National Institute of Child Health and Human Development [NICHD], 2000); the RAND Corporation report on reading comprehension, titled *Reading for Understanding: Toward an R&D Program in Reading Comprehension* (Snow, 2002); and the Australian report, *Teaching*

Table 5.1. Key information about four major summary reports

Report document(s)	Date	Type	Producer	Sponsor(s)	Focus/ key question(s)	Companion document(s)
Preventing Reading Difficulties in Young Children (Snow, Burns, & Griffin, 1998)	1998	Research-based consensus	National Research Council, National Academies of Science and Engineering	U.S. Department of Education; U.S. Department of Health and Human Services	How does reading develop, and how can that development be promoted?	Yes
Report of the National Reading Panel: Teaching Children to Read: An Evidence-Based Assessment of the Scientific Research Literature on Reading and Its Implications for Reading Instruction: Reports of the Subgroups (National Institute of Child Health and Human Development [NICHD], 2000)	2000	Meta-analysis and synthesis	Widmeyer Communications and IQ Solutions	NICHD	What instructional methods are most effective in teaching children to read?	Yes
Reading for Understanding: Toward an R&D Program in Reading Comprehension (Snow, 2002)	2002	Research-based consensus	RAND Corporation	U.S. Department of Education	What do we know, and what should the future research focus be, regarding reading comprehension?	No
Teaching Reading: Report and Recommendations, National Inquiry into the Teaching of Literacy (Commonwealth of Australia, 2005)	2005	Research-based consensus	Commonwealth of Australia	Commonwealth of Australia	What are the optimal approaches to reading instruction and literacy development for the children of Australia?	No

Reading: Report and Recommendations, National Inquiry into the Teaching of Literacy (Commonwealth of Australia, 2005). There are other panel reports that are equally valuable: the National Early Literacy Panel (NELP) report that is currently in progress (n.d.), the National Literacy Panel for Language Minority Children and Youth (NLP; August & Shanahan, 2006), and the President's Commission on Excellence in Special Education (2002) report.

Why Are Each of These Major Reports Important to Teaching Reading?

These reports were all written by panels of experts, yet each one is unique and important to teaching reading. The PRD report (Snow et al., 1998) is a report by the National Research Council (NRC) of the National Academies of Science and Engineering. It is generally referred to as a consensus report. The panel of scientists, convened by the NRC, considered research and presentations by other experts in the field, and then they discussed the major issues and reached some general agreement about the research they had read or heard about and wrote a report. The PRD report generally addressed the issues of how best to prevent reading problems in children.

The report of the NRP (NICHD, 2000) is an evidence-based report that was commissioned by Congress to specifically address the question of which instructional approaches could best achieve what the PRD report (Snow et al., 1998) said was necessary to teach children to read. Since the question was one of effectiveness of instructional approaches, this panel developed a methodology with inclusion and exclusion criteria, and within their methodology they restricted the literature to be included to experimental and quasi-experimental studies. Using that methodology, they reviewed, analyzed, and synthesized relevant research studies. When it was possible, they conducted meta-analyses. Otherwise they simply wrote research syntheses.

Reading for Understanding: Toward an R&D Program in Reading Comprehension (Snow, 2002) was prepared by a study group of experts convened by the RAND Corporation at the behest of the U.S. Department of Education. The U.S. Department of Education asked RAND to examine how to improve the quality of educational research funded by the government. The study group was gathered to develop a research framework regarding the most important issues in literacy and to develop a research agenda. The report was considered timely and important because of the increasing demands for strong literacy skills in high school graduates, the increasingly poor performance of U.S.

students in reading in international comparisons, the achievement gaps between different demographic groups within the United States, and the fact that even with considerable funding for educational remediation and intervention, effects on student achievement were uncertain. The study group considered research and drafted a report, solicited review of that draft document by non–study group experts in reading comprehension, presented the draft at national meetings and solicited input via the Internet, and then revised the report based on these various sources of input. From that perspective it can be considered a consensus report rather than a systematic research synthesis. The report did introduce an important way of thinking about reading comprehension, which is significant not only in calling for future research in this area but also in planning improved instruction in reading comprehension.

   Teaching Reading: Report and Recommendations, National Inquiry into the Teaching of Literacy (Commonwealth of Australia, 2005) is the report of an independent committee appointed by the Australian Minister of Education, Science, and Training to review current practice in teaching literacy to Australian school children. While highly similar to the U.S. panel reports in its call for evidence-based instructional practices, this report focused primarily on teacher preparation. The panel solicited written submissions from various state, territorial, and nongovernmental education authorities as well as individuals. It also drew on the expertise of the panel members, visited a cross section of schools, conducted a study of teacher preparation courses at Australian institutions of higher education, and conducted a literature review. The panel goals included the following:

> Identifying the extent to which prospective teachers are provided with reading teaching approaches and skills that are effective in the classroom, and hav[ing] the opportunities to develop and practice the skills required to implement effective classroom reading programs….[I]dentifying the ways in which research evidence on literacy teaching and policies in Australian schools can best inform classroom teaching practice and support teacher professional learning. (Commonwealth of Australia, 2005, p. 6)

The panel also sought to examine the effectiveness of assessment methods currently in use for progress monitoring. The recommendations that appear later in this chapter are the result of its work toward these objectives.

   All four reports mentioned in this section hold valuable information that can be used to inform instruction in the classroom. But they do not exhaust the supply of governmental and scholarly works from which such information can be obtained. They are foundational reports. The PRD (Snow et al., 1998) and the NRP (NICHD, 2000) reports have served as the basis of reading legislation, including the Reading Excellence Act (PL 105-277) and No Child Left Behind Act of 2001 (PL 107-110). Both of these public laws urged or required evidence-based practice in U.S. schools.

Finally, there are other panel reports that are equally valuable but address specific areas of reading. First, the NELP report that is currently in progress (NELP, n.d.) is a panel report, with the panel convened by the National Center for Family Literacy under contract from the federal National Institute for Literacy. The report presents research information on prereading skills and abilities in the preschool period and may be of interest to some kindergarten teachers and those who wish to have additional background about the earlier learning that can facilitate beginning reading. The NLP report (August & Shanahan, 2006), developed under contract from the U.S. Department of Education, addressed reading in English language learners (ELLs). It offered important information about teaching bilingual students and students whose English ability is still developing or just beginning. It is a resource of which all teachers should be aware, since most teachers are likely to have ELLs in their classes at some point during their teaching careers. Also mentioned in the following sections of the chapter is the President's Commission on Excellence in Special Education report (2002). This report deals with the process of identifying students and determining their eligibility for special services and how to give enough attention to the delivery of evidence-based instruction for students in special education.

What Other Reports, Compilations, and Meta-Analyses May Be Useful to Teachers?

There are also other reports, summaries, or compilations that may be highly useful. One that is worthy of mention is the *Handbook of Reading Research* (Kamil, Mosenthal, Pearson, & Barr, 1999). This report consists of invited chapters by well-known authors summarizing research in specific areas of reading. The research is selected using less formal criteria than federal panel reports, and while generally thorough and scholarly, some chapters may be less systematic. However, the fact that this report is updated periodically makes it a useful resource.

Finally, individual researchers or teams of researchers often publish meta-analyses and/or syntheses of research on specific aspects of reading and writing instruction. These publications provide a good way to access information on multiple studies and to find convergent evidence on a topic. New information is continuously being published. We urge teachers to read and, where possible and appropriate, incorporate new information into their repertoire of classroom techniques. But we also urge a critical reading and discussion with colleagues of such information before and during its incorporation into instructional practice.

What Are the Key Findings of the Preventing Reading Difficulties in Young Children Report?

The PRD report (Snow et al., 1998) offered recommendations based on available research at the time in several key areas, including preschool, kindergarten, Grades 1–3, teacher education and professional development, ELLs, reading instruction, and children with persistent reading difficulties. All of the recommendations are founded on the critical issue of the need to provide excellent reading instruction to all children. The PRD report stated that this instruction is most effective when begun early, and when elementary school children arrive at school with the prerequisite skills and motivation to succeed in literacy.

The panel indicated that primary-grade reading instruction must include all areas of reading: the alphabetic principle, sight words and decoding, reading fluency, and comprehension. The panel stated that "explicit instruction that directs children's attention to the sound structure of oral language and to the connections between speech sounds and spellings" (Snow et al., 1998, p. 6) is needed to help children who have not mastered letter–sound relationships (i.e., the alphabetic principle) or who have difficulty applying these relationships to decoding unfamiliar words; that is, the panel recommended explicit phonics instruction. The panel also recommended building both conceptual and linguistic knowledge and comprehension skills, using direct instruction for comprehension strategies (e.g., summarizing the main idea, predicting events, drawing inferences from what has been read, monitoring one's own understanding or misunderstanding). According to the panel, in order to provide timely instructional intervention for children having difficulty, both word recognition skills and fluency should be assessed on a regular basis. The panel stated that primary-grade students should be writing letters, words, and sentences, and that invented spelling could help children understand sound segmentation and sound–spelling relationships, but that conventionally correct spellings should be taught through focused instruction and practice. The panel recommended that students be encouraged to read independently and be given opportunities to read and reread texts with assistance in class.

Specific recommendations were made in the PRD report regarding preschool and kindergarten. Specifically, all children, but especially those placed at risk, such as those from low-income families, should have access to contexts or environments that promote the early language and literacy skills that have been identified as important predictors of later reading success (Snow et al., 1998). Preschool programs should be planned to provide such opportunities; that is, such programs should stimulate verbal interaction and overall language development, increase vocabulary, and familiarize children with early book reading. Recognition and production of letters and familiarity with the purposes of reading were also cited as an important part of the preschool experience. Teachers and parents of preschool children should have information about the skills children should be developing at these ages and what to do if they are not acquiring them.

Teacher education and professional development were deemed to be of critical importance in the panel's recommendations (Snow et al., 1998). Teachers must understand how children learn to read and what the developmental precursors of reading are, in order to support and appropriately instruct children in learning to read. Teachers also should be familiar with and knowledgeable about current research on reading in order to integrate new methods and change their teaching strategies.

The PRD panel also made specific recommendations regarding ELLs. The panel recommended that children should be taught how to read in their native language while acquiring oral proficiency in English where feasible; that is, if a sufficient number of children speak the same home language, and teachers are available who can speak that language and offer materials in that language, those students should learn how to read in their native language (Snow et al., 1998). They also recommended that for those children for whom native language instruction is not available, the focus of instruction should be on oral English proficiency, with postponement of formal English reading instruction until an adequate level of English proficiency is attained, although what constitutes an adequate level was not defined. More recent research has indicated that this postponement is not necessary; students can and do learn both oral and written English at the same time when entering the primary grades or higher without English oral proficiency (see McCardle & Chhabra, 2006). The panel emphasized the value of bilingualism and biliteracy and recommended supporting bilingual abilities whenever possible.

Another key area for which recommendations were made by the panel is resources (Snow et al., 1998). The panel recommended manageable class sizes; low student–teacher ratios; sufficient amounts of high-quality materials and good libraries, school classrooms, and school buildings. Although the panel made the strong point that high-quality instruction could prevent most reading difficulties, they made specific recommendations for students exhibiting significant reading difficulties. For such children, the panel recommended that supplementary instructional services, coordinated closely with classroom reading instruction, be provided by reading specialists or other specialists qualified to provide reading services. The panel emphasized that while volunteer tutors can play an important role, volunteer tutors should not be responsible for primary reading instruction or intervention with students with persistent reading difficulties.

How Can This Information Guide Classroom Decision Making or Planning?

The panel who prepared the PRD report (Snow et al., 1998) wanted as one of its primary goals to translate the research-based findings into advice for teachers, parents, and others involved in helping children learn to read. To meet this goal, a companion document to the panel report was produced very soon after the report publication. This document, *Starting Out Right: A Guide to Promoting Children's Reading Success* (Burns, Griffin, & Snow, 1999), available on the Internet as a free download or for purchase in hard copy from the National Academies Press, is aimed at parents, teachers, and child care providers. It contains an introduction and four chapters, with a menu of the chapters provided in the introduction so that readers can choose the chapter they feel will be most informative to them. The four major chapters provide an introduction to the reading process, information on what children need in order to arrive in kindergarten well prepared to learn to read, elements of effective instruction for kindergarten and early elementary classrooms, and information on reading difficulties. The book not only explains techniques to use with young children, but it also provides examples and lists of books and resources.

In producing this document, the National Research Council's Division of Behavioral and Social Sciences and Education demonstrated what appears to have become a very helpful trend. Subsequent reports have nearly always included companion documents, including teacher guides to implementation, parent brochures, and other information written for nonresearchers in less technical language and often with helpful practical examples.

What Are the Key Findings of the National Reading Panel Report?

The NRP report (NICHD, 2000) summarized research selected to answer the question of what works in reading instruction. The panel followed a rigorous methodology in the literature search and in the selection of the types of studies that would be considered. Because the panel members were asked by the U.S. Congress to address the particular question of what instructional methods are effective in teaching children to read, the panel members limited their selections to experimental and quasi-experimental studies addressing instruction in the five components of reading: PA, phonics, fluency, vocabulary, and comprehension. Of more than 100,000 studies found in the original literature searches, the panel members narrowed the number to just a few hundred relevant studies, and then they examined those articles. Where the panel members were able to perform meta-analyses, they did. Otherwise they synthesized the literature. The panel members wrote five reports, addressing the findings about instruction in the five major components of reading.

One of the topics studied was alphabetics, which includes both PA and phonics instruction. Children must understand that the words in their oral language are composed of small segments of sound and then must learn the letter–sound correspondences that represent these in print, in order to learn to read. The NRP (NICHD, 2000) found that teaching children to manipulate phonemes in words was highly effective under a variety of teaching conditions with a variety of learners across a range of grade and age levels; teaching PA, especially with the use of letters, was effective in improving children's reading compared to instruction that did not include PA. While PA does not constitute a complete reading program, it is an important part of developing and understanding the alphabetic system. Phonics instruction, also a part of alphabetics, is a way of teaching early reading skills that stresses the acquisition of letter–sound correspondences and their use in reading and spelling. The NRP found that systematic phonics instruction is also effective for students in kindergarten through sixth grade, including both typically developing readers and those having difficulty learning to read. Kindergartners who received systematic phonics instruction were better able to read and spell words; first graders had the same results but also demonstrated significant improvement in their ability to comprehend text. Systematic synthetic phonics instruction was shown to have a positive and significant effect with children of different ages, abilities, and socioeconomic backgrounds. (For more detail, see Chapter 7 on alphabetics.)

While phonics instruction is an essential part of reading instruction, the NRP (NICHD, 2000) emphasized that there are other components that are just as important to a successful classroom reading program, such as fluency. Fluent readers are those who read orally with speed, accuracy, and proper expression. The NRP concluded that repeated oral reading that included guidance from teachers, peers, or parents had a significant and positive impact on word recognition, fluency, and comprehension across a range of grade levels. However, in examining the literature on the role of independent silent reading, the NRP found no conclusive evidence that encouraging students to read independently had any effect on reading fluency. Therefore, if silent reading is used in the classroom, it should be complemented by guided oral reading.

The ultimate goal of reading is to understand text. Vocabulary is an essential part of that process. The NRP found that vocabulary instruction does lead to gains in comprehension, but methods must be appropriate for the age and ability of the reader (NICHD, 2000). Several specific techniques were found to be effective in enhancing vocabulary, including preteaching vocabulary, restructuring, providing multiple exposures to words, and using computers. The panel also found that substitution of easy words for more difficult words can assist low-achieving students (although this must be done with care and used as an interim measure to help those students ultimately learn the more difficult words).

Comprehension is an active process that requires an intentional and thoughtful interaction between the reader and the text. Comprehension instruction includes having teachers prepare students with comprehension strategies and guide them in applying these to all types of text. The NRP found that comprehension can be improved by teaching students to use specific cognitive strategies to fully understand text; teaching a combination of strategies was shown to be more effective than teaching single strategies (NICHD, 2000). Seven types of comprehension instruction, when used as part of a multistrategy method, were shown to improve comprehension in readers without reading difficulties: comprehension monitoring, cooperative learning, use of graphic and semantic organizers (e.g., story maps), question answering, question generation, story structure, and summarization.

How Can This Information Guide Classroom Decision Making or Planning?

The National Institute for Literacy (NIFL) is a federal agency tasked with the dissemination of research-based evidence on reading instruction. When the NRP report was published, NIFL developed its first evidence-based document on reading instruction for teachers. Based on the NRP findings, *Put Reading First: The Research Building Blocks for Teaching Children to Read* (Partnership for Reading, 2003) provides definitions of terms, examples of how research findings might be actually implemented in a classroom, and suggestions for teachers. Compared to the 350-page NRP report (NICHD, 2000), *Put Reading First* is a handy little booklet that a teacher can carry along and easily use. This and NIFL's other dissemination documents for teachers, parents, and the public can be found online; they are downloadable, but there is also a toll-free telephone number to call to order hard copies of these publications. There are several parent publications that teachers may find helpful as handouts to help parents and other adults learn how they might support and facilitate children's learning of literacy.

The International Reading Association (IRA) also produced a volume to assist teachers in implementing the findings of the NRP. *Evidence-Based Reading Instruction: Putting the National Reading Panel Report into Practice* (IRA, 2002) is a compilation of articles from the IRA journal *The Reading Teacher*, grouped by the five essential reading components in the NRP report, along with summaries of NRP findings for each major section. There is also a section called "Putting It All Together" which comprises papers that address two or more of the essential components, and an appendix that contains the IRA's position paper on evidence-based practice.

What Are the Key Findings of the RAND Report?

In the introduction to the RAND report (Snow, 2002), there were several key points made. First, delaying comprehension instruction until later elementary grades can cause disadvantage to students; a focus on comprehension is important throughout reading instruction and from the very beginning. Such instruction should be systematic and sustained. Latino and African American students often attend schools with fewer resources, less focus on academics, and fewer experienced teachers. Performance expectations are often lower. These factors all contribute to these student populations having poorer reading comprehension, and thus to the achievement gap between these groups and Caucasian students. ELLs face reading challenges in the later grades when they encounter texts that use sophisticated vocabulary and syntax that they may not have mastered. Early decoding ability is not sufficient for children to become successful readers; this is clearly an essential beginning to reading, but reading instruction does not end at the end of third grade. It must continue throughout a student's schooling. One reason teacher preparation programs have not focused more on comprehension instruction is the small research base on which to build instructional practice.

Possibly the most important aspect of this report is the panel's view about reading comprehension as not only the logical end point of reading instruction but also the interaction of reader, text, and activity (Snow, 2002). While this idea may seem self-evident, it is important because it breaks reading comprehension into three aspects, any one of which can change. Thus reading comprehension may be very different depending on what is being read, how it is being read (e.g., orally or silently, under pressure, for pleasure), and what the reader brings to the task. A student may be a highly proficient reader but may have limited vocabulary or background knowledge in a particular area to be able to grasp the meaning of a particular text. The report defined the term *reading comprehension* as "the process of simultaneously extracting and constructing meaning through interaction and involvement with written language" (p. xiii). The report emphasized that the process of learning to read and developing strong reading comprehension takes place not only in the classroom but also in the larger context of the student's life. Instruction must to some extent take that larger context into account.

Another portion of the RAND report, "Developing a Research Agenda," described what researchers know about reading comprehension, reading comprehension instruction, and teacher preparation (Snow, 2002). Reading comprehension instruction designed to enhance reading fluency supports gains in reading fluency, as one might expect, but it also enhances word recognition skills and results in moderate reading comprehension gains. The panel cited the NRP finding (NICHD, 2000) of insufficient evidence of a causal connection between sustained silent reading as an effective technique to develop fluency. Instructional strategies, such as concept mapping and story mapping, generating questions, summarizing, identifying the big ideas in stories, and using graphic techniques, foster reading comprehension by promoting self-monitoring in reading comprehension. The RAND report also called for explicit instruction in comprehension strategies, which have been shown to enhance student learning, especially for low-achieving students, by providing clear explanations, encouraging sustained attention to task, activating prior knowledge, breaking tasks into smaller steps, and providing opportunities for practice that incorporate frequent feedback.

How Can This Information Guide Classroom Decision Making or Planning?

While there are no companion teacher guides emanating from the RAND report (Snow, 2002), Sweet and Snow (2003) produced a book,

Rethinking Reading Comprehension, which took the information in the RAND report a step further and explicitly discussed implications for the classroom. Chapters by many of the members of the RAND study group presented information about comprehension instruction for adolescents and for ELLs, collaborative teaching of comprehension, and individual differences and explained how these factors may affect reading comprehension what students need to know to be able to understand coherence relations in expository and narrative text.

What Are the Key Findings of Australia's *Teaching Reading* Report?

In Australia's *Teaching Reading* report (Commonwealth of Australia, 2005), the Australian panel cited the findings of the NRP report (NICHD, 2000) and strongly encouraged basing instructional practice on research evidence. The Australian panel made 18 recommendations. Several of these recommendations generally addressed literacy instruction for all students and called for teachers to be educated using rigorous, evidence-based strategies that have been shown to effectively improve children's literacy development. The panel stated that these evidence-based strategies should include systematic, direct, and explicit phonics instruction so that children can break the alphabetic code and should include integrated support of oral language, vocabulary, grammar, fluency, reading comprehension, and use of new technologies. Furthermore, reading instruction should be comprehensive, diagnostic, and age appropriate. The panel called for every child to be assessed upon entry to school and in Grades 3, 5, 7, and 9. The panel also recommended an assessment of individual progress to be completed twice annually during the first 3 years of school.

The panel was clear that reading should be the key focus of elementary school teacher preparation, and that preparation should include an evidence-based, integrated approach to the five major components of reading (Commonwealth of Australia, 2005). In addition, the panel recommended that teachers study child and adolescent development and inclusive approaches to literacy teaching. Secondary school teacher training should include content-area literacy coursework. Teacher certification should include a demonstration of the personal literacy skills necessary for one to be an effective teacher as well as a demonstration of effective literacy teaching ability. Schools, professional organizations, and institutions of higher education should provide ongoing professional development to help teachers continue to keep up with changes and developments in evidence-based instruction.

The Australian panel said that all schools should have a literacy specialist who can facilitate a whole-school literacy plan, support staff development, assist classroom teachers in their own professional development, and help ensure that progress monitoring includes the individual plans for children experiencing reading difficulties (Commonwealth of Australia, 2005). The panel called for rigorous training of specialists and recommended that graduate schools provide curricula for training literacy specialists to support the skills and knowledge base of teachers.

Regarding diversity and ELLs, the panel recommended that literacy be taught to all grades and by all teachers across the curriculum to meet the needs of children from diverse backgrounds and locations. Further, the panel recommended that special national programs be established to link theory and practice so that preservice teachers are well prepared to teach reading and other subjects to diverse groups of children effectively. Building on the home language and literacy practices, programs, guides, and workshops should be developed for parents and caregivers to enable them to support their children's literacy development.

With their call for national standards for literacy instruction, the panel urged the relevant organizations to collaborate in their development and implementation as well as on issues of teacher registration and recognition of accomplished teaching in literacy (Commonwealth of Australia, 2005). In addressing school reform to implement evidence-based literacy instruction, the panel recommended that all education leaders examine their approaches. The panel also recommended that the implementation of explicit, whole-school literacy programs be planned, developed, and monitored collaboratively by schools and parents.

At the national level, it is important to be able to track students as they move between districts and territories. The panel recommended the establishment of confidential unique identifiers to allow children's performance to be tracked even when they change schools or relocate geographically (Commonwealth of Australia, 2005). Further, the panel recommended that this new approach should be aligned at all governmental levels—national, state and territorial—and should be supported by all levels of Australian government.

How Can This Information Guide Classroom Decision Making or Planning?

While there are no specific companion documents that we have been able to discover based on this report, the fact that this report adopted and reinforced the findings and recommendations of the PRD (Snow et al., 1998) and NRP (NICHD, 2000) reports should reinforce the confidence that we have in these findings and their worthiness to inform practice.

What Are the Key Findings of the National Early Literacy Panel Report?

The National Center for Family Literacy, under contract from the National Institute for Literacy, established a panel to evaluate and report on the research evidence on reading and prereading abilities and activities in the preschool period. Although the NELP report has not yet been published, panel representatives have made presentations on some of the findings, and preliminary results are summarized on the panel's web site (NELP, n.d.). The panel is addressing what skills and abilities in children from birth to age 5 predict later reading outcomes, and what programs, environments, settings, and child characteristics contribute to or inhibit the development of reading skills and abilities. To date the panel members have reported preliminary findings on predictors of later decoding, reading comprehension, and spelling. The panel's preliminary findings included strong evidence for the importance of alphabetic knowledge, phonological awareness (PA), rapid naming tasks (e.g., letter, digits, objects, or colors), being able to write one's own name, and phonological short-term memory. Global oral language skills and concepts about print have been less consistently found to be good predictors, once PA and alphabet knowledge were controlled for. The panel's findings have also encouraged explicit attempts to build alphabetic awareness and oral language, share books with young children, and use home, preschool, and kindergarten interventions, as these actions can be valuable for later language and literacy skills. The full report is anticipated in 2008.

How Can This Information Guide Classroom Decision Making or Planning?

Although the NELP (n.d.) report is not yet published, there are already efforts underway to develop companion documents. For example, a guide to adult literacy instruction has been developed for teachers of the adult components of family literacy programs, to help parents develop their own literacy in conjunction with assisting their children to develop literacy skills. This document is available on the Internet from the National Center for Family Literacy and the National Institute for Literacy. Other companion documents intended to guide practices in preschool programs will doubtless be developed, all aimed at helping prepare preschoolers to enter kindergarten ready for more formal instruction in reading.

What Are the Key Findings from the National Literacy Panel for Language Minority Children and Youth Report?

Both the NRP and PRD reports (NICHD, 2000; Snow et al., 1998) explicitly called for information on teaching ELLs to read. Much earlier, the NRC had produced a report, *Educating Language Minority Children* (August & Hakuta, 1998), on that topic. That report, too, called for additional research and additional reporting on this topic. As a result, under contracts from the National Institute for Literacy and the Institute of Education Sciences, with additional support from the U.S. Department of Education Office of English Language Acquisition and the NICHD, the Center for Applied Linguistics and SRI International established the National Literacy Panel for Language Minority Children and Youth (NLP). Their report, *Developing Literacy in Second-Language Learners* (August & Shanahan, 2006), was edited by one of the authors of the earlier NRC report on the same topic, Diane August, and by NLP chair Timothy Shanahan, who was also a member of the NRP. Their extensive report serves as a benchmark for educating ELLs in the United States. The report consisted of four major sections and presents syntheses of various types of research on key topics. These sections addressed literacy development in ELLs, the relation of sociocultural context and literacy development, instructional approaches and professional development, and student assessment. The major findings from the NLP included the importance of focusing reading instruction on the major components of reading identified by the NRP. According to the NLP report, explicit work in these areas is particularly beneficial for ELLs. Instruction in these fives areas is considered necessary but not sufficient for language minority students learning to read; oral English proficiency is also critical. Oral language and literacy proficiency in the first language can facilitate literacy in English. The extent to which this is true and in which areas will depend in part on the characteristics of the first language, but literacy in one language certainly conveys some advantage to literacy development in a second language. The importance of taking sociocultural context into account is also emphasized.

How Can This Information
Guide Classroom Decision Making or Planning?

While the NLP report is relatively recent, there are already efforts in progress to produce companion documents to promote classroom implementation. The International Reading Association (IRA) is producing a practice guide, and the IRA, in partnership with NICHD and other federal agencies and organizations, convened meetings of practitioners and researchers to provide input on a document specific to classroom reading instruction for ELLs, based on parts of the NLP report and with updated information. In addition, a web-based document for teachers that offers information gleaned from research that can be applied in teaching ELL students is available on the web site of Teachers of English for Speakers of Other Languages (http://www.tesol.org). A research synthesis should be published in 2008.

What Are the Key Findings
of the President's Commission on
Excellence in Special Education Report?

It is important to note that while research on overall reading instruction received a great deal of attention in terms of major national reports, special education was not being ignored. In a special report titled *A New Era: Revitalizing Special Education for Children and Their Families*, the President's Commission on Excellence in Special Education (2002) made certain points about special education in the United States. The Commission reported that there had been too much focus on the process of identifying students and determining their eligibility for special services and not enough attention given to the delivery of evidence-based instruction. The Commission criticized the "wait to fail" model of identifying students with disabilities and made four major recommendations. First, they recommended early identification and early intervention (using research-based intervention programs) to prevent learning disabilities whenever possible, adding that the identification process for children with disabilities should be simplified. The Commission also recommended the use of response to intervention (RTI) models for the identification and assessment process and for progress monitoring, and the use of universal design in accountability tools to ensure that all assessments are designed to allow for necessary accommodations and modifications (see Chapter 15 for a more in-depth discussion of RTI). The Commission also made recommendations about future research and its dissemination.

They specifically called for the U.S. Department of Education, Office of Special Education and Rehabilitation Services to support demonstration and dissemination programs that focus on the adoption of scientifically based practices, including continuing teacher education.

How Can This Information Guide Classroom Decision Making or Planning?

While there are no companion documents for *A New Era: Revitalizing Special Education for Children and Their Families* (President's Commission on Excellence in Special Education, 2002), the report itself offered some useful information for teachers and parents. In particular, the sections on assessment and accountability, flexibility, and parental empowerment provided relevant background. Teachers may also find the section on special education research and dissemination interesting, as the panel called for greater use of demonstration programs and dissemination of information specifically through continuing education for teachers. The Office of Special Education and Rehabilitative Services has a special web site (http://idea.ed.gov/) that offers many resources about identification and service provision under Individuals with Disabilities Education Improvement Act of 2004 (PL 108-446). Among the many topics addressed are instructional materials accessibility, evaluation, highly qualified teachers, and statewide and district assessments. Most topics have a handy issue brief included and free documents that can be downloaded.

How Can This Information from Panel Reports and Accompanying Documents Guide Classroom Decision Making or Planning?

The information in all of the reports mentioned in this chapter can serve as resource material for classroom teachers. This chapter was meant as an overview of these reports. In the following chapters we go into detail about the specific findings of each of the major reports and their companion documents, which served as some of our key source material for those chapters. We will also provide scenarios based on use of this information to illustrate how implementation of the findings might play out in classrooms. We encourage educators to obtain all of the free companion documents for examples and ideas, refreshers on the information in the larger reports, and in some cases, handouts to parents. These handouts can help parents understand why teachers use certain classroom strategies, how children are being instructed and monitored, and what parents can do to reinforce the skills teachers are helping children to develop.

ONLINE RESOURCES

August, D., & Shanahan, T. (Eds.). (2006). *Developing literacy in second-language learners: Report of the national literacy panel on language-minority children and youth.* Mahwah, NJ: Lawrence Erlbaum Associates. Retrieved March 25, 2008, from http://www.cal.org/natl-lit-panel/reports/Executive_Summary.pdf

Commonwealth of Australia. (2005). *Teaching reading: Report and recommendations, national inquiry into the teaching of literacy.* Retrieved December 28, 2007, from http://www.dest.gov.au/nitl documents/report_recommendations.pdf

National Early Literacy Panel (NELP). (n.d.). *Synthesizing the scientific research on development of early literacy in young children.* Retrieved January 17, 2008, from http://www.nifl.gov/partnershipforreading/family/ncfl/NELP2006Conference.pdf

National Institute of Child Health and Human Development. (NICHD). (2000). *Report of the National Reading Panel. Teaching children to read: An evidence-based assessment of the scientific research literature on reading and its implications for reading instruction: Reports of the subgroups* (NIH Publication No. 00-4754). Washington, DC: U.S. Government Printing Office. Retrieved March 25, 2008, from http://www.nationalreadingpanel.org

Snow, C. (Ed.). (2002). *Reading for understanding: Toward an R&D program in reading comprehension.* Washington, DC: RAND Corporation. Retrieved March 25, 2008, from http://www.rand.org/pubs/monograph_reports/MR1465/MR1465.pdf

Snow, C.E., Burns, M.S., & Griffin, P. (Eds.). (1998). *Preventing reading difficulties in young children.* Washington, DC: National Academies Press. Retrieved March 25, 2008, from http://books.nap.edu catalog/6023.html

Towne, L., Wise, L., & Winters, T. (Eds). (2004). *Advancing scientific research in education.* Washington, DC: National Academies Press. Retrieved March 25, 2008, from http://www.nap.edu/catalog/11112.html

REFERENCES

August, D., & Hakuta, K. (1998). *Educating language minority children*. Washington, DC: National Academies Press.

August, D., & Shanahan, T. (Eds.). (2006). *Developing literacy in second-language learners: Report of the national literacy panel on language-minority children and youth*. Mahwah, NJ: Lawrence Erlbaum Associates.

Burns, M.S., Griffin, P., & Snow, C.E. (1999). *Starting out right: A guide to promoting children's reading success*. Washington, DC: National Academies Press.

Commonwealth of Australia. (2005). *Teaching reading: Report and recommendations, national inquiry into the teaching of literacy*. Retrieved December 28, 2007, from http://www.dest.gov.au/nitl/documents/report_recommendations.pdf

Individuals with Disabilities Education Improvement Act of 2004, PL 108-446 20 U.S.C. §§ 1400 *et seq.*

International Reading Association. (2002). *Evidence-based reading instruction: Putting the National Reading Panel report into practice*. Newark, DE: International Reading Association.

Kamil, M., Mosenthal, P., Pearson, P., & Barr, R. (Eds.). (1999). *Handbook of reading research* (Vol. 3). Mahwah, NJ: Lawrence Erlbaum Associates.

McCardle, P., & Chhabra, V. (2006). Commentary. *Elementary School Journal*, 107(2), 239–248.

National Early Literacy Panel (NELP). (n.d.). *Synthesizing the scientific research on development of early literacy in young children*. Retrieved January 17, 2008, from http://www.nifl.gov/partnershipforreading/family/ncfl/NELP2006Conference.pdf

National Institute of Child Health and Human Development. (NICHD). (2000). *Report of the National Reading Panel. Teaching children to read: An evidence-based assessment of the scientific research literature on reading and its implications for reading instruction: Reports of the subgroups* (NIH Publication No. 00-4754). Washington, DC: U.S. Government Printing Office.

No Child Left Behind Act of 2001, PL 107-110, 115 Stat. 1452, 20 U.S.C. §§ 6301 *et seq.*

Partnership for Reading. (2003). *Put reading first: The research building blocks for teaching children to read (Kindergarten through Grade 3)*. Washington, DC: Author.

President's Commission on Excellence in Special Education. (2002). *A new era: Revitalizing special education for children and their families*. Washington, DC: U.S. Department of Education, Office of Special Education and Rehabilitative Services. Retrieved on December 28, 2007, from http://www.ed.gov/inits/commissionsboards/whspecialeducation/reports.html

Reading Excellence Act, PL 105-277, 112 Stat. 2681-337, 20 U.S.C. § 6661a *et seq.*

Snow, C. (Ed.). (2002). *Reading for understanding: Toward an R&D program in reading comprehension*. Washington, DC: RAND Corporation.

Snow, C.E., Burns, M.S., & Griffin, P. (Eds.). (1998). *Preventing reading difficulties in young children*. Washington, DC: National Academies Press.

Sweet, A.P., & Snow, C.E. (Eds.). (2003). *Rethinking reading comprehension: Solving problems in teaching of literacy.* New York: Guilford Press.

Towne, L., Wise, L., & Winters, T. (Eds.). (2004). *Advancing scientific research in education.* Washington, DC: National Academies Press.

What Does Research Say About the Major Components of Reading?

● ●

"There is a consensus among researchers about the critical elements for effective reading instruction...the integration of explicit instruction in the alphabetic principle, reading for meaning, and opportunity to learn. These critical elements are present in classroom instruction that prevents reading difficulties as well as in effective small-group and one-on-one interventions."

(B.R. Foorman, J.I. Breier, & J.M. Fletcher, 2003, p. 613)

The National Reading Panel (NRP) took the five major areas that were commonly agreed on as being important to reading and reviewed, meta-analyzed where possible, and synthesized the research on these five areas (National Institute of Child Health and Human Development [NICHD], 2000). Evidence-based reading instructional practice was built on these five major components of reading: phonemic awareness (PA), phonics, fluency, vocabulary, and reading comprehension.

In this section, we present the five major components of reading, plus writing and spelling, and discuss the relationship they bear to reading. Reading requires a strong basis of language ability, including vocabulary and listening comprehension. These skills, like much of language, seem to be acquired almost magically. Children with no sensory or cognitive deficits acquire language rapidly during the preschool period. In fact, reading development used to be compared to language acquisition and termed a natural process. However, researchers and educators now know that while language development proceeds successfully in most children as they interact with adults and other children, reading is an ability that must be learned (Lyon, 2000). Despite the fact that language is well underway by the late preschool years, there are aspects of language that will also need instruction.

The topic of vocabulary is discussed in Chapter 6. Vocabulary is an example of a language aspect that needs to be developed. As children begin school, they will also begin to encounter words that often are not familiar to them. As they progress in the academic atmosphere of classrooms, language will become increasingly complex—in fact, the language of the classroom and the textbook is often referred to as *academic language.* Children in school encounter vocabulary and expressions as well as sentence structures that are quite different from the language of everyday social interaction. Thus, teaching children vocabulary and providing them experiences through activities and reading materials to enrich and enlarge their vocabularies is an important part of ensuring that they become successful readers.

Two other components of reading that were addressed by the NRP are PA and phonics. The NRP determined that PA is an important, foundational skill for reading, but that for school-age children learning to read, PA instruction is most effective when combined with letters (NICHD, 2000). *Phonics,* the study of the letter–sound relations and how letters and groups of letters combine to form words, builds upon those PA and letter–sound recognition skills. Chapter 7, titled "Alphabetics," addresses these issues. We chose to use the term *alphabetics* when naming this chapter since that is the term used by the NRP, and since it addresses the combination of PA, the alphabetic principle, and phonics, aspects of reading that are foundational skills for reading in alphabetic languages.

Chapter 8 addresses what research recommends to improve reading fluency. *Fluency* is a term used in language as well as in reading. Being able to speak fluently has different meanings to various people: not stuttering to a speech-language pathologist, being able to speak a foreign language smoothly without having to stop and look up words in a dictionary to a teacher of foreign languages, or being able to recognize words and read sentences aloud quickly and accurately with good expression to a reading teacher. Reading fluency was often thought to be something that simply occurred without instruction when students got good enough at reading. It does require practice, but researchers now know that guided practice can help children become fluent readers, and that gaining fluency is important to reading comprehension.

Chapter 9, titled " Reading Comprehension," addresses the goal (and indeed the very essence) of reading. Comprehension is part of reading instruction from the earliest stages of word recognition through high school and even college. As early as second grade, educators begin teaching students to be strategic in their reading: to monitor their own reading process, to relate what they are reading to what they already know, to look for specific types of information in different types of text, and to summarize and think about what they read. By high school, educators expect students to be able to read, learn new information, and critically evaluate what they have read from various sources and relate this information in a coherent whole. This requires skilled instruction and teachers with expertise in all of these reading comprehension strategies themselves.

Chapters 10 and 11 address two abilities that were not taken up by the NRP but are closely related to and can clearly enhance reading ability: spelling and writing. Spelling is not only a skill that is useful in writing, but it is also a skill that can have a quite positive impact on reading. If students know how to spell English words, it can help them with meaning as they are more likely to realize that the words contain certain root words, prefixes, and suffixes that affect meaning. Many English words are spelled with predictable patterns. Teaching those patterns and how to spell the exceptions (which in their own right are often predictable if something is known about their origin) can help students connect the letters they see in print with the words they spell. Writing is a way of reprocessing what has been read, of solidifying mental representations of information, and of expressing what the reader has learned. It also helps readers understand how authors develop texts, considering their message, choices of words, and organization of ideas. Writing is a complex ability that clearly benefits from instruction and can have a beneficial influence on reading comprehension. Chapters 10 and 11 present information on how teachers can help students use those strategies.

REFERENCES

Foorman, B.R., Breier, J.I., Fletcher, J.M. (2003). Interventions aimed at improving reading success: An evidence-based approach. *Developmental Neuropsychology, 24*(2–3), 613-639.

Lyon, G.R. (2000, January/February). Why reading is not a natural process. *LDA Newbriefs, 38* (4).

National Institute of Child Health and Human Development (NICHD). (2000). *Report of the National Reading Panel. Teaching children to read: An evidence-based assessment of the scientific research literature on reading and its implications for reading instruction: Reports of the subgroups* (NIH Publication No. 00–4754.). Washington, DC: U.S. Government Printing Office.

Vocabulary

KEY CONCEPTS

- Vocabulary development is very important to reading comprehension and consists of several aspects of learning, including oral language vocabulary, sight words, concepts, conceptual development, and the use of context clues.

- In order to develop students' ability to use new words and concepts, conceptual knowledge must be developed through multiple thoughtful encounters with words; this can be achieved through reading, writing, and talking about words.

- Vocabulary instruction promotes students' knowledge of words, how to use words, and how to learn new words.

The first-grade teachers at the elementary school agreed that students coming to the first grade have difficulty learning sight words and do not know the meaning of many of the words they can sound out. The teachers found research that indicated the importance of oral language in reading. They were reminded by what they found out: Young students cannot make sense of a word in print if they do not know what the word means. The teachers decided to read more to students and tried to provide more opportunities for students to talk rather than allowing them to give simple one- or two-word answers to questions. They also introduced a new word each week, specifically one that students were not likely to have in their oral vocabulary. For example, one week the word was *compromise*. In addition to using activities that build vocabulary, the teachers developed a plan to engage parents of students in kindergarten and the primary grades in home activities to develop oral vocabulary. They also worked with upper-grade teachers to provide extra credit to students who helped younger siblings with vocabulary activities that included songs and games.

What Does Vocabulary Development Mean to Researchers and Educators?

Vocabulary development related to reading can encompass several areas: oral vocabulary, sight words, concept development, and the use of context clues.

Oral vocabulary refers to the words students use in their oral communications. For young children, it usually includes words, such as *mother, bed, food,* and the like. It is developed initially before a student enters school and continues to grow throughout a person's life. Oral vocabulary is based on experiences and language learned from interactions, including listening to and talking to parents, siblings, and playmates, as well as listening to and viewing media, such as radio, television, movies, and computer-based information and entertainment.

Sight word vocabulary refers to words that are common or high-use words, for which students have concepts but which may be difficult to decode even when students have mastered letter–sound correspondences. Students need to learn to recognize sight words quickly in order to gain reading fluency and be able to attend to the meaning of what they are reading. Sight words include function words like *a, the, for* and *and,* and words that may not follow the regularities of English phonology and are not easily revealed through decoding (*through, tough, pint*). Eventually, sight words also include the frequently encountered words in reading as students begin to automatically recognize words they decode; this process of automaticity is discussed in Chapter 8. Sight words are essential for fluency in reading.

Vocabulary instruction that develops new concepts or links familiar concepts with new words focuses on another type of vocabulary. This development of conceptual knowledge related to words is essential for reading comprehension, especially as students become more mature and read more content-related material. This type of vocabulary knowledge is developed through multiple exposures to the words and thoughtful encounters with them, reading and talking about them, and using them in speech and writing rather than memorization and drills (Stahl, 2003).

What Does Some of the Research Say About Vocabulary and Word Knowledge in General?

There is a large amount of research on vocabulary development. In a much-cited study of young children's language development, Hart and Risley (1995) indicated that many economically disadvantaged preschoolers come to kindergarten with far smaller vocabularies than more advantaged children. This uneven start can make learning to read more difficult. Because the early years are a period of very rapid language development, including vocabulary, catching up can be difficult. Building a vocabulary of words about the world around a child is an important preschool activity, but it is a continuing area of growth throughout life.

Several reviews of vocabulary research indicate that *word knowledge* is multidimensional and is built over time through repeated encounters with words. Word knowledge includes both definitional and contextual information. There are multiple meanings for some words and connotations that are important aspects of knowing a word and how to use it or understand it (Nagy & Scott, 2000). Language learners, whether young children or older learners in Grades 4–12 learning a new language, sometimes use words incorrectly, because they know the definition but not how to use the word in a sentence. For example, a student might say, "I want to acquaint him," meaning, "I want to get to know him." The meaning fits, but the word does not work in this context, because of properties of the word that students usually learn from use. Effective vocabulary instruction provides opportunities to extend word knowledge beyond the ability to match a word to a definition or synonym.

Nagy and Scott (2000) reviewed research on another aspect of word knowledge, a general awareness of words and how words operate, how letters map to sounds and words and the different aspects of word meaning that are part of that knowledge. Another aspect of word knowledge is called *morphological awareness*. Morphemes are the meaning-bearing units in words, and knowledge of these units correlates with reading ability. Root words are morphemes, and teaching root words, their meanings, and how they contribute to the meanings of other words improves reading comprehension (Nagy & Scott, 2000; see also Chapter 10 on spelling to learn more about roots and morphemes).

In considering what research says about language awareness, Nagy and Scott (2000) indicated the importance of knowledge about how words work in sentences as being another aspect of word knowledge that is important for developing a rich vocabulary that contributes to reading comprehension.

What Does Research Say About Vocabulary and Its Relation to Reading?

There is clear evidence that reading ability is linked to vocabulary size (Baumann, Kame'enui, & Ash, 2003). Stahl and Fairbanks (1986) did a meta-analysis of vocabulary research and concluded that vocabulary instruction did improve reading comprehension. They also pointed out that there were differences in the effectiveness of instructional strategies, with drill and practice on definitions alone not significantly effective in improving comprehension; however, instruction that involved students using the words in context as well as considering their definitions produced gains in comprehension.

Mezynski (1983) analyzed eight vocabulary studies and concluded that factors in effective vocabulary instruction include the breadth of word knowledge, the degree of active processing, and the amount of practice with new words. Broad knowledge of a word includes definition(s), how the word is used in sentences, examples and nonexamples of the concept, semantic associations, such as *cow-animal*, synonyms, and antonyms. In clarifying levels of processing, Stahl (1985) suggested three levels: *association*, which involves associating a word with a definition or context, essentially a rote activity; *comprehension*, which requires the use of word knowledge for such activities as understanding the word in context or classifying the word; and *generation*, which entails the producing of novel responses to words through such activities as sentence generation or paraphrasing definition. Others have agreed that there are various levels of knowledge about a word

(Baumann et al., 2003; Beck, McCaslin, & McKeown, 1980; Kame'enui, Dixon, & Carnine, 1987).

Several studies have indicated that students can often figure out a word's meaning from context and can learn words from encountering them in reading (Baumann et al., 2003). There is research that indicates that wide reading can help students improve their vocabulary (Snow, Burns, & Griffin, 1998). Certainly the large vocabularies adult readers have are not the result of instruction on all of those words, but of encountering many of the words repeatedly in reading and conversational contexts. Stanovich, West, Cunningham, Cipielewski, and Siddiqui (1996) concluded that even poor readers can gain vocabulary and conceptual information from exposure to print. There is also a link between being read to at home and reading achievement (Cain, 1996). Encountering words in multiple contexts is important in building knowledge of the different aspects of their meaning that specific contexts evoke (Stahl, 2003). The *habitat* of the squirrel is different from the *habitat* of a Native American before Columbus arrived, which in turn is different from the *habitat* of a child living in a suburban home. The first calls to mind a forest, the second calls to mind an undeveloped country, and the third calls to mind a suburban neighborhood.

What Does Research Indicate About Vocabulary Instruction and Its Effectiveness?

Research presented in the National Reading Panel (NRP) report indicated that vocabulary learning does lead to improved comprehension (National Institute of Child Health and Human Development [NICHD], 2000) and that instruction in vocabulary is important. Research is inconclusive about the best instructional approaches for vocabulary development, but there is research that indicates the effectiveness of various approaches (Baumann et al., 2003; Kamil, 2004; NICHD, 2000). Looking across studies of effective vocabulary instruction, Blanchowicz and Fisher summarized the general implications of the research as supporting four principles:

1. That students should be active in developing their understanding of words and ways to learn them

2. That students should personalize word learning

3. That students should be immersed in words

4. That students should build on multiple sources of information to learn words through repeated exposures (2000, p. 504)

Research on vocabulary instruction can be roughly placed in two general categories: research on how to teach word meanings and research on how to teach students to learn new words (Graves, 1986; Baumann et al., 2003). The NRP report (NICHD, 2000) indicated that explicit instruction can be highly effective, and the methods they reviewed indicated that instructional methods should include active engagement in word learning and multiple repetitions to help students consolidate learning of words, and that use of computers and multimedia can be effective in vocabulary instruction (Kamil, 2004; NICHD, 2000). Stahl and Kapinus (2001) have suggested that a complete program in vocabulary development would include teaching words, teaching about words, and teaching an appreciation of words. In teaching new words, again there are two suggested categories of strategies: those for teaching new words for familiar concepts, and those for teaching new concepts that go with new words (Baumann et al., 2003; Graves, 1986).

Students can learn to connect words to definitions or synonyms when the teacher provides instruction, but this instruction does not usually result in better comprehension of text containing the taught words. However, the *key word* method (Levin, McCormick, Miller, Berry, & Pressley, 1982; McDaniel & Pressley, 1989) is an effective strategy for teaching words by association that also enhances comprehension of passages containing the taught words (Baumann et al., 2003). The key word method involves having students make a visual image connecting part of the word to its meaning (Pressley, Levin, & McDaniel, 1987). Students are told the word meaning and asked to imagine a picture in their minds for that meaning. They can also make sentences that contain the target word and demonstrate its meaning (Atkinson, 1975; Rowher, 1973). The key word method of vocabulary development has been heavily researched with results strongly supporting its effectiveness with different types of words and different types of students (Baumann et al., 2003; NICHD, 2000).

Approaches for teaching new concepts include various ways to show relations among aspects of a concept, such as *semantic mapping* and *semantic feature analysis*. These strategies have been shown to be effective for both teaching vocabulary and improving the comprehension of passages containing the taught words (Baumann et al., 2003). The new conceptual information must be linked to the learner's own background knowledge and experiences. Semantic mapping and feature analysis help students make explicit links between new and old information related to a word's meaning.

McKeown, Beck, Omanson, and Pople (1985) determined that an intensive, rich vocabulary program that involves writing and thinking about words promotes learning of concepts and improves reading comprehension scores. Stahl, Burdge, Machuga, and Stecyk (1992) and the NRP report (NICHD, 2000) confirmed the effectiveness of rich instructional programs for vocabulary development. Such programs include multiple types of activities for students to use, talk about, and learn about words. For example, students might use a card with the word and its definition on one side and the word used in two or three sentences on the other. Students might make a semantic map of the word or do a semantic feature analysis. They might discuss the relationship between the new word and other words that could be synonyms, antonyms, semantically related, or not related at all. These various activities provide multiple exposures to the word, opportunities to think about the properties of the word, and access to a growing understanding of words in general as well as specific words.

The NRP report found four studies that indicated that computers were an effective platform for delivering vocabulary instruction (NICHD, 2000). However, this is an area where further research is needed. While computers can provide interesting, effective instruction for learning the meanings of words, there is no conclusive evidence at this point that computer-based vocabulary work in general improves reading comprehension. Certainly, it seems more challenging to design computer-based vocabulary instruction that goes beyond linear drills and activities, to promote the thinking, discussions, and learning about vocabulary that are captured in rich classroom vocabulary programs. It is important to remember that computers are tools, and that just as each instructional approach that teachers can use in the classroom must be studied for its effectiveness, so each new computer software program for teaching students specific aspects of reading, such as vocabulary, must also be studied for its effectiveness.

Differences in age and ability can have a significant effect on how well students learn vocabulary from instructional activities (NICHD, 2000). For example, one study (McGivern & Levin, 1983) found that the key word approach showed significant effects with fifth-grade students. However, students with lower ability had greater gains than students with higher ability, although the strategy was more difficult for students with lower ability to use.

Teaching words from a specific passage before students read the passage enhances both vocabulary learning and reading comprehension. It not only provides an introduction to new words and their meanings, but also helps students recall what they know about the topic of the passage in relation to the vocabulary and make a connection to their own knowledge and experience as they read the passage (NICHD, 2000). Teaching students general strategies for learning new words is another aspect of vocabulary instruction that contributes to making them better readers (Baumann et al., 2003).

What Are Some of the Specific Instructional Strategies that Have Been Effective in Developing Knowledge of Words and Concepts?

There are several effective instructional strategies that can be used in developing new word and concept knowledge. Some of these strategies are mentioned in this section, with examples of how to use them.

Multiple Sentences

Having students use words in multiple sentences is one sound instructional strategy for the development of new words and concepts (Coomber, Ramstad, & Sheets, 1986). Often teachers have students use a word in one sentence, which can require either definitional knowledge or contextual knowledge but frequently not both. Having students use a word in two or three sentences provides multiple encounters with the word and promotes the use of a broader knowledge of the word than is needed to use it in one sentence.

Semantic Mapping

Semantic maps require students to graphically show the relation of the meaning of the word to various aspects of the concept it represents and to other concepts. One type of semantic map is structured, requiring the students to provide the information (Schwartz & Raphael, 1985). See Figure 6.1 for an example of the structure of a semantic map.

Word Pair Chart

This activity, developed by Pearson and Johnson (1978), involves having students think about the relationships among words. It requires the use of both contextual and definitional information and some careful thinking. Its potential to promote vocabulary knowledge is not so much in filling out the chart, but in the discussion of why certain relationships were chosen. For instance, students might decide that opposites also go together since they are sometimes points on a continuum such as *hot* and *cold, near* and *far*. See Table 6.1 for word pair chart examples.

How Do Teachers Decide What Words to Teach?

Of course, it is not possible for a classroom teacher to teach all of the words students need to learn, especially using multiple activities to

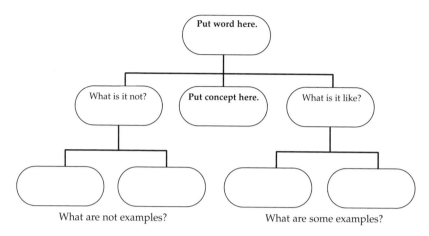

Figure 6.1. Structured semantic map. (From Schwartz, R.M., & Raphael, T. [1985]. Concept of definition: A key to improving students' vocabulary. *The Reading Teacher, 39*, 98–203; adapted by permission.)

provide multiple exposures. There are some guidelines for deciding what words to teach, not based directly on research but from researchers who developed rich instructional programs for vocabulary learning (Beck & McKeown, 1985). These researchers suggested that teachers think of vocabulary as being in three tiers. The first tier includes basic, high-frequency words, such as *car, cake, house,* and *street.* These words do not require direct instruction to learn their meanings. Another tier consists of low-frequency words that are applicable to specific content or contexts. Some words in this tier would be *adagio, meson,* and *fractile.* The meanings of these words are best taught when they are needed for understanding specific passages or lessons. The third tier contains words frequently encountered or employed by mature language users. This tier might include such words as *novice, facility, lair,* and *prestige.* This is the group of words for which instruction is likely to yield benefits for vocabulary knowledge and reading comprehension.

Table 6.1. Word pair chart

	Same	Opposite	Go together	No relation
Desert–nomad			X	
Nomad–wanderer	X			
Nomad–settler		X		
Desert–city				X
Star–energy			X	

From Stahl, S.A., & Kapinus, B. (2001). *Word power: What every educator needs to know about teaching vocabulary.* Washington, DC: National Education Association; adapted by permission.

In addition to selecting words to teach based on their frequency of use, Beck and McKeown (1985) also suggested grouping words in semantic categories to facilitate use of learning strategies involving the identification of associations among words. For example, a category of people might include *virtuoso, rival, accomplice,* and *philanthropist.*

Teaching students about the origins of words in the English language as well as teaching them how morphemes and affixes (prefixes and suffixes) can combine with words to change word meanings and build new words is also effective in enhancing student vocabulary. Moats (2005) and Henry (2003) indicated that this can begin as early as Grade 2. In the upper elementary and middle school grades, knowledge of Latin and Greek root words and combining forms (affixes and Greek combining forms) can result in a virtual vocabulary explosion, which can be very helpful with content area vocabulary in other classes, such as math, science, and social studies. Much more detail is offered in Chapter 10.

What Does Research Tell Us About the Relationship of Oral Language and Listening Vocabulary to Reading Comprehension?

Beimiller (2003) indicated that elementary students' reading levels are limited by their listening vocabulary. For upper elementary students, lack of vocabulary knowledge is related to increasing problems with reading, "even if they have good reading (word identification) skills" (p. 23). Beimiller concluded, "Thus, early delays in oral language come to be reflected in low levels of reading comprehension, leading to low levels of academic success" (p. 23). But this need not be the case. A rich program in vocabulary development that involves the development of oral language, conceptual knowledge, knowledge about words, and an awareness of words can improve students' vocabulary and reading success (Baumann et al., 2003). In addition, teaching students about the English language as part of spelling and language arts instruction can certainly have an impact on both everyday vocabulary use as well as on more academic words and concepts. Having students use new words in writing helps to consolidate their knowledge of and comfort using these words. (See also our discussions in Chapter 10, on spelling, and in Chapter 11, on writing.)

What Additional Research Is Needed About Vocabulary Development and Instruction?

As with all areas of reading instruction, more research is needed on vocabulary development and instruction. Table 6.2 lists a sampling of some areas where additional work is needed. This is not a complete listing, as much research is needed in many areas of vocabulary development for children and students of all ages, from preschool through adulthood, and for all types of learners, including both monolingual and English language learners, students with special needs, and older students from high school through adult education programs.

What Resources Are Available for More Information on Teaching Vocabulary?

The web sites for the International Reading Association (IRA; http://www.reading.org) and the National Council of Teachers of English (NCTE; http://www.ncte.org) have resources and information on vocabulary instruction. Excellent books on vocabulary instruction

---

What we know from research

- Vocabulary knowledge is related to reading comprehension.
- Students require multiple exposures to learn words.
- Students require both definitional and contextual information to begin to fully understand a word.
- Wide reading contributes to vocabulary growth.
- Direct instruction in the meaning of words improves vocabulary knowledge and reading comprehension
- Instruction in the meaning of root words, prefixes, and suffixes enhances vocabulary knowledge and reading comprehension.
- Students learn some words incidentally through reading and other exposures (e.g., media).
- A rich instructional program that focuses on vocabulary can be effective in teaching concepts and improving comprehension.

(continued)

Table 6.2. *(continued)*

> ### What we need to know from additional research
>
> - What does it mean to know a word?
>
> - What is the nature of knowledge of and about words?
>
> - What instructional strategies are more effective for teaching vocabulary, and with which students?
>
> - What is the nature of the relation between vocabulary and comprehension?
>
> - Are there strategies to help students enhance their vocabulary while reading for pleasure without detracting from the enjoyment of reading?
>
> - What are effective methods for teaching students about using morphemes and context to independently learn new words?
>
> - What are the relative contributions of different types of activities for building vocabulary, and how can we improve vocabulary growth for students at different vocabulary levels?
>
> - What types of words and contexts increase vocabulary acquisition from reading and other exposures?
>
> - What role can computer programs play in enhancing vocabulary, and which instructional approaches are optimal for computer presentation?

Table 6.2.   Vocabulary research needs

include *Bringing Words to Life* by Beck, McKeown, and Kucan (2002) and *Vocabulary in the Elementary and Middle School* by Johnson (2001), which offer both research-based theory and instructional strategies for teachers to use. *Words Their Way* by Bear, Invernizzi, Templeton, and Johnston (2004) has lessons and background on phonics, vocabulary, and spelling and includes a CD and a web site for further teacher ideas and support. *Creating Strategic Readers: Techniques for Developing Competency in Phonemic Awareness, Phonics, Fluency, Vocabulary, and Comprehension* by Ellery (2005) has a section full of instruction strategies to build vocabulary. And we feel compelled to note that there are many other resources that may be available, and more are being published all the time. We have offered only a sampling of those with which we are personally familiar.

HOW MIGHT RESEARCH ON TEACHING
• • • VOCABULARY PLAY OUT IN THE CLASSROOM? • • •

Mr. Wells noticed that his seventh-grade students were having difficulty reading their science texts and could not remember important science terms. He checked some resources and found that students need from four to seven exposures to a word to learn it. He also learned that students need opportunities to work with a word in various contexts that call for the use of both definitional and contextual information about the word. He noticed that many of the science terms the students needed to know were built from Greek base words. Mr. Wells decided on a multipronged approach. He developed some homework activities, such as writing multiple sentences, making semantic maps, and developing word pairs to help students learn the science vocabulary. In class, he presented a series of short lessons on Greek combining forms, developed in collaboration with the language arts teacher, who agreed to reinforce the lessons in language arts class as well. Mr. Wells found that classroom follow-up discussions of the homework were sometimes lively and offered another instance for students to encounter and work with the words. He began to make a point of explicitly teaching the root words, prefixes, and suffixes of some of the science terms. The students seemed motivated and encouraged by their new knowledge and began to construct a giant semantic map of their science terms on one wall of the classroom. After 6 weeks of these activities, Mr. Wells noticed that students were comprehending their science texts better and improving their overall understanding of science content.

REFERENCES

Atkinson, R.C. (1975). Mnemotechnics in second language learning. *American Psychologist, 30*, 821–828.

Baumann, J.F., Kame'enui, E.J., & Ash, G.E. (2003). Research on vocabulary instruction: Voltaire redux. In J. Flood, D. Lapp, J.R. Squire, & J.M. Jensen (Eds.), *Handbook of research on teaching in the English language arts* (pp. 752–785). Mahwah, NJ: Lawrence Erlbaum Associates.

Bear, D.R., Invernizzi, M., Templeton, S., & Johnston, F. (2004). *Words their way* (3rd ed.). Upper Saddle River, NJ: Pearson.

Beck, I.L., McCaslin, E.S., & McKeown, M.G. (1980). *The rationale and design of a program to teach vocabulary to fourth-grade students* (LRDC Publication1980/25). Pittsburgh: University of Pittsburg, Learning Research and Development Center.

Beck, I.L., & McKeown, M.G. (1985). Teaching vocabulary: Making the instruction fit the goal. *Educational Perspectives, 23*, 11–15.

Beck, I.L., McKeown, M.G., & Kucan, L. (2002) *Bringing words to life: Robust vocabulary instruction*. New York: Guilford Press.

Beimiller, A. (Spring, 2003). Oral comprehension sets the ceiling on reading comprehension. *American Educator, 27*, 23.

Blanchowicz, C.L.Z., & Fisher, P. (2000). Vocabulary instruction. In M.L. Kamil, P.B. Mosenthal, P.D. Pearson, & R. Barr (Eds.) *Handbook of reading research* (Vol. III., pp. 503–523). Mahwah, NJ: Lawrence Erlbaum Associates.

Cain, K. (1996). Story knowledge and comprehension skills. In C. Cornoldi & J. Oakhill (Eds.), *Reading comprehension difficulties: Processes and intervention* (pp.167–192). Mahwah, NJ: Lawrence Erlbaum Associates.

Coomber, J.E., Ramstad, D.E., & Sheets, D.R. (1986). Elaboration on vocabulary learning: A comparison of three rehearsal methods. *Research in the Teaching of English, 20,* 281–293.

Ellery, V. (2005). *Creating strategic readers: Techniques for developing competency in phonemic awareness, phonics, fluency, vocabulary, and comprehension.* Newark, DE: International Reading Association.

Graves, M.E. (1986). Vocabulary learning and instruction. In E.Z. Rothkopf (Ed.), *Review of research in education.* (Vol. 13, pp. 49–89). Washington, DC: American Educational Research Association.

Hart, B., & Risley, T.R. (1995). *Meaningful differences in the everyday experience of young American children.* Baltimore: Paul H. Brookes Publishing Co.

Henry, M.K. (2003). *Unlocking literacy: Effective decoding and spelling instruction.* Baltimore: Paul H. Brookes Publishing Co.

Johnson, D.D. (2001). *Vocabulary in the elementary and middle school.* Needham Heights, MA: Allyn & Bacon.

Kame'enui, E.J., Dixon, D.W., & Carnine, R.C. (1987). Issues in the design of vocabulary instruction. In M.G. McKeown & M.E. Curtis (Eds.), *The nature of vocabulary acquisition* (pp. 129–145). Mahwah, NJ: Lawrence Erlbaum Associates.

Kamil, M.L. (2004). Vocabulary and comprehension instruction: Summary and implications of the National Reading Panel findings. In P. McCardle & V. Chhabra (Eds.), *The voice of evidence in reading research* (pp. 213–234). Baltimore: Paul H. Brookes Publishing Co.

Langer, S.K. (1942). *Philosophy in a new key: A study in the symbolism of reason, rite, and art.* Cambridge, MA: Harvard University Press.

Levin, J.R., McCormick, C.B., Miller, G.E., Berry, J.K., & Pressley, M. (1982). Mnemonic versus nonmnemonic vocabulary learning strategies for children. *American Educational Research Journal, 19,* 121–136.

McDaniel, M.A., & Pressley, M. (1989). Keyword and context instruction of new vocabulary meanings: Effect on text comprehension and memory. *Journal of Educational Psychology, 81,* 204–213.

McGivern, J.E., & Levin, L.R. (1983). The knowledge-keyword method and children's vocabulary learning: An interaction with vocabulary. *Contemporary Education Psychology, 8,* 46–54.

McKeown, M.G., Beck, I.L., Omanson, R.C., & Pople, M.T. (1985). Some effects of the nature and frequency of vocabulary instruction on the knowledge and use of words. *Reading Research Quarterly, 20,* 522–535.

Mezynski, K. (1983). Issues concerning the acquisition of knowledge: Effects of vocabulary training on reading comprehension. *Review of Educational Research, 53,* 253–279.

Moats, L. (2005, Winter). How spelling supports reading: And why it is more regular and predictable than you may think. *American Educator, 12,* 42–43.

Nagy, W.E., & Scott, J.A. (2000). Vocabulary processes. In M.L. Kamil, P.B. Mosenthal, P.D. Pearson, & R. Barr (Eds.), *Handbook of reading research* (Volume III, pp. 269–284). Mahwah, NJ: Lawrence Erlbaum Associates.

National Institute of Child Health and Human Development. (2000). *Report of the National Reading Panel. Teaching children to read: An evidence-based assessment of the scientific research literature on reading and its implications for reading instruction: Reports of the subgroups* (NIH Publication No. 00-4754). Washington, DC: U.S. Government Printing Office.

Pearson, P.D., & Johnson, D.D. (1978). *Teaching reading comprehension.* New York: Holt, Rinehart, & Winston.

Pressley, M., Levin, J.R., & McDaniel, M.A. (1987). Remembering versus inferring what a word means: Mnemonic and contextual approaches. In M.G. McKeown & M.E. Curtis (Eds.), *The nature of vocabulary acquisition* (pp. 107–127). Mahwah, NJ: Lawrence Erlbaum Associates.

Rohwer, W.D. (1973). Elaboration and learning in childhood and adolescence. In W.H. Reese (Ed.), *Advances in child development and behavior* (Vol. 8, pp. 1–57). New York: Academic Press.

Schwartz, R.M., & Raphael, T. (1985). Concept of definition: A key to improving students' vocabulary. *The Reading Teacher, 39,* 98–203.

Snow, C.E., Burns, M.S., & Griffin, P. (Eds.) (1998). *Preventing reading difficulties in young children.* Washington, DC: National Academies Press.

Stahl, S.A. (1985). To teach a word well—a framework for vocabulary instruction. *Reading World, 15,* 16–27.

Stahl, S.A. (2003, Spring). How words are learned incrementally over multiple exposures. *American Educator, 27,* 18–19.

Stahl, S.A., Burdge, J.L., Machuga, M.B., & Stecyk, S. (1992). The effects of semantic grouping on learning word meaning. *Reading Psychology, 13,* 19–35.

Stahl, S.A., & Fairbanks, M.M. (1986). The effects of vocabulary instruction: A model-based meta-analysis. *Review of Educational Research, 56,* 72–110.

Stahl, S.A., & Kapinus, B. (2001). *Word power: What every educator needs to know about teaching vocabulary.* Washington, DC: National Education Association.

Stanovich, K.E., West, R.F., Cunningham, A.E., Cipielewski, C., & Siddiqui, S. (1996). The role of inadequate print exposure as a determinant of reading comprehension problems. In C. Cornoldi & J. Oakhill (Eds.), *Reading comprehension disabilities* (pp. 15–32). Mahwah, NJ: Lawrence Erlbaum Associates.

Alphabetics

KEY CONCEPTS

- Alphabetics, phonics, and letter–sound correspondences are necessary but not sufficient for learning to read.

- Explicitly teaching children decoding skills is an important step in ensuring that all students learn to read.

- Systematic phonics is effective in teaching students to read and spell and has the greatest effect when delivered early, during kindergarten and first grade.

This chapter discusses phonemic awareness (PA) and phonics, but the PA that is most useful to students in the elementary grades is linked to knowing the letters of the alphabet and their correspondence to sounds. So we chose to call the chapter "Alphabetics." We might have also called it "Decoding," since once students can recognize the letter–sound correspondences of English and have learned the regularities of English spelling, they are breaking the code of print and have some of the essential skills that will speed them on the path to reading. But *decoding* is sometimes used just as an alternate term for phonics. Thus we chose to use the term *alphabetics*, as does the National Reading Panel (NRP) report (National Institute of Child Health and Human Development [NICHD], 2000), to group together those phonological skills that are necessary but not sufficient for learning to read.

What Does Research Indicate About Alphabetics Instruction?

There are two alphabetic components of reading instruction: PA and phonics. These components are useful in teaching individuals to read in alphabetic languages. Alphabetics instruction has been found to be essential to reading, regardless of whether one uses decoding, analogy, prediction, or sight reading, as we will describe in the sections that follow. It is also essential to writing and spelling.

Phonemic Awareness

A *phoneme* is the smallest meaningful unit of sound in a language. Phonemes themselves do not necessarily have meaning (unless a word consists of a single phoneme, such as *a* or *oh*), but they can change the meaning of a word. For instance, changing the first sound in *cat* to /b/ changes the word, and the two words mean very different things. Because sound comes out in an unsegmented stream, students must learn to segment the sounds. To learn to read, children must learn to link these sounds to letters or groups of letters called *graphemes*. PA is the awareness of phonemes, that is, the ability to recognize and manipulate phonemes in spoken words (Lieberman, Shankweiler, Fischer, & Carter, 1974). Ehri (2004) described seven tasks that demonstrate PA ability: *isolation* (i.e., recognizing individual sounds within words), *identity* (i.e., picking out the common sound in different words), *categorization* (i.e., picking out the odd or different

Table 7.1. Tasks that demonstrate phonemic awareness ability

Task	Example
Phoneme isolation	What is the first sound in *bat*? (/b/)
Phoneme identity	Which sound is the same in *bird, ball,* and *boy*? (/b/)
Phoneme categorization	Which word does not belong: *cat, car, dog*? (*dog*)
Phoneme blending	What word do these sounds make: /s/ /k/ /u/ /l/ (school)
Phoneme segmentation	How many phonemes are there in *ship*? (3 phonemes)
Phoneme deletion	Say *snooze* without the /s/. (news)
Onset-rime manipulation	sh-*op*, sn-*ooze*, *j*-*ump*

sound in a group of words), *blending* (i.e., combining a sequence of separately pronounced sounds to make a known word), *segmentation* (i.e., breaking a word into its individual component sounds, often using tapping, counting, or positioning blocks or other markers for each sound), *deletion* (i.e., recognizing the word that is left after removing a specific phoneme) and *onset-rime manipulation* (i.e., isolating, identifying, blending, or deleting the onset, or first sound or blend that precedes the vowel of a syllable or rime). See Table 7.1 for examples.

The NRP produced a report that included subgroup reports on each of the five major components of reading: PA, phonics, fluency, vocabulary, and comprehension (NICHD, 2000). In the section on PA instruction, they reported the results of a meta-analysis of several studies, with the overall finding that explicit PA instruction has a positive impact, not only on improving PA skills but also on reading and spelling. (These same findings are also summarized in Ehri, 2004.) PA instruction produced a lasting effect that was observable on follow-up several months after the training was completed and was seen on both standardized tests and on tests developed by researchers. Two aspects of PA instruction were clear in the overall findings. First, it was clear that PA can be taught; that is, explicit instruction definitely improves children's PA. Second, PA instruction that uses actual letters is more effective than PA using sound alone or using blank tokens (e.g., movable blocks) to represent the sound units. The panel went into greater detail, examining the conditions under which PA training was most effective, and it is these findings that are most helpful in actual classroom practice.

The NRP report (NICHD, 2000) examined the impact of PA instruction on three groups: typically achieving readers, children who were at risk of reading difficulties (as indicated by low PA skills) below second grade, and readers who were defined as low-achieving students in Grades 2–6 (where *low achieving* was defined as reading below grade level). PA instruction was found to have a positive impact on PA skills and on word reading, pseudoword reading, and, to some extent, reading comprehension. For the typically achieving and at-risk children, PA instruction also appeared to transfer to spelling ability, but this was not true for the older, low-achieving students. The panel speculated that PA training may not have helped to improve spelling ability in readers with disabilities because their spelling skills are much harder to remediate than are their reading skills. Ehri (2004) suggested that these older students may have needed more than just PA instruction to improve their spelling. Other student characteristics were also examined. Both low and mid-to-high socioeconomic status students benefited from PA instruction. In addition, the panel examined studies of PA instruction in students learning English and other alphabetic languages and found stronger effects for students learning English. They speculated that one possible explanation may be that English is a more difficult (less regular) orthography in terms of the letter–sound correspondence than their native language. For example, a language, such as Spanish, in which the letter–sound correspondence is much closer to one-to-one, is said to have a more transparent orthography, which makes some aspects of learning to read easier. And not all English language learners (ELLs) come from a background of an alphabetic language. Clearly, the issue of ELL students is one that deserves its own specific research. (In fact, a major panel report has been published that has synthesized the available research on this group of students [August & Shanahan, 2006].)

In addition to student characteristics, the panel also examined training characteristics. One of these, the use of letters in PA training, is mentioned in the previous section. They also looked at group size, length of training, number of skills taught, and who delivered the instruction. Group size was considered in three categories: individual tutoring, small-group instruction containing 2–7 students, and whole-class instruction. Small-group instruction was found to be more effective than either of the other two. More research is needed to determine why this is so. However, Ehri (2004) reasoned that perhaps students paid more attention because they wanted to do as well as their peers in the group, or that they learned not only due to the instruction directly but also indirectly from watching their fellow students perform.

In the PA studies examined by the NRP, total training time ranged from an hour to 75 hours (NICHD, 2000). The panel broke studies into four time blocks (1–4.5 hours, 5–9.3 hours, 10–18 hours, and 20–75 hours). Based on their findings, it appears that the two middle blocks of time are optimal, and that spending more than 18 hours teaching PA is less effective. The major message seems to be that explicit instruction can accomplish what is needed in a moderate amount of time and that more instruction is not necessarily better when it comes to PA. Clearly, time spent on instruction is only one factor, and it is important that the time allocated to instruction actually be spent on instruction. Foorman and colleagues found that often teachers spend a great deal of time in classroom management when the time is allocated in their instructional plan to a particular focus within reading or language arts (Foorman & Schatschneider, 2003; Foorman et al., 2006; Saunders, Foorman, & Carlson, 2006). Others have also commented on the importance of measuring the quality and quantity of time allotted to specific tasks within a reading/language arts block to understand instructional effectiveness (Allington, 1991; Saunders et al., 2006). While the NRP report said that their findings should not be used to dictate instructional time periods, we would recommend that about 15–20 minutes a day of the reading/language arts instructional block be spent on PA training for students in kindergarten, first, or second grade who have not already mastered these skills, and that it be linked to letter sounds. Of course, as teachers continue with phonics and other aspects of reading instruction, it should become apparent which students have mastered PA, and individualized review work that incorporates PA and phonics would then be helpful to those students needing assistance.

Number of skills taught was another variable that the NRP report considered, since it could have a bearing on the effectiveness of PA instruction (NICHD, 2000). The panel members separated the studies into those that taught single PA skills, two skills, or more than two. (See Table 7.1 for a listing of these individual skills.) They found that focusing PA instruction on one or two skills was more effective than teaching multiple skills. They offered the possible explanation that children taught many different ways to manipulate the sounds in words may have become confused about which one to use when tested after training. They also offered that when teaching multiple skills, perhaps each individual skill received less time and attention, and that perhaps the studies that taught multiple skills were teaching higher level PA skills to older students who were having difficulty with PA. Instruction focusing on two particular PA skills, blending and segmentation, showed stronger effects than instruction in more than two skills. As Ehri (2004) pointed out, blending helps children decode unfamiliar words, and segmenting helps children form connections to remember how to read and spell words. These are highly functional skills that seem to complement one another.

A final issue concerned who was teaching PA in the studies examined by the NRP (NICHD, 2000). Much attention has been given in research to fidelity of implementation of particular programs. That is, if a program is developed by researchers who do the instruction themselves or deliver it via specially trained research assistants, how much training will be required and what special skills might be needed that teachers may not have had the opportunity to acquire? So the question often asked is whether teachers will have equal success with the program. Therefore, the panel considered it important to compare studies in which teachers delivered the PA instruction to those in which researchers or research assistants delivered the instruction. They found that both groups were effective in delivering PA instruction. In addition, there were studies that demonstrated that computers can be effectively used in training students on PA skills. Ehri (2004) eloquently highlighted why the effects of the studies are probably an underestimate. Ehri said it this way:

> In these experiments, reading was only measured as an outcome. Teachers did not intervene to help children use their phonemic awareness [PA] skills to read. If student transfer to reading occurred, the process was unassisted. This contrasts with normal classroom instruction, in which teachers not only teach PA but also teach children how to apply it in their reading and give students practice doing this. Under the latter circumstances, much bigger effects on reading would be expected. (2004, p. 166)

PA instruction is part of alphabetics. As we said in the beginning of this chapter, alphabetics instruction has been found to be essential to reading, regardless of whether one uses decoding, analogy, prediction, or sight reading. *Decoding* is the process of converting letters to sounds and blending them to form words. It is sometimes referred to as *sounding out words*. Decoding may involve not only phoneme isolation, identification, and blending, but also onset-rime segmentation. Children may also read unfamiliar words by analogy. That means that they apply knowledge of words that are familiar but share onset or rime with the unfamiliar word; clearly this approach requires PA. Readers may approach unfamiliar words in context using prediction; that is, using letters in the word and the information in the text can help to logically predict what the word must be. However, this is a less reliable method than using decoding or analogy. Familiar words are read by sight. People used to believe that one could learn to read by memorizing all the words, and that reading sight words relied almost entirely on memory. Ehri (1992) demonstrated that sight word learning depends on applying knowledge of letter–sound correspondences. For words to become automatized (recognized quickly and accurately), the reader must be able to analyze all the letters and match them up to phonemes in pronunciation (Ehri & Saltmarsh, 1995).

What Is Known, and What Additional Research Is Needed About Phonemic Awareness?

Although research has provided some good information about PA, there are always new questions to consider. Table 7.2 summarizes some of what is known through completed research and offers suggestions for new directions for future research.

Basically, what we know about teaching PA is this. Most children do require instruction, but PA is generally learned best when instruction ranges from 5 to 18 hours and when the sound manipulation is paired with letters. PA is most effective for at-risk children below second grade, for typically achieving readers, and for low-achieving readers from Grades 2 through 6. PA instruction is not only effective in helping students with alphabetics, but it also has a positive impact on reading for all three groups of students and on spelling for at-risk and typically achieving students. It appears to be insufficient for improving spelling in children with reading disabilities beyond Grade 2. Teaching

---

What we know from research

- PA instruction transfers to reading and, for younger students, spelling.
- It is more effective to teach PA with letters.
- It is more effective to teach PA in small groups (2–7 students).
- Blending and segmentation are key skills.
- Teachers are effective in delivering PA instruction.
- Computers can be helpful in PA training.
- Socioeconomic status does not make a difference; PA training is effective for students from all socioeconomic backgrounds.

What we need to know from additional research

- What do teachers need to know to effectively integrate PA instruction with other elements of beginning reading instruction?
- What are the processes and conditions that make small-group instruction effective?
- What are the motivational properties of PA training, and how can teachers enhance motivation and interest if these are lacking?
- How can computers be used in PA training in ways to maximize transfer to spelling and reading?

Table 7.2. Phonemic awareness (PA) research needs

one or two skills is more effective than teaching multiple skills, and in particular, teaching blending and segmenting seems to be most useful. Socioeconomic status does not make a difference; children from both low and mid-to-high socioeconomic backgrounds benefit from PA instruction. PA instruction is part of alphabetics, which is essential to reading, regardless of whether one uses decoding, analogy, prediction, or sight reading. Thus, PA instruction is foundational to reading, and children will benefit from explicit, systematic instruction in this important skill.

HOW MIGHT TEACHING PHONEMIC
• • • AWARENESS PLAY OUT IN THE CLASSROOM? • • •

Mrs. Brown had a class of kindergarten students who needed a great deal of development of their oral language and concepts as well as work on PA. She delivered instruction in PA during the time she devoted to reading activities but knew her students would need practice to reinforce this skill. She decided to use her science lessons as a means of developing concepts and oral vocabulary as well as guided practice in PA skills. She showed the students pictures of animals, and together they made a list of animals they have seen or read about. They also made a list of what animals do: live someplace, eat, sleep, have babies, and move around in characteristic ways. After she made the lists on the board, she read the name of an animal and asked students to identify the beginning sound in the word. The next day she had the class review what they discussed and the list. She read the names of three animals: *camel, cat,* and *coyote.* "What sound do you hear in all of these words?" she asked. Students responded, and she continued to pick groups of words that have the same sounds at the beginning.

The next day, she helped the students begin a chart of the animals, with information about what each animal ate, where it lived, and what its babies were called. She introduced the words *habitat* and *prey.* Students described habitats, animals that are prey, and those animals that look for prey. They also counted the sounds in these new words. Then Mrs. Brown wrote words from the chart and had students practice counting the phonemes. She went on to help the students understand the terms *wild* and *tame* and to classify the animals according to those terms. She wrote the word *tame* on the board and then asked what word they would have if they changed the *t* to *g.* She went on to do the same with the word *wild.* Mrs. Brown saw that linking this practice to a topic all of the children seemed interested in made the skills practice fun and engaging for them.

Phonics

Phonics is an instructional method that teaches the correspondence between alphabet letters in written language and the phonemes of spoken language and how to use them to read and spell words. The goal of phonics instruction is to help children learn about the alphabetic system of a language so that they can use that knowledge to decode new words and become skilled at recognizing familiar words quickly and accurately, to enable reading. Phonics instruction is referred to as *systematic phonics* when all of the major letter–sound correspondences are taught, including short and long vowels and vowel and consonant digraphs, in a clearly defined sequence, and usually with practice applying knowledge of these correspondences in reading words. Within systematic phonics, there are several different instructional approaches: *synthetic, analytic, phonics through spelling, phonics in context,* and *analogy phonics*.

In *synthetic phonics*, children learn to convert letters to sounds, and then synthesize or blend them to form words. *Analytic phonics*, starting from the word rather than the sound in isolation, teaches children to analyze letter–sound correspondence after having identified the words. *Phonics through spelling* teaches students to transform sounds into letters to write words, as the name implies. In *phonics in context*, students are taught to combine use of letter–sound correspondence with context cues to identify unfamiliar words in text. *Analogy phonics* uses analogy with known written words or parts of words to identify unfamiliar words. Clearly, many phonics programs may incorporate two or more of these approaches.

What Were the Findings of the National Reading Panel Regarding Phonics?

Phonics was the second of the five major components of reading studied by the NRP, as Part II of Alphabetics (NICHD, 2000). As in the PA report, the panel conducted a meta-analysis of experimental and quasi-experimental studies to determine the effectiveness of phonics instruction. The studies they examined compared systematic phonics instruction with low or no phonics instruction. The major overall finding was that systematic phonics instruction helps children learn to read more effectively than do programs that teach little or no phonics, and that, while it is effective for children from kindergarten through

Grade 6, this instruction appears to be most effective when begun early (kindergarten and first grade). This finding reiterates and confirms what Chall (1967) and several subsequent reviews (e.g., Adams, 1990; Anderson, Hiebert, Wilkinson, & Scott, 1985) have concluded: Early, systematic phonics instruction leads to better reading achievement than does phonics instruction that is delivered later and in a less systematic way.

Systematic phonics instruction was found to be effective across a variety of conditions and characteristics. The panel examined results comparing different age and ability groups of students, low versus middle socioeconomic groups, for three different major types of programs: one-to-one tutoring, small-group instruction, and whole-class instruction. Systematic phonics instruction, like PA instruction, was found to be effective for students from both low and middle socioeconomic groups. This is important because it tells us that even students who may enter school at some disadvantage usually can and do learn when taught using systematic phonics methods. Unlike the findings for PA, for phonics instruction there were no major differences depending on whether the instruction was delivered in one-to-one tutoring, in small groups, or as whole-class instruction.

The NRP report considered the impact of systematic phonics instruction on six outcome measures: decoding real words, decoding pseudowords, word identification including some irregular words, spelling words, reading text orally, and comprehending text (NICHD, 2000). Overall, systematic phonics instruction had a greater impact on all six outcomes than did reading programs that included low or no phonics instruction. Students in the studies were divided by age and grade into younger (kindergarten and first grade) and older (Grades 2–6) groups. Systematic phonics instruction had a significant impact on both younger and older students. However, the contribution to reading growth was larger for younger readers who had little prior reading ability than for older students who had already had some reading instruction and had developed some reading skills. The effects were equally strong for kindergarten and first graders.

Older students included typically developing readers, low-achieving readers, and students with reading disabilities. There were few studies of typically developing readers; more than three fourths of the comparisons involved readers with reading disabilities or readers who were low achieving. More research is needed to determine why the overall effect of systematic phonics instruction, although significant compared to control groups, was lower for the older students. However, the NRP report offered several possible explanations (NICHD, 2000). One is that it may be more difficult for students to learn phonics if they have already developed other, less effective approaches to word recognition. Another is that remediating students who have reading disabilities or who are low-achieving readers is particularly challenging. For example, students with auditory processing problems might have difficulty with phonics instruction and need more individualized help with this skill. As to individual reading outcomes, the NRP report found that older students benefited more from systematic phonics instruction than from instruction that included low or no phonics, for word and nonword reading but not for spelling or text comprehension.

To determine if there were any differences between low-achieving students and those with reading disabilities receiving systematic phonics instruction, the NRP report examined results separately for these two groups (NICHD, 2000). For students with reading disabilities, despite the fact that the effect was small, systematic phonics instruction helped them comprehend text more successfully than did the nonsystematic programs without phonics. However, systematic phonics instruction was not effective in improving reading comprehension for low-achieving readers. Ehri (2004) speculated that the lower or zero effect size for comprehension and spelling for older readers may reflect the greater need that these students have for specific instruction focused on comprehension strategies and background knowledge, and for spelling instruction targeted to individual words.

In order to examine whether the specific type of systematic phonics program made a difference, the NRP divided the programs into three categories: synthetic phonics programs; analytic phonics programs; and a miscellaneous category including spelling, basal phonics programs, and some researcher-developed programs focused on word analysis (NICHD, 2000). They found that all three were more effective than nonsystematic or no phonics programs. Thus, a variety of approaches are effective, with the important common factor being that they are systematic; however, systematic phonics instruction is especially beneficial when a synthetic approach is used.

The NRP report also examined specific phonics programs, to offer additional information about what the particular advantages of those programs might be (NICHD, 2000). For phonics instruction in kindergarten, the NRP panel discussed Stuart's (1999) study, which compared use of Jolly Phonics (Lloyd, 1993) and instruction centered around a big-book instruction approach (Holdaway, 1979). While the big-book instruction did include some discussion of letters and sounds and was described as fun and imaginative in the original report, the panel noted that it was not systematic. Jolly Phonics, used in the United Kingdom for 4- and 5-year-old students (their first year of formal schooling), used meaningful pictures, stories, and actions to reinforce a systematic approach to letter sound and formation, blending for reading, sound identification for reading, and a focus on high-frequency irregularly spelled words. The panel described this program as promoting "playful, creative, flexible teaching that fits well with whole language practice and leads directly to authentic reading and writing" (NICHD, 2000, p. 2-125). In this study, the at-risk kindergartners taught with Jolly Phonics were able to read more words and pseudowords and write more words than were the children taught using the big-books approach. There was no differential effect on comprehension between the two approaches, but the advantage of having kindergartners better prepared to use alphabetic knowledge when they enter first grade seems clear.

In discussing the Jolly Phonics program, the panel highlighted the value of using mnemonics to teach letter–sound correspondence, citing not only this but also other programs that have demonstrated successful mnemonics use with young children (Ehri, Deffner, & Wilce, 1984; Wendon, 1992). The panel commented that techniques, such as the use of memory aids, are valuable to speed up learning and help prepare kindergartners for reading instruction. The association between sounds and the letters they represent is arbitrary and meaningless; without some meaningful association this can be a difficult task for young children. Using interesting characters or incorporating the learning in games that are fun helps promote learning and should make letter learning happen more quickly and with greater ease.

Another kindergarten phonics program discussed by the NRP report (NICHD, 2000) in some detail is that of the program introduced by Vandervelden and Siegel (1997). In this program, intervention is tailored to the individual child's level of knowledge. Since kindergartners enter the classroom with widely varying levels of knowledge about letters and sounds, this intervention can help fill in gaps for children with low PA skills and letter–sound correspondence. The authors of the study provided one-on-one tutoring for those with the least knowledge on entry, instructed those at the next level in pairs, and worked with small groups at the next level. The experimental treatment included 15 children, and there were 15 children in a control group who received the same instructional delivery format (i.e., tutoring, pairs, or small group) but with the usual classroom activities as their focus. The children receiving phonics outperformed the controls on tests of PA, letter–sound correspondence, and on matching speech to print for words and pseudowords. They did less well on reading high-frequency words, suggesting that perhaps PA is a better focus than word reading and spelling for kindergarten children. Since this program was only 12 weeks long, it also may be that more time or a more optimal design is needed to establish the link from PA and letter–sound correspondence to independent word reading (i.e., for moving beyond matching the oral to the printed word to actually recognizing words in print).

The panel also offered a detailed discussion of two longer phonics programs that ran for 2.5–3 years. The first was studied by Blachman and colleagues and involved instruction with low socioeconomic, inner-city children beginning in kindergarten and lasting through first grade, and, for those who did not complete it in first grade, continuing to second grade (Blachman, Ball, Black, & Tangel, 1994). Control students were taught using a basal reader that included a phonics workbook that students completed independently. At the beginning of the program, students knew on average only two letter sounds and could not write their names. By the end of kindergarten, they knew on average 19 letter names and 13 letter–sound correspondences. Both kindergartners and first graders outperformed students in the control conditions. The core program involved 30-minute lessons and a five-step program emphasizing the alphabetic code by teaching new correspondences (vowels were highlighted in a different color); teaching phoneme analysis and blending; reading regular, irregular, and high-frequency words from flash cards (to support automaticity); reading decodable text; and writing words and short sentences to dictation. The program was systematic, and by the end of the program children had been introduced to all syllable types. The program integrated vocabulary and reading comprehension, with increasing work with text as vocabulary development allowed. Teachers were given assistance in program implementation through monthly in-service sessions.

Several features were noted as possibly explaining the advantage of this program over the basal program in teaching children alphabetics and word reading skills (Blachman et al., 1994). One was consistency and continuity, in that the program continued for more than 2 years; student learning was reinforced by consistency in the program elements and in the practice it provided them in applying what they learned; tests were included to help teachers determine who needed more work on certain aspects of alphabetics. The program involved a developmental sequence and was tailored to enable all students to complete it. The consistency of teacher in-services as well as the variety of types of reading and writing in which students applied their skills also seemed to contribute.

The second comprehensive phonics program was a tutoring program using synthetic phonics as compared to embedded phonics instruction (Torgesen et al., 1999). These two different phonics programs were compared to a tutoring control group and a classroom control group. The programs lasted 2.5 years; the comprehensive systematic phonics program involved explicit PA and synthetic phonics (PASP) taught by tutors beginning in kindergarten. Children were selected based on poor PA and letter knowledge. Students were taught auditory discrimination using an existing program (Lindamood &

Lindamood, 1984) and learned to track sounds in words with aware-ness of articulatory gestures and with colored blocks and letters. There was a heavy focus on decoding skills, although some attention focused on word and text reading. The embedded phonics program began with whole-word recognition, and letter–sound correspondence was taught using sight words.

Torgesen et al. (1999) taped lessons to document the proportion of time spent on letter sounds, sight word instruction, and reading or writing connected text. The PASP tutors spent approximately triple the amount of time on PA and letter sounds, but about half the time on sight words and connected text compared to the embedded phonics tutors. The two phonics instruction groups were similar in speed and accuracy of word reading, but the PASP group outperformed the embedded phonics group on PA, decoding accuracy and efficiency, and word reading accuracy. Thus, they concluded that systematic, intensive synthetic phonics training was more effective in teaching word reading skills compared to embedded phonics and control groups.

There were some striking findings in the Torgesen et al. (1999) study beyond the effectiveness of the phonics instruction. They had selected those most at risk for reading difficulties to be in the study, but this group included two different types of potentially poor readers: children with high IQs who were therefore expected to not have diffi-culty reading but were performing poorly, and students with lower IQs for whom it was expected that they would have some difficulty. What the researchers observed in their careful study of these children was that certain variables in addition to instruction helped to explain stu-dent performance. These included parent education and occupation, behaviors in the classroom (activity level, attention, adaptability, and socialization skills), and phonological capabilities (PA, short-term memory, naming speed), but not IQ. Thus these researchers concluded that the IQ–achievement discrepancy was not relevant in determining which students needed or would benefit from reading intervention.

Finally, the NRP (NICHD, 2000) reported on a set of studies of modified versions of Reading Recovery (RR; Greaney, Tunmer, & Chapman, 1997; Santa & Hoien, 1999; Tunmer & Hoover, 1993). Gre-aney and colleagues gave poor readers in Grades 2–5 in New Zealand a 12-week RR lesson augmented with explicit letter–phoneme pattern instruction after they had learned the majority of their letters. Students were taught to read pairs of nouns containing rimes and then to read the rimes within the words. These researchers demonstrated that those who received rime training outperformed controls on tests of word and pseudoword reading but not on reading comprehension; findings indi-cated that rime–analogy phonics instruction produced greater word recognition growth than did the whole-word reading program used to teach the control group. Tunmer and Hoover (1993) conducted a similar study but augmented the RR with more systematic phonics instruction. The children studied were the poorest readers in the first grade. They showed enormous growth in phonics and word reading abilities compared to the standard control group, and they achieved the same amount as students in the unmodified RR group but in significantly fewer tutoring sessions. Santa and Hoien (1999) also provided RR modified with systematic phonics instruction to at-risk first graders. The phonics instruction included word study to develop PA and decoding skills; children were taught to spell words and to use analogy to recognize unfamiliar words. Compared to students receiving small-group guided reading instruction, the modified RR students showed greater growth in word reading and in reading comprehension. This illustrated that teaching phonics with larger units along with phonemes can be effective.

Taken together, the meta-analyses and comparisons of moderating variables as well as in-depth examination of individual studies indicated several very positive things about systematic phonics instruction. Systematic phonics instruction is effective in teaching students to read and spell, but has the strongest effect when delivered early (i.e., in kindergarten and first grade). Systematic phonics instruction helped beginning readers acquire and use the alphabetic system to read and spell words both in isolation and in text. Phonics instruction contributed to their ability to read real and pseudowords, read regular and irregular words, comprehend text, and read orally. Systematic phonics instruction was effective for low versus middle socioeconomic students, and was effective whether delivered via one-to-one tutoring, small-group instruction, or full-classroom instruction. It was effective in improving word and nonword reading for older students, but not spelling. For students with reading disabilities, but not for low-achieving students, systematic phonics instruction was effective in improving text comprehension. While all types of systematic phonics instruction are more effective than instruction that includes nonsystematic or no phonics instruction, systematic phonics instruction produces stronger effects when the approach is synthetic.

What Additional Research Is Needed on Phonics Instruction?

The phonics research that is available does offer some practical information to help in the classroom, which is discussed in more detail in the next section. Table 7.3 summarizes some of what is known through completed research and offers suggestions for new directions for future research, since there are always new questions to be answered.

What we know from research

- Systematic phonics instruction is effective in teaching children to read words and nonwords, spell, comprehend text, and read orally.
- Synthetic phonics is stronger than other methods.
- Phonics instruction is more effective if introduced earlier, in kindergarten and first grade.
- Phonics can be effectively taught to individual children, small groups, or whole classes.
- Socioeconomic background of students does not make a difference; phonics instruction is effective for students from low and middle socioeconomic groups.
- Using memory aids (mnemonic pictures, gestures, or other activities) can aid rate and ease of letter–sound correspondence learning for kindergarten children.

What we need to know from additional research

- How does phonics ability relate to spelling ability for elementary and middle grade students?
- Is the small difference between synthetic and other methods that is revealed in research reliable?
- Does student motivation play a role in learning phonics?
- What makes whole-class phonics instruction effective?
- Why are small groups more effective for phonemic awareness instruction but not for phonics?
- What are the optimal approaches to remediating older students who have decoding difficulty?
- Why do older students make less rapid progress with systematic phonics instruction than younger, more novice readers? Does this have to do with unlearning ineffective practices or with learning differences in older students?

Table 7.3.   Phonics research needs

How Is Phonics Important to Reading?

Basically, we have known from Chall's (1967) review of research that phonics is important to reading and that it is most effective when delivered early and systematically. This has been reconfirmed in a meta-analysis of more recent literature by the NRP (NICHD, 2000). Researchers and educators know that systematic phonics instruction is more effective than nonsystematic instruction or instruction that does not include phonics; systematic phonics instruction is effective in improving word reading, nonword reading, spelling, reading comprehension, and oral reading. Systematic phonics instruction is most effective for kindergarten students and first graders who have little or no reading ability, and when the approach is a synthetic phonics approach. It is not effective in improving spelling for low-achieving readers in Grades 2–6.

Ehri (2004) outlined implications of these NRP analyses and what we know generally about teaching reading for classroom instruction. Students need to acquire PA, especially segmenting and blending. They need to know the names and shapes of the letters of the alphabet, the sounds the letters represent, and the major phoneme–grapheme correspondences. Kindergarten teachers must ensure that their students enter first grade with good PA and alphabet knowledge as well as familiarity with the reading process. Students need to be taught to decode the spelling of words and practice that decoding with familiar words, so they can recognize them automatically. They need to learn meanings associated with the spelling of these words, so the spelling and meaning are bonded in their memories.

The important ingredients of systematic phonics instruction include the following: There must be a plan for teaching all of the major letter–sound correspondences, including vowels and digraphs. *Synthetic phonics* means teaching students to transform graphemes into phonemes and blend them into words. They can begin with two letters and then move to longer sequences. From there students can learn larger units, again by decoding and blending. The larger units should be planned to enable the students to read new words. They should also apply these alphabetics skills to reading stories. Usually these are decodable texts targeted to the sound–letter correspondences and rime units the students have mastered. Gradually, as they master alphabetics, richer and more interesting texts can be introduced.

Ehri (2004) also listed some ineffective practices that should be avoided. These included extensive reliance on worksheets for teaching phonics. Another is having students memorize and recite complex rules; having them recognize the patterns by reading and writing words to illustrate the rules is a better approach. Finally, teaching phonics in isolation is not an effective practice. Students need the opportunity to apply their alphabetic knowledge, to practice what they have learned in reading and writing. Teachers must have sufficient depth of knowledge of PA and systematic phonics to teach them effectively, to know what to expect of students, to monitor student progress, and to adapt instruction to ensure student learning. Phonics is not a complete reading program, but it is one part. It must be integrated with instruction in other areas of reading, such as fluency and comprehension.

HOW MIGHT TEACHING
• • • PHONICS PLAY OUT IN THE CLASSROOM? • • •

Ms. Winn teaches first grade. She wanted to be sure students developed concepts and oral vocabulary related to social studies as well as their reading skills. She decided to use her social studies time to do both. Although she introduced phonics generalizations during the reading block of time for her class, she reinforced the skills and provided opportunities for application during her social studies lessons. She saw this as an ideal time to work on vocabulary. The students were learning about communities, and their vocabulary included several words that she wanted to work on with them: *community, city, town, street, home, store, business, neighbor, service,* and *dependence.* She discussed the term *community* with students, and they named types of communities and their characteristics. She then asked students to look at the first syllable in community. What sound does the *o* make? What other words have that sound? She wrote the words *come, some, Tom, hop,* and *stop* on the board. Then she asked students what was the same and what was different about the letters that come after the *o* in these words. What did they notice that is strange or different? The students noted that some words have a silent *e* with an *o* that is not long. They talked about these words that did not follow the rule of a vowel followed by a consonant and silent *e* producing a long vowel sound. They went back and listed some more words that did follow the rules.

Spelling and Reading

How Is Spelling Related to Reading?

Both reading and spelling rely on the same underlying knowledge: *alphabetics,* or the relationship between sounds and letters. Instruction in spelling can contribute to reading ability. Reading and spelling build and rely on the same mental representation; Snow, Griffin, and Burns (2005) argued that the real value of spelling is that being able to spell a word solidifies that mental representation so that it is more accessible for reading. According to Moats (2005/2006), students who are not proficient spellers are likely to restrict their writing to words they can spell, thus limiting their ability to express themselves. Spelling instruction is important and positively influences both reading and writing. (For more detail about spelling, see Chapter 10 on spelling and Chapter 11 on writing.)

Are There Documents That May Be Useful in the Classroom Based on Alphabetics Research?

Based on the findings of the NRP report, there have been various follow-up documents produced specifically for teachers (NICHD, 2000). To bring the evidence presented in the NRP report to teachers in somewhat nontechnical language, but with greater detail than in the summary of that report, McCardle and Chhabra (2004) edited a book, *The Voice of Evidence in Reading Research.* In addition to information about PA, phonics, and the other major components of reading (fluency, vocabulary, and comprehension), this book addressed various aspects of research that teachers should know about, and how both legislation and policy in reading have been developed.

The National Institute for Literacy published *Put Reading First: The Research Building Blocks for Teaching Children to Read* (Partnership for Reading, 2003b). This handy free document offers definitions and examples and was meant as a guide to classroom implementation. While it was targeted to teachers of students in kindergarten through Grade 3, others may find it provides helpful information about the five major components of reading addressed by the NRP report (NICHD, 2000) when working with older students who are struggling with reading. It's written in clear, understandable language. A second parallel document teachers may find helpful to share with parents is *A Child Becomes a Reader* (Partnership for Reading, 2003a), which contains helpful explanations and ideas for parents, also free upon request.

The International Reading Association also produced a useful document based on the NRP report (NICHD, 2000): *Evidence-Based Reading Instruction: Putting the National Reading Panel Report into Practice* (International Reading Association, 2002). This publication provides guidance for teachers about the requirements of the Reading First legislation as well as how to implement evidence-based practice in the classroom when teaching reading. It is a helpful resource for classroom teachers.

HOW MIGHT TEACHING PHONICS AND
• • • CRITICAL THINKING SKILLS PLAY OUT IN THE CLASSROOM? • • •

Mr. Piper wanted his first-grade students to develop critical thinking skills as well as phonics skills. He frequently planned instruction and practice activities that would do both. For example, he gave two words, such as *pin* and *hand,* and then asked what rule fits how the vowels sound in the middle of the words. Then he asked whether each of a few subsequent words fit the rule, pronouncing each word as he wrote it: *tin, find, fin, fan, pan, hand, sand, send,* and *mind.* Students responded with a thumbs up if the word fit the rule and a thumbs down if it did not. Students gave explanations for their responses. Mr. Piper directed the students to look for and describe a pattern for the words that did not fit the first pattern: *find* and *mind.* Then he asked for other ways the words could go together based on their sounds, then on their meanings. Finally, he asked students to work in groups of three to make up new words using the letters of the words on the board. Students were given letter tiles for this last task.

In addition to practicing the application of their phonics knowledge, Mr. Piper's students were analyzing, synthesizing, comparing and contrasting, and generating new rules and words. This was phonics in which the students were engaged and learning. It was not drill, but thoughtful practice.

REFERENCES

Adams, M.J. (1990). *Beginning to read: Thinking and learning about print.* Cambridge, MA: MIT Press.

Allington, R.L. (1991). Children who find learning to read difficult: School responses to diversity. In E.H. Hiebert (Ed.), *Literacy for a diverse society* (pp. 237–252). New York: Teachers College Press.

Anderson, R.C., Hiebert, E.F., Wilkinson, I.A.G., & Scott, J. (1985). *Becoming a nation of readers.* Champaign, IL: Center for the Study of Reading.

August, D., & Shanahan, T. (Eds.). (2006). *Developing literacy in second-language learners: Report of the National Literacy Panel on language-minority children and youth.* Mahwah, NJ: Lawrence Erlbaum Associates.

Blachman, B. (1999). Phonological awareness. In M. Kamil, P. Mosenthal, P. Pearson, & R. Barr (Eds.), *Handbook of reading research* (Vol. 3). Mahwah, NJ: Lawrence Erlbaum Associates.

Blachman, B., Ball, E., Black, R., & Tangel, D. (1994). Kindergarten teachers develop phoneme awareness in low-income, inner-city classrooms: Does it make a difference? *Reading and Writing: An Interdisciplinary Journal, 6,* 1–18.

Chall, J. (1967). *Learning to read: The great debate.* New York: McGraw-Hill.

Ehri, L. (1992). Reconceptualizing the development of sight word reading and its relationship to recoding. In P. Gough, L. Ehri, & R. Treiman (Eds.), *Reading acquisition* (pp. 107–143). Mahwah, NJ: Lawrence Erlbaum Associates.

Ehri, L.C. (2004). Teaching phonemic awareness and phonics: An explanation of the National Reading Panel meta-analyses. In P. McCardle and V. Chhabra (Eds.), *The voice of evidence in reading research* (pp. 153–186). Baltimore: Paul H. Brookes Publishing Co.

Ehri, L., Deffner, N., & Wilce, L. (1984). Pictorial mnemonics for phonics. *Journal of Educational Psychology, 76,* 880–893.

Ehri, L., & Saltmarsh, J. (1995). Beginning readers outperform older disabled readers in learning to read words by sight. *Reading and Writing: An Interdisciplinary Journal, 7,* 295–326.

Foorman, B.R., & Schatschneider, C. (2003). Measurement of teaching practices during reading/language arts instruction and its relationship to student achievement. In S. Vaughn & K.L. Briggs (Eds.), *Reading in the classroom: Systems for observing teaching and learning* (pp. 1–30). Baltimore: Paul H. Brookes Publishing Co.

Foorman, B.R., Schatschneider, C., Eakin, M.N., Fletcher, J.M., Moats, L.C., & Francis, D.J. (2006). The impact of instructional practices in Grades 1 and 2 on reading and spelling achievement in high poverty schools. *Contemporary Educational Psychology, 31,* 1–29.

Greaney, K., Tunmer, W., & Chapman, J. (1997). Effects of rime-based orthographic analogy training on the word recognition skills of children with reading disability. *Journal of Educational Psychology, 89,* 645–651.

Holdaway, D. (1979). *The foundations of literacy.* Sydney, Australia: Ashton-Scholastic.

International Reading Association. (2002). *Evidence-based reading instruction.* Newark, DE: International Reading Association. Retrieved June 17, 2007, from http://www.reading.org/Library/Retrieve.cfm?D=10.1598/0872074609.intro&F=bk460-intro-na.pdf

Lieberman, I.Y., Shankweiler, D., Fischer, F.W., & Carter, B. (1974). Explicit syllable and phoneme segmentation in the young child. *Journal of Experimental Child Psychology, 18,* 201–212.

Lindamood, C.H., & Lindamood, P.C. (1984). *Auditory discrimination in depth.* Austin, TX: PRO-ED.

Lloyd, S. (1993). *The phonics handbook.* Wilston, VT: Jolly Learning.

McCardle, P., & Chhabra, V. (2004). *The voice of evidence in reading research.* Baltimore: Paul H. Brookes Publishing Co.

Moats, L.C. (2005). How spelling supports reading: And why it is more regular and predictable than you may think. *American Educator, 12(22),* 12–43.

National Institute of Child Health and Human Development. (2000). *Report of the National Reading Panel. Teaching children to read: An evidence-based assessment of the scientific research literature on reading and its implications for reading instruction: Reports of the subgroups* (NIH Publication No. 00-4754). Washington, DC: U.S. Government Printing Office.

Partnership for Reading. (2003a). *A child becomes a reader.* Washington, DC: Author.

Partnership for Reading. (2003b). *Put reading first: The research building blocks for teaching children to read (Kindergarten through Grade 3).* Washington, DC: Author.

Santa, C., & Hoien, T. (1999). An assessment of early steps: A program for early intervention of reading problems. *Reading Research Quarterly, 34,* 54–79.

Saunders, W.M., Foorman, B.R., & Carlson, C.D. (2006). Is a separate block of time for oral English language development in programs for English learners needed? *Elementary School Journal, 107,* 181–198.

Snow, C.E., Griffin, P., & Burns, M.S. (Eds.). (2005). *Knowledge to support the teaching of reading: Preparing teachers for a changing world.* San Francisco: Jossey-Bass.

Stuart, M. (1999). Getting ready for reading: Early phoneme awareness and phonics teaching improves reading and spelling in inner-city second-language learners. *British Journal of Educational Psychology, 69,* 587–605.

Torgesen, J., Wagner, R., Rashotte, C., Rose, E., Lindamood, P., Conway, T., et al. (1999). Preventing reading failure in young children with phonological processing disabilities: Group and individual responses to instruction. *Journal of Educational Psychology, 91,* 579–593.

Tunmer, W., & Hoover, W. (1993). Phonological recoding skill and beginning reading. *Reading and Writing: An Interdisciplinary Journal, 5,* 161–179.

Vandervelden, M., & Siegel, L. (1997). Teaching phonological processing skills in early literacy: A developmental approach. *Learning Disability Quarterly, 20,* 63–81.

Wendon, L. (1992). *First steps in Letterland.* Cambridge, UK: Letterland Ltd.

CHAPTER 8

Fluency

KEY CONCEPTS

- Reading fluency is important to reading comprehension.

- Instruction in the form of guided repeated oral reading can help students improve their reading fluency.

- While extensive reading provides good practice for children, there is insufficient evidence to indicate that practices, such as sustained silent reading, should be given instructional time in place of other methods that have evidence of effectively improving reading fluency.

Mrs. Green had two fifth-grade students who read very slowly and labori-
ously. They both had a limited set of words they recognized on sight.
Although their ability to figure out words using phonics was solid, they
were spending too much time figuring out words that they should have
been recognizing by now. She realized that these students needed to
develop their repertoire of sight words. She decided to build that vocabulary in several ways. One way was to have the students begin a personal
collection of sight words. She had them write words they needed to know
on index cards on one side. On the back, she had them write a sentence
that used the word in a meaningful context (Gaskins, 2004). The students
practiced reading the words and using them in sentences, working with
each other and their parents as well as with the teacher. She also had
the students sort the cards in ways that focused on similar word parts
so that words like *card, cart,* and *Carmen* would be grouped together.
She also had them sort the cards in meaningful groups: descriptive
words, actions, and so forth. Finally, she had them practice reading with
expression in materials that are at their reading level.

Fluency is generally defined in reading as the ability to read text rapidly
and accurately with conversational prosody or expression. It relies
heavily on good word recognition skills, but good decoding or word
recognition skills are not enough to guarantee reading fluency. It also
takes practice. While researchers and educators have known this for a
long time (Samuels, 1997; Samuels, 2006), in 2000 when the National
Reading Panel (NRP) published its report (National Institute of Child
Health and Human Development [NICHD], 2000), this was an often-
neglected or insufficient part of classroom reading instruction.

What Does the Research Literature Say in General About Reading Fluency?

There is longstanding agreement that a major step in children's learning to read is the ability to read *fluently,* that is, the ability to read aloud
accurately, at a conversational rate, with expression. Chall (1996)
referred to this as the third stage of reading, coming after children have
established concepts of print and know the names and sounds of letters
of the alphabet and can decode (or segment sounds and recognize the
regularities of the sound–spelling relationship). Fluency is an important step in developing good reading comprehension. Children who

labor over individual words are so focused on the task of word recognition that they are rarely able to gain the meaning of the sentence they are wading through.

Fluency may sound simple, but the following description as stated in the NRP report of what it involves makes it clear that fluency is not just a matter of speed. It is also a very important part of reading:

> In its early conception, it was recognized that fluency requires high-speed word recognition that frees a reader's cognitive resources so that the meaning of a text can be the focus of attention...Fluency may also include the ability to group words appropriately into meaningful grammatical units for interpretation (Schreiber, 1980, 1987). Fluency requires the rapid use of punctuation and the determination of where to place emphasis or where to pause to make sense of text...Fluency helps enable reading comprehension by freeing cognitive resources for interpretation, but it is also implicated in the process of comprehension as it necessarily includes preliminary interpretive steps. (NICHD, 2000, p. 3-6)

Fluency includes various processes or behaviors that teachers can look for. The NRP examined these aspects and cited various research studies which laid out the characteristics of reading fluency (NICHD, 2000). As noted above, speed, accuracy, and expression are among these. But researchers have also noted that fluency requires *automaticity*—meaning that reading should be able to be carried out fluently without conscious attention, effortlessly, and without interfering with other processes that are occurring at the same time, such as attention to meaning. Researchers have also agreed that fluency results from extended practice, and Ackerman (1987) included in his description that fluency is developed through extensive practice that takes place under consistent conditions. Logan (1997) made the point that fluency should be viewed as a continuum, as something that develops gradually over time. While it may appear that some children catch on almost overnight, or make large sudden gains, studies have shown that there is a gradual, continual improvement over time in reading speed. This is also why researchers like to study change over time and examine the trajectory or curve of growth, rather than only measure skills before and after an intervention, and why teachers monitor progress periodically rather than just at the beginning and end of the year or semester. Reading speed, and other aspects of fluency or of any skilled behavior that becomes automatized, shows gradual improvement over time.

Decoding and comprehension may be seen as competing for cognitive resources. Human memory does have some limitations, and while researchers do not fully understand those limits, it seems clear that for children who are nonfluent readers, the process of word recognition slows them down and takes up resources that are necessary for comprehension. The reading task for fluent readers is easier. When word recognition has become automatic, cognitive resources are available for grouping words into phrases and sentences, which enables the reader to better understand the text. This automaticity frees up cognitive resources for tasks like drawing inferences. Eye movement research also supports this; readers actually do fixate on each word, but as they become more skilled at reading, they also improve their rate and their ability to span more information in a single fixation. In other words, they do not skip over words but can take in more than a single word on each fixation. Rayner, a leading and well-known researcher on eye movement in reading, and his colleagues found that fast readers make shorter fixations, take in larger spans (longer saccades), and tend to make fewer regressions or looks back at the same material than do slow readers (Rayner, 1978, 1986, 1998; Rayner & Duffy, 1988; Rayner, McConkie, & Zola, 1980; Rayner & Pollatsek, 1994). Faster and more accurate reading comes with practice.

Knowing that practice is important to the development of reading fluency is not enough. It is also important to know what types of practice, under what conditions, can most effectively and efficiently, with best use of both student and teacher time in the classroom, result in the largest gains in this ability, which thereby supports higher level reading achievement.

All sources agree with the commonsense notion that practice improves reading fluency. And many would agree that at least some of that practice should be oral reading. Probably the most commonly known procedure for oral reading, at least until the past few years, was round robin reading (Opitz & Rasinski, 1998). However, it is important to realize that round robin reading actually offers children far less practice than other methods; children spend more time listening to other children read and awaiting their turn than practicing reading. Thus it is the least effective technique for improving all aspects of fluency: accuracy, speed, and expression. Even when it is accompanied with fairly high-quality guidance, students have little opportunity to improve their oral reading since they do not usually reread the same text (NICHD, 2000). Stahl (2004) cited an old observational study (Gambrell, Wilson, & Gantt, 1981) that indicated that children reading in round robin approaches only read about 6 minutes a day, and children doing less well in reading often read even less (2 minutes per day or less) in this context; this approach therefore offers even less practice for those who need it most!

What Does Research Indicate Related to the Role of Fluency and Its Instruction in Learning to Be a Proficient Reader?

In *Preventing Reading Difficulties in Young Children* (PRD; Snow, Burns, & Griffin, 1998), the panel discussed the importance of fluency to comprehension. One study described an experimental intervention that is a mixture of vocabulary, comprehension strategies, and fluency (Stahl, Heubach, & Cramond, 1997). In this study, teachers read text aloud to introduce it to students; discussed the story; mapped it with story maps, charts, and diagrams; and reviewed vocabulary used (Stahl et al., 1997). In addition, they encouraged students to reread the story aloud with parents at home and with partners in class. For those needing additional help, teachers read the story aloud and had children echo read behind them. Overall, this integrated approach to promoting comprehension while building fluency seemed to be successful with the majority of children. The PRD panel highlighted the importance of fluency in reading, recommending that it be a focus of reading instruction that is monitored to ensure rapid response to any difficulties children have with attaining the skill of fluency reading.

The NRP report dedicated an entire chapter to reading fluency (NICHD, 2000). Based on their knowledge of the field and the very thorough literature searches performed, the NRP read and analyzed studies in order to address what specific instructional techniques were effective in building reading fluency in children. The panel reviewed research studies published from 1990 to 1998 that met their criteria for selection (based on topic and research quality). They examined two specific approaches: 1) those that used repeated oral reading or guided oral reading techniques and 2) those that encouraged recreational or independent reading.

First, the NRP examined 14 studies that examined guided repeated oral reading (NICHD, 2000). These studies used pre- and posttests to measure the immediate effect of guided repeated oral reading of passages on reading fluency or comprehension of those passages. The studies did not examine the impact on reading passages on which students had not had this guided repeated reading practice; this is not to say there was no effect on the students' reading of novel passages, only that this was not measured. However, on what was measured in these studies—increased fluency and, in some cases, reading comprehension—there were demonstrable improvements in student performance. The procedures varied from study to study; for example, some required students to practice for a set amount of time or to a set criterion, some included reading along with someone reading the same text, some included previewing through listening, and some provided specific feedback to students during oral reading. Especially when children heard the text before or when teachers previewed the text with the students, reading fluency and comprehension were improved by guided repeated reading. Together the 14 studies examined for immediate effects included 752 students ranging from first grade to college age and both good and poor readers. Gains were found for both good and poor readers.

The NRP also examined 17 experimental studies that, in addition to pre- and posttests, used control groups and reported sufficient information to be included in a meta-analysis (NICHD, 2000). Specifically, the NRP stated "repeated reading procedures had a clear impact on the reading ability of nonimpaired readers at least through Grade 4, as well as on students with various kinds of reading problems throughout high school" (NICHD, 2000, p. 3-17). The NRP made the point that fluency is developmental—that is, students are encountering increasingly difficult texts as they develop as readers, so a student who is quite fluent with third-grade reading materials may be slower and more halting with more difficult texts. A student may have automatized word recognition for most words in third-grade texts, but when reading a higher level text may encounter words that are unfamiliar and may force him or her to fall back on decoding skills for those words. In addition, the NRP pointed out that good and poor readers may gain different things from repeated oral reading. They cited Faulkner and Levy (1999), who demonstrated that poor readers learned more in the area of vocabulary while better readers became better at reading with appropriate expression.

The children in the guided repeated reading conditions in the studies that underwent meta-analysis gained more than the control students in both reading fluency and comprehension, although the results were stronger for fluency (NICHD, 2000). Nonetheless, it was clear that fluency does have a positive effect on reading comprehension.

The NRP (NICHD, 2000) also examined 12 studies that used single-subject design. The pattern of findings for these studies as a group confirmed and reinforced what had been shown both in the immediate effects studies and the meta-analysis: that guided repeated oral reading has value in improving reading fluency.

While there were not enough studies that compared two different repeated reading approaches to make strong statements about whether some methods were better than others, a few specific approaches were singled out. Rashotte and Torgesen (1985) showed that students made more improvement using passages that shared a lot of words than with passages that did not; this finding tends to support the Faulkner and

Levy (1999) result that what seems to be learned first in repeated reading approaches, at least for poor readers, is vocabulary. The NRP report also discussed several studies using partner reading (NICHD, 2000). The advantage of this approach is that, with little or no additional training, classroom teachers could implement this technique successfully, and that in fact parents or peer tutors with a few hours' training could also use the procedure.

The NRP's bottom line on guided repeated reading is that it does help improve students' reading abilities, at least through fifth grade, but also for older students who have reading difficulties (NICHD, 2000). There are two key parts to guided repeated reading: It not only provides practice reading since the student rereads the same text multiple times, but specific feedback is also provided.

Stahl (2004) recapped the NRP findings but added new evidence from his own team's work on fluency. He made the important point that fluency is important to comprehension but does not guarantee that a student will improve in reading comprehension. In his 2004 chapter, he described a fluency program that he and colleagues had developed called *fluency-oriented reading instruction* (FORI). While they felt it was a promising approach to gains in reading fluency, they had not evaluated it using a control group; thus it was not published in a peer-reviewed journal and was not included in the NRP report. In a major study of FORI that did include a control group, which was underway at the time of his writing the 2004 book chapter, Stahl offered preliminary findings. The program used a redesigned basal reading lesson, a free reading period at school, and a home reading program. A sample lesson plan was included in his chapter and is included here as Figure 8.1, which offers two levels: one for students at or above grade level and one for students approaching grade level. This approach is adaptable for students at different levels. Kuhn (2000), a colleague of Stahl, found that children reading a different book each day had better success on a measure of reading comprehension than those who read the same book repeatedly. This was incorporated into a wide-reading variation of FORI and studied in a much larger sample. Stahl's group found that for children reading at the preprimer level, experimental FORI students outperformed the control group (Stahl, 2004). As the school underwent schoolwide reform, the study had to be restructured and became a comparison of the repeated reading FORI and the wide-reading condition; the students in the wide-reading FORI outperformed both historical controls and the FORI repeated reading students. Stahl's conclusion was that both variations, which were similar in their outcomes, were effective. He interpreted this as suggesting that what made the difference for students was the increased amount of reading and the support given

	Monday	Tuesday	Wednesday	Thursday	Friday
		For students reading at or above grade level			
Basal lesson	**Teacher introduces story.** Teacher reads story to class and discusses it with students. Teacher reviews key vocabulary and gives comprehension and other story-focused exercises. *Option:* Teacher develops graphic organizers. *Option:* Students do activities from class text.	**Students read and practice story.** *Option:* Students do partner reading.	**Students read and practice story.** *Option:* Students do partner reading.	**Students do extension activities,** such as writing in response to the story.	**Students do extension activities,** such as writing in response to the story. *Option:* Teacher keeps running records of children's reading.
Choice reading	Students read a book of their choosing.	Students read a book of their choosing.	Students read a book of their choosing.	Students read a book of their choosing.	Students read a book of their choosing.
Home reading	Students read 15–30 minutes in a book of their choosing.	Students read the story to parents or other reader.	Students read 15–30 minutes in a book of their choosing.	Students read 15–30 minutes in a book of their choosing.	Students read 15–30 minutes in a book of their choosing.

	Monday	Tuesday	Wednesday	Thursday	Friday
	For students approaching grade-level reading				
Basal lesson	**Teacher introduces story.** Teacher reads story to class and discusses it with students. Teacher reviews key vocabulary and gives comprehension and other story-focused exercises. *Option:* Teacher develops graphic organizers. *Option:* Teacher uses prepared audiotape.	**Students read and practice story.** *Option:* Teacher and students do echo reading.	**Students read and practice story.** *Option:* Students do partner reading.	**Students do extension activities,** such as writing in response to the story. *Option:* Students do partner reading. *Option:* Students do activities from class text.	**Students do extension activities,** such as writing in response to the story. *Option:* Students do activities from class text. *Option:* Teacher keeps running records of children's reading.
Choice reading	Students review the story and choose a book of their choosing.	Students read a book of their choosing.	Students read a book of their choosing.	Students read a book of their choosing.	Students read a book of their choosing.
Home reading	Students spend 15–30 minutes in a book of their choosing.	Students read the story to parents or other reader.	Students read the story to parents or other reader.	Students read the story to parents or other reader.	Students spend 15–30 minutes with a book of their choosing.

Figure 8.1. Fluency-oriented reading instruction (FORI) divided into two instructional groups. (Note: both groups use reading material appropriate to grade level.) (From Stahl, S. [2004]. What do we know about fluency?: Findings of the National Reading Panel. In P. McCardle & V. Chhabra [Eds.], *The voice of evidence in reading research* [p. 201]. Baltimore: Paul H. Brookes Publishing Co.; reprinted by permission.)

during that reading. He concluded that fluency can and should be taught as part of an effective reading program. Figure 8.1, originally published in Stahl (2004), provides a nice example of how one might work on fluency with students at or above grade level and students

What we know from research

- Reading fluency facilitates and supports reading comprehension (Snow, Burns, & Griffin, 1998).
- Fluent reading does not guarantee comprehension (Stahl, 2004).
- Accuracy is a better indicator in the early grades (Grades 1–2); rate remains a significant indicator (Stahl, 2004).
- Fluency is correlated with comprehension achievement in Grade 4, while accuracy is not (Pinnell et al., 1995).
- Fluency and comprehension are related, but the nature of the relationship is complex, sometimes even reciprocal (Stahl & Heubach, 2005; Stecker, Roser, & Martinez, 1998).
- Reading connected text, not isolated words, can improve both fluency and comprehension (National Institute of Child Health and Human Development [NICHD], 2000).
- Practice reading and specific feedback on that reading are crucial elements in improving students' reading fluency (NICHD, 2000).
- Different amounts of free reading time seem to have different effects on more and less proficient readers (Samuels, 2006).

What we need to know from additional research

- What elements of guided repeated reading are most responsible for improved fluency?
- What are the particular contributions of the components of guided reading (i.e., oral reading, guidance, repetition, text factors)?
- What is the optimal timing and duration of guided repeated reading to best help students develop reading fluency?
- How should instruction be modified to address the different needs of older students in developing sufficient fluency or accuracy when it is not acquired?
- What is the nature of the relationship between fluency and comprehension?
- How does comprehension facilitate fluency?
- What are the optimum lengths of time and conditions for self-selected silent reading in order to improve fluency and comprehension?

Table 8.1. Fluency research needs

approaching grade level. Table 8.1 provides information on fluency research needs.

Is It Possible to Help Students to Become More Fluent Readers Just by Having Them Read More?

Encouraging students to read more is widely recommended and intuitively appealing. Logically one would think this was a great idea. However, this seemingly simple and straightforward approach was the topic of great controversy when the NRP report was published in 2000 (NICHD, 2000). The NRP was tasked with reporting on what works—that is, what evidence there was of the effectiveness of specific instructional approaches. This meant looking at experimental and quasi-experimental studies. They did examine the research literature on approaches to encouraging students to read. What they found was that most of the studies on these approaches reported correlations between reading more and reading better. However, with only correlational data, it is impossible to say that one of these two associated things causes the other. Do students who are better readers read more because they enjoy reading? Or does reading more make them better readers? Another problem with searching for experimental evidence of whether encouraging students to read more will actually affect their reading achievement is that most of the studies that had been done up to 1999 did not measure the actual amount of increased reading; while they did tend to measure reading comprehension, few measured fluency.

The NRP concluded that there was insufficient experimental research evidence to recommend encouraging students to read more as an instructional practice (NICHD, 2000). This is not to say it should not happen, nor does it mean that there is no research of any type supporting this approach, but it should not replace other reading instruction. It is also important to note that the panel did not say it would not improve student reading, but rather that there is no experimental or quasi-experimental evidence that it does or does not improve student reading. The panel stated it this way:

> Although several reviews of the literature have concluded that procedures like sustained silent reading (SSR) work simply because reading achievement does not decline once they are instituted, that is not a sound basis on which to recommend such procedures as effective. (NICHD, 2000, p. 3-27)

Stahl, who served as a consultant to the NRP and who also conducted research on reading fluency, summarized his thoughts on this controversy and the role of reading practice:

> Although the research reviewed by the NRP (NICHD, 2000) does not support the use of SSR, common sense suggests that children should have some time during the day to read books of their own choosing, if only for motivational purposes (see Turner, 1995). However, I suggest that teachers actively monitor children's reading, both by going around the room to make sure that children are on task and by asking questions about what children are reading, and encouraging children to read books of an appropriate level...In short, reading practice may be useful for children, but like guided repeated reading, the practice needs to be actively monitored and guided by the teacher and should involve reading books at an appropriate level of difficulty. (Stahl, 2004, p. 207)

We agree with the NRP and Stahl. It is clear that students should read, in school and out, and that more reading is better because they will learn more vocabulary, enhance their knowledge of the world, and gain important practice. In addition, one researcher concluded in his review of research on wide reading that "other forms of evidence and scholarly review provide sufficient basis for strongly advocating and recommending its promotion" (Pikulski, 2006, p. 87). However, based on the NRP findings, it is also clear that independent reading should not be employed at the expense of other instructional practices. And we heartily endorse Stahl's final plea, that teachers guide and monitor student reading, including their independent reading.

How Can Teachers Tell If Students Are Progressing in Reading Fluency?

The NRP report (NICHD, 2000) lists several informal procedures that teachers can use in the classroom to assess fluency. These include informal reading inventories, miscue analysis, pausing indices, running records, and reading speech calculations. All involve having students read orally. Both the Gray Oral Reading Test (Wiederholt & Bryant, 1992) and the Comprehensive Test of Phonological Processing (Wagner, Torgesen, & Rashotte, 1999) are standardized measures that can also be used for this purpose.

There are also some other ways that classroom teachers can track student growth in fluency.

Curriculum-Based Measurement

Curriculum-based measurement (CBM) measures fluency using materials from the school reading program with a standardized process: Directly observe and record 1 minute of oral reading accuracy and the number of words. Fluency is reflected by the number of words read accurately in that 1 minute, which can be changed to a percentage of number correct divided by total words read in that one minute. Oral reading performance should be observed repeatedly over time using different but equivalent passages (Deno & Marston, 2006).

Miscue Analysis

Miscue analysis involves having a student read a passage and recording the exact mistakes, repetitions, skipping of words, and rate. Look for patterns in the errors that are made, such as omitting the endings of words, using the initial sounds but not paying attention to the rest of a word, or substituting words that do not make sense in the context of the passage (Clay, 2002; Harp, 2000).

Timed Readings of Short Texts

Timed readings of short texts can be woven into classroom routines. Both the teacher and the student keep track of the increase in rate of words read in short texts. Ask students to retell what they read, since reading words without comprehension is not true reading fluency.

HOW MIGHT THIS RESEARCH ON
• • • FLUENCY PLAY OUT IN THE CLASSROOM? • • •

Mr. Johns had several students in his second-grade class who read almost every word of a selection accurately but who had no expression. While these students were fluent in reading words, they were not fluent in reading words in a way that indicates an awareness of their meaning. He decided both to encourage wide reading to build their vocabulary and to provide guided practice in oral reading. He had the students prepare a short passage from self-selected books they were reading and read the passage to a partner. He circled the room during silent reading time and during the shared reading time, offering suggestions, such as feedback on expression or help with meaning in order to improve expression or pacing. He also provided feedback, asked questions, and made observational notes. He watched for improvement and for areas where students needed additional instruction or help.

REFERENCES

Ackerman, P.L. (1987). Individual differences in skill reading: An integration of psychometric and information processing perspectives. *Psychological Bulletin, 102,* 3–27.

Chall, J. (1996). *Stages of reading development.* (2nd ed.). Orlando, FL: Harcourt Brace & Co.

Clay, M.M. (2002). *An observation survey: Of literacy achievement* (2nd ed.). Portsmouth, NH: Heinemann.

Deno, S.L., & Marston, D. (2006). Curriculum-based measurement of oral reading: An indicator of growth in fluency. In S.J. Samuels & A.E. Farstrup (Eds.), *What research has to say about fluency instruction* (pp. 179–203). Newark, DE: International Reading Association.

Faulkner, H.J., & Levy, B.A. (1999). Fluent and nonfluent forms of transfer in reading: Words and their message. *Psychonomic Bulletin and Review, 6,* 111–116.

Gambrell, L.B., Wilson, R.M., & Gantt, W.N. (1981). Classroom observations of task-attending behaviors of good and poor readers. *Journal of Educational Research, 74,* 400–404.

Gaskins, I.W. (2004). Word detectives. *Educational Leadership, 81*(6), 70–73.

Harp, B. (2000). *The handbook of literacy assessment and evaluation* (2nd ed.). Norwood, MA: Christopher-Gordon.

Kuhn, M.R. (2000). *The effects of repeated readings and non-repeated readings on comprehension and fluency.* Unpublished doctoral dissertation, University of Georgia, Athens.

Logan, G.D. (1997). Automaticity and reading: Perspectives from the instance theory of automatization. *Reading and Writing Quarterly, 13,* 123–146.

National Institute of Child Health and Human Development. (2000). *Report of the National Reading Panel. Teaching children to read: An evidence-based assessment of the scientific research literature on reading and its implications for reading instruction: Reports of the subgroups* (NIH Publication No. 00-4754). Washington, DC: U.S. Government Printing Office.

Opitz, M.F., & Rasinski, T.V. (1998). *Good-bye round robin.* Portsmouth, NH: Heinemann.

Pikulski, J.J. (2006). Fluency: A developmental and language perspective. In S.J. Samuels & A.E. Farstrup (Eds.), *What research has to say about fluency instruction* (pp. 70–93). Newark, DE: International Reading Association.

Pinnell, G.S., Pikulski, J.J., Wixson, K.K., Campbell, J.R., Gough, P.B., & Beatty, A.S. (1995). *Listening to children read aloud.* Washington, DC: U.S. Department of Education Office of Educational Research and Improvement.

Rashotte, C.A., & Torgesen, J.K. (1985). Repeated reading and reading fluency in learning disabled children. *Reading Research Quarterly, 20,* 180–188.

Rayner, K. (1978). Eye movements in reading and information processing. *Psychological Bulletin, 85,* 618–660.

Rayner, K. (1986). Eye movements and the perceptual span in beginning and skilled readers. *Journal of Experimental Child Psychology, 41,* 211–236.

Rayner, K. (1998). Eye movements in reading and information processing: 20 years of research. *Psychological Bulletin, 124,* 372–422.

Rayner, K., & Duffy, S.A. (1988). Online comprehension processes and eye movements in reading. In M. Daneman, G.E. MacKinnon, & T.G. Waller (Eds.), *Reading research: Advances in theory and practice* (pp. 13–16). New York: Academic Press.

Rayner, K., McConkie, G.W., & Zola, D. (1980). Integrating information across eye movements. *Cognitive Psychology, 12,* 206–226.

Rayner, K., & Pollatsek, A. (1994). *The psychology of reading.* Mahwah, NJ: Lawrence Erlbaum Associates.

Samuels, S.J. (1997). The method of repeated readings. *Reading Teacher, 32,* 403–408.

Samuels, S.J. (2006). Toward a model of reading fluency. In S.J. Samuels & A.E. Farstrup (Eds.), *What research has to say about fluency instruction* (pp. 24–46). Newark, DE: International Reading Association.

Schreiber, P.A. (1980). On the acquisition of reading fluency. *Journal of Reading Behavior, 12,* 177–186.

Schreiber, P.A. (1987). Prosody and structure in children's syntactic processing. In R. Horowitz & S.J. Samuels (Eds.), *Comprehending oral and written language.* New York: Academies Press.

Snow, C.E., Burns, M.S., & Griffin, P. (Eds.). (1998). *Preventing reading difficulties in young children.* Washington, DC: National Academies Press.

Stahl, S. (2004). What do we know about fluency?: Findings of the National Reading Panel. In P. McCardle & V. Chhabra (Eds.), *The voice of evidence in reading research* (pp. 355–382). Baltimore: Paul H. Brookes Publishing Co.

Stahl, S.A., & Heubach, K.M. (2005). Fluency-oriented reading instruction. *Journal of Literacy Research, 37,* 26–60.

Stahl, S., Heubach, K., & Cramond, B. (1997). *Fluency-oriented reading instruction.* Washington, DC: National Reading Center and U.S. Department of Education, Office of Educational Research and Improvement, Educational Resources Information Center.

Stecker, S.K., Roser, N.L., & Martinez, M.G. (1998). Understanding oral reading fluency. In T. Shanahan & F.V. Rodriguez-Brown (Eds.), *47th Yearbook of the National Reading Conference* (pp. 295–310). Chicago: National Reading Conference.

Turner, J.C. (1995). The influence of classroom context on young children's motivation for literacy. *Reading Research Quarterly, 30,* 410–441.

Wagner, R., Torgesen, J., & Rashotte, C.A. (1999). *Comprehensive test of phonological processing (CTOPP).* Austin, TX: PRO-ED.

Wiederholt, J.L., & Bryant, B.R. (1992). *Gray Oral Reading Test (GORT).* Austin, TX: PRO-ED.

CHAPTER 9

Reading Comprehension

KEY CONCEPTS

- Reading comprehension is the goal of reading instruction, and a complex ability that develops over a long period of time, beginning at the word level and continuing to develop into adulthood.

- Reading comprehension is the ability to understand written language at several levels: words in print, the relationships of those words in sentences, and how sentences and then groups of sentences (paragraphs and larger chunks of text, such as chapters and stories) work together to provide information the reader uses to build an understanding of text.

- Many aspects of reading are essential to ensure that students develop good reading comprehension, including decoding, fluency, vocabulary, background knowledge, and motivation.

Mrs. Jennings noticed that Jeremy, a well-behaved, intelligent third grader, seemed to have difficulty responding to questions about what he read. She asked Jeremy to read part of a story from the basal out loud. Jeremy did an excellent job, reading accurately and with reasonable fluency. However, when she asked Jeremy to tell her about what happened in the passage, he could not do so. It was clear that he was not able to comprehend what he read in spite of reasonable skills in word recognition. Mrs. Jennings realized that Jeremy needed to work on comprehension.

The importance of reading comprehension cannot be downplayed—it is the very essence of reading, its ultimate goal. It is *why* individuals read. It is also where people most often fail in reading. The much-noted "fourth-grade slump," in which students who have mastered beginning reading skills (i.e., phonemic awareness [PA], phonics, alphabetics) fall behind in school, is thought to be due in large part to a failure in reading comprehension. There are several ways that comprehension can be approached and several taxonomies for teaching and assessing comprehension. We emphasize those that have been addressed in large research syntheses and are supported by theory. There are several useful practices that are supported by research as being useful in the classroom.

As noted in other chapters in this book, vocabulary and reading fluency are fundamental to reading comprehension. Lack of background knowledge can impede comprehension. There are several research-based approaches for developing comprehension, including *reciprocal teaching* (Palincsar & Brown, 1984; Palincsar, Brown, & Martin, 1987), which is described in the scenario at the end of this chapter, and for teaching comprehension strategies that are effective in building reading comprehension. Unlike the basic decoding skills and reading fluency, reading comprehension instruction is not only the job of the reading or language arts teacher, but it also falls within the domain of content-area teachers; for example, the science, history, mathematics, and literature teachers all need to teach students the special vocabulary used in their content areas, and point out aspects of text construction that may aid comprehension and oral and written communication in their content areas. Content-area teachers teach and reinforce academic language and writing skills that will enable students to learn content and to demonstrate what they have learned. Researchers know that students who are not explicitly taught comprehension strategies are unlikely to develop them spontaneously (National Institute of Child Health and Human Development [NICHD], 2000).

How Is Comprehension Defined, and How Can Research Guide Comprehension Instruction?

Very simply (although reading comprehension is neither a simple concept nor simple to teach), *reading comprehension* is the ability to understand written language at several levels: words in print, the relationships of those words in sentences, and how sentences and then groups of sentences, paragraphs, chapters, and stories work together to provide information the reader uses to build an understanding. *Comprehension* includes the ability to build understanding across large pieces of text, such as entire articles, chapters, and books. In addition to using the words or meaning cues in text, comprehension involves using the organization of text to support understanding. All of this happens through an active process that can and should be taught. Reading comprehension results from a reader's interaction and engagement with text. Students who comprehend well can construct a mental representation of what they read, hold it in memory, relate it to background information, revise it when inconsistencies are detected, and communicate the meaning of the text accurately in writing or speaking.

The National Reading Panel (NRP) pointed out in the introduction to the subgroup report on text comprehension instruction (NICHD, 2000) that it was only in the 1970s that we recognized that comprehension is not just a passive process of understanding that happens when an individual reads. Rather, it is an active process where an engaged reader uses intentional thinking to construct meaning through interaction with a text. The RAND study group (Snow, 2002) in fact defined *reading comprehension* in terms of the active engagement between reader and text. Ironically, prior to the 1970s, most instruction on reading comprehension was done in the content areas rather than as part of reading instruction. Since then, we have come to focus more on the process of reading comprehension and the theory that readers actively use their own background knowledge and the information in the text to construct a mental representation of the meaning of the text as they read it. This mental representation is a basis for understanding, remembering, and using what is read (Cote & Goldman, 2004; Tierney & Pearson, 1994). Students can be taught strategies that facilitate these mental processes. Therefore, as a field, we have begun to focus attention on how best to assist students in developing those strategies and understanding the processes they need to use.

Comprehension is described by the NRP as a cognitive process that "integrates complex skills and cannot be understood without examining the critical role of vocabulary learning and instruction and its development, [and] interactive strategic processes are critically necessary to [its] development" (NICHD, 2000, p. 41).

The RAND study group (Snow, 2002) defined reading comprehension similarly, as

> The process of simultaneously extracting and constructing meaning through interaction and involvement with written language. Reading comprehension consists of three elements: the *reader* who is doing the comprehending, the *text* that is to be comprehended, and the *activity* in which the comprehension is a part. (p. 11)

The RAND group also pointed out that this three-way interrelationship occurs within a larger sociocultural context that both shapes and is shaped by the reader as she or he interacts with the text repeatedly during reading. Teachers must be prepared to instruct students in how to comprehend, and this means guiding and structuring that interaction among reader, text, and activity.

There are many abilities and capacities that the reader must have. Of course, the reader must be able to decode the printed material of the text, which requires the components of reading we have already discussed in earlier chapters—PA, phonics, the alphabetic principle, vocabulary, and the ability to read fluently. In addition, the reader must have certain cognitive capacities, including attention, memory, and the ability to analyze and draw inferences. These last two, being able to analyze information and draw inferences, are learned and can be taught. In addition, readers must have motivation, including interest in reading the material and a purpose for reading it as well as a sense of self-efficacy as a reader (see Chapter 12 on motivation and engagement). Finally, the reader must have vocabulary knowledge and some background knowledge in order to understand what is being read. Interest and motivation, attention, and how much relevant background knowledge or depth of familiarity with vocabulary a student has will vary with the type of text and the particular text being read, and will change over time during reading. After all, one of the underlying purposes for reading any text is to gain new knowledge and insight. So the reader brings many things to the task of reading and gains many things through the experience of reading.

One goal of a teacher in instructing students in strategies for comprehension is to try to ensure, as much as possible, that a part of what happens in the reader as part of his or her interaction with text is *not* frustration, loss of interest and motivation, and failure. Instruction in reading comprehension is giving students the tools to prevent reading failure. (Of course, this is also true of reading instruction in the fundamental decoding skills.)

The reader is changeable. What about the text? There are many types of text, so while a single text does not change while we read it, readers must be familiar with what to expect from various types of text. Consider how different poetry, an editorial essay, a novel, a web page, and a recipe look; how differently they are organized; and how differently a person goes about reading each one. Texts do become more accessible as readers interact with and tease them apart during and after the reading process. The vocabulary used, the sentence structure, the organization, and the amount of background knowledge required all affect how easy or difficult a text will be for a reader to interact with and comprehend. Teachers can prepare students for the different types of text, and can build expectations about the material in advance, which can be very helpful in understanding them. In addition, teachers can give students the tools they will need in analyzing text to build their mental representations.

This leaves the third dimension: the activity itself. Very important to the activity of reading is purpose, which can be externally imposed, through assignment by a teacher, or internal, a text that is undertaken out of an interest in a particular subject. In either case, once the reader is engaged in the text, she or he may encounter new information that can change the purpose or change the activity as she or he engages more or less actively. If the reader is not particularly interested in the information, or is resentful or resistant to the assignment, this can lead to incomplete comprehension. If she or he sees the relevance of the activity, this can contribute to deeper interaction with the text and thus better comprehension. Goals of the activity may be, for example, that the reader seeks to repair something and must learn how it works and why it may not be working, or wants to build something and so wants to learn what tools and materials are needed and the sequence of tasks most likely to enable success. The activity's goal may be learning for its own sake, learning in order to apply that knowledge, or simply the enjoyment of engaging with text (settling down with a good novel). All of these can have other, longer term, beneficial consequences, such as increased vocabulary, gaining new incidental knowledge, or discovering a new interest.

All reading occurs in a sociocultural context. Much of the reading we are talking about in this book occurs in school, in an instructional context. But it is also in a social context of peers, within the cultures of school and of a student's own ethnic and linguistic cultures. All of this influences learning, reading, and how instruction is both delivered and received. Taking all of these factors into account while teaching reading comprehension must seem to some like being asked to pat their heads, rub their stomachs, and execute a complex dance step all at the same time. Yet educators master these techniques over time and integrate them into their repertoire of instructional skills. Our point here is that this information does affect how well educators communicate with students, how well students grasp what educators are trying to teach them, how relevant it may seem to the tasks they are attempting, and how they feel about their own performance and success or lack of success in tasks. The many contexts play a very important role in student learning, and thus in success in teaching.

What Do Researchers and Educators Know About Reading Comprehension?

Before addresssing the meta-cognitive reading strategies that the NRP found to support comprehension (NICHD, 2000), and that the RAND study group (Snow, 2002) advocated teaching, we should review some of the many things that are known to influence reading comprehension. Both the NRP in its subgroup reports and the RAND group, in building the basis for their outline of what research is needed in reading comprehension, highlighted what is already known.

First, as noted in Chapter 8 on reading fluency, instruction that improves fluency has a positive impact on word recognition and comprehension. Fluency is built through practice reading, and while there are many techniques to accomplish this, the most effective seems to be guided repeated oral reading, either with a teacher or with peers. Listening to the story read aloud in person or on tape can be helpful, but it is the practice of reading the same story repeatedly that is most helpful. Although reading more is always good practice, simply encouraging students to read silently does not have the same effect of improving reading fluency as does guided repeated oral reading.

Second, vocabulary (addressed in Chapter 6) is crucial to understanding. As the RAND study panel noted, the relationship of vocabulary to reading comprehension is complex, influenced not only by knowledge of words and their meanings and by instructional opportunities but also by cultural context and background knowledge (Snow, 2002). There is evidence that providing students with numerous books to read at home and at school and working to promote language development can have a positive impact on growth in vocabulary. While more research is needed about the specific effects of various instructional approaches to expanding vocabulary on reading comprehension, it is clear that vocabulary is foundational to comprehension, so vocabulary growth is beneficial for students generally and is therefore an area that should always be held in mind in any instructional setting or activity.

It is important to keep in mind, as stated in Chapter 6, that vocabulary instruction must focus on more than definitions and one-shot encounters with words if it is to support students' comprehension. Just as students need to be fluent in recognizing words, they need to be fluent in accessing the concepts behind the words. That access is seldom achieved by going over definitions one time before or after reading.

Providing students with additional background information, previewing vocabulary that may be new to them, and discussing key concepts as well as activating students' prior knowledge of a topic area through discussions prior to and after reading a text all support reading comprehension. While all students may benefit from such instructional activities, these can be especially helpful for students who are struggling or doing poorly in reading comprehension. As the RAND study group pointed out, instruction for high-achieving students often addresses higher order thinking, while teachers tend to focus more on factual reading for lower achieving students and tend to interrupt them more (Snow, 2002). It is important to deal with concepts, inferencing, linking background knowledge to the text at hand, and critical thinking about the ideas in the text with all students. Those who struggle more with the act of reading itself will require even more explicit instruction in these areas.

Student choice in reading materials can positively affect motivation to read and thus will promote better reading comprehension. Clearly, teachers can and should guide the choices of student reading materials; this can be done by determining the available selections from which choices are made. Teachers can determine what books are made available, whether broadly or within a given topic area for a particular assignment, and can provide lists of potential choices. Available materials should include texts at various levels of difficulty; students need not only materials that are within their ability but also some that present a challenge. Students who can choose books of greater interest to them within a topic will be more motivated not only to read the text but also to actively use the strategies they know to comprehend the text.

Finally, knowledge about text genre is an important factor in reading comprehension, and instruction in the diversity of types of text can facilitate reading comprehension. This comes into play when students are taught cognitive strategies. As the RAND study group pointed out, readers unaware of structure will likely not have a plan of action for a particular text and may gain information from that text in a random manner, whereas those who are aware of the way a text is structured are better able to organize information as they read, based on their knowledge of text structure and their expectations based on that knowledge (Snow, 2002). Both explicit instruction about the structure of different genres of text as well as strategy instruction can help students in learning about and using text structure to comprehend the information they read.

What Are Comprehension Strategies, and What Evidence Is There of Their Effectiveness for Instruction in Reading Comprehension?

Comprehension strategies are procedures that readers apply to guide their reading or writing. The NRP examined the research literature on reading comprehension (NICHD, 2000). They did not find enough similar studies with detailed information on effect sizes to allow meta-analyses. However, their analysis and synthesis of the existing literature revealed 16 categories of instructional focus; there was evidence that classroom instruction in the use of seven strategies was effective in improving the reading comprehension of typically developing readers (NICHD, 2000). Those seven strategies are described in the sections that follow, and methods for teaching them are provided in Table 9.1.

Table 9.1.   Goals of the National Reading Panel strategies and how they might be taught to students based on research

Strategy	Sample methods
1. *Comprehension monitoring*—to develop awareness of the cognitive processes used in reading, to be able to realize when not understanding the text that is being read, and to know how to fix the situation.	The teacher demonstrates and then teaches students to formulate what is causing the students problems understanding. The teacher teaches students to use think-aloud procedures to identify when problems occurred, to look back in text for information to solve problems, to restate text in more familiar terms, and to look ahead in text for information to solve a problem.
2. *Cooperative learning*—to teach students to complete reading tasks together to become more independent readers, and to develop social skills related to learning and literacy.	Students are taught and then allowed to practice partner reading, summarization of paragraphs, turn-taking in making predictions, word recognition, describing story structure, and summarizing the story.

Strategy	Sample methods
3. *Graphic organizers*—to use visual representation to aid memory of content and organization of information in a text.	The teacher shows students how to graph or map ideas in a structure using graphic metaphors (e.g., umbrella as main idea with related ideas under it), maps with the main idea in the center and related concepts around it, or box diagrams (e.g., problem, action, and results boxes to fill in).
4. *Story structure*—to teach students that a story has a beginning, a middle, and an end. Students should practice retelling what happened in each section. By Grade 2, students should be able to identify characters, settings, problems, and solutions. Story maps are one way of helping students organize the components of a story graphically.	The teacher demonstrates with the class how to represent the events of a story in visual form with students finding the key events in a narrative text. The teacher then provides opportunities for students to practice, providing guidance and feedback as needed. Students learn how to answer *who, where, when, what,* and *how* questions about the story. Students also learn how to construct a map of the setting, problem, goal, action, and outcome.
5. *Question answering*—to teach students to focus on specific content, to facilitate reasoning (*how* or *why* questions), and to look back in the text when students cannot answer questions (i.e., content questions) as well as to distinguish between those questions that require the integration of background information and those that call on recognition or repetition of what was read.	The teacher asks questions during the reading of the text and has students look back for answers if they cannot answer correctly after the first reading. The teacher also has students analyze questions as to whether they require literal information from the text or the drawing of inferences by combining background knowledge with information from the text. It is essential to include open-ended questions that have different possible answers that require revisiting the text to justify one's response, questions that require critical thinking and analysis, and questions that support substantive engagement and discussion rather than supplying the response that the teacher already has in mind.
6. *Question generation*—to enable students to become independent, active readers by learning to pose and answer questions about the text; to teach the student to generate *why, how, when, where,* and *which* questions in order to increase awareness of whether the material is being understood. (Teachers can also use this strategy to monitor student comprehension.)	The teacher asks students to generate questions that integrate information from different parts of the text passage read. The teacher then asks students to evaluate their own questions as to whether the questions contain important information, are integrative, and can be answered based on what is in the text. Teachers provide feedback on question quality and teach students to evaluate their own questions. It helps to provide students with a framework for answering questions (e.g., using information that is presented in the text, using the text information plus their own knowledge, and using their own knowledge alone; Raphael, 1986).
7. *Summarization*—to teach students to identify the central ideas in a text, to use prior knowledge to make inferences, and to generalize as well as to express related ideas in a succinct, well-organized way.	The teacher instructs and then guides students in summarizing, omitting trivial and redundant details, using superordinates in order to generalize, identifying topic sentences, and generating topic sentences where they are not explicitly found.

Strategy 1: Comprehension Monitoring

Readers' ability to check whether what they are reading is making sense and whether they are accomplishing their purposes for reading, such as locating relevant information for a task, is referred to as *comprehension monitoring*. It also includes the ability to apply "fix-up" strategies when comprehension is not going well. In five of seven studies, students trained in comprehension monitoring showed improvements on standardized tests of reading comprehension and the ability to remember the content of the text they had read. Also known as metacognitive awareness, the goal of this strategy is to help students develop an awareness of the cognitive processes involved in reading so that they will be able to recognize when they do not understand the material they are reading and try to change that situation. Several of the other specific strategies described can be used to support comprehension monitoring.

Strategy 2: Cooperative Learning

Often also described as collaborative learning, *cooperative learning* means having students work together to achieve their individual and common goals (Harris & Hodges, 1995). This approach in reading comprehension instruction involves having peers interact about using reading strategies, building and analyzing their understanding of the text, and instructing and informing each other. Cooperative learning has been shown to improve learning of the strategies and to improve reading comprehension. In addition, it gives students more control and responsibility for their own learning.

Strategy 3: Graphic Organizers

Teaching students to organize information they are reading into graphic representations, or *graphic organizers,* is a helpful strategy to promote comprehension. To benefit, students must have some skill in reading and writing. Use of graphic organizers for the ideas presented in a text and their relationships to each other can help students understand relationships among ideas in a text, and can improve memory for content. This strategy also shows promise for use in content area instruction (social studies and science).

Strategy 4: Story Structure

A set of instructional strategies focusing on *story structure* can be used to help students understand narrative texts. By teaching the organization of stories, such as beginning, middle, and end, teachers help students use the temporal organization in stories to support their comprehension. Knowing about the components of stories, including character, setting, problem, and solution, helps students comprehend stories by looking for salient aspects. A specific type of graphic organizer, story maps, can be used to help students understand or show their own understanding of stories. Poor readers show greater improvement from this type of training. While story structure can be taught without visual/graphic representation, making story maps seems to help weaker students understand the structure of a story or text. Because stories are a staple of early elementary reading, instruction in story structure is especially important at this stage.

Strategy 5: Question Answering

Question answering, or the strategy in which the teacher asks the students questions about the text, assists students in learning from text. Students also should learn what to do if they cannot answer the content questions posed, and to recognize questions they can answer from their own knowledge, questions they can answer strictly from the text, and questions that require the generation of inferences or conclusions. One systematic technique for helping students understand how to go about answering questions is to teach question–answer relationships (QAR), developed and researched by Taffy Raphael and others (Raphael & McKinney, 1983; Raphael & Pearson, 1985; Raphael & Wonnacott, 1985). The evidence for effectiveness of this strategy is primarily that students improved on experimenter-developed tests of questions; the NRP found no studies that used standardized or other general tests. This strategy was shown to be most useful in improving reading comprehension when taught in combination with other strategies.

Strategy 6: Question Generation

This strategy involves asking students to generate questions about the text, which requires them to find key ideas and important information in the text in order to formulate questions. The evidence of this strategy's effectiveness came from individual studies as well as from Rosenshine, Meister, and Chapman's (1996) meta-analysis. It is not clear how much this single strategy contributes to improved reading comprehension on standardized measures, although students did well on experimenter-developed measures. This strategy seems to be most useful in combination with other strategies

Strategy 7: Summarization

The process of *summarization* involves relating the smaller ideas in a piece of text or an entire text to build and articulate a general understanding of the text. While initially this may appear to be more of a writing strategy than a reading strategy, it can also be done orally, and it has been shown to have beneficial effects on reading comprehension. When well instructed in summarizing, students learn to identify the main ideas in a text but leave out extraneous details. They develop the ability to generalize from examples rather than including those examples, to include ideas related to the main idea, and to eliminate redundancy. In addition, students are more likely to remember what was read if they write a summary of it. Summarization can improve note-taking ability and make students more aware of the structure of the text.

Cognition and Metacognition

In referring to reading strategies and strategy instruction, there are two important dimensions to consider: cognition and metacognition. While it is sometimes difficult and not always necessary to distinguish between the two, knowing and understanding the differences in these concepts can help teachers as they analyze students' performance and plan instruction.

   Cognition refers to mental functions that are usually included in most lists of reading and thinking skills, such as understanding, summarizing, comparing, inferring, and analyzing. *Metacognition* refers to what a person is aware of or does related to those cognitive skills. For example, a reader might be making an inference about a historical event. As the reader continues reading, he or she becomes aware that the previous inference does not make sense with respect to the new information in the text. This awareness of a misinterpretation of the text, or awareness of a breakdown of the cognitive process of inferring, is metacognition. It is essential that students learn to check whether what they are reading makes sense—metacognitive awareness of comprehension—and how to fix the situation by such strategies as rereading, reading more slowly, and rethinking previous inferences and conclusions.

How Are Comprehension Strategies Taught?

Meaning does not simply exist or jump off the page for students. They must actively construct it. To do this, they need instruction on how to monitor their understanding and employ cognitive strategies that will enable them to construct that meaning. Students who are good comprehenders have a purpose for reading and notice when something they are reading is not clear, does not make sense, or does not seem to fit with what they know of the world, and they are able to do something about that. They are not only able to correct the situation when they do not understand text; they are able to read more efficiently. That is, they can organize the information they gain and summarize it, so that they consolidate that information in memory, which increases their own store of background knowledge. Thus they grow not only in reading but in learning from the text they are reading.

Instruction specifically focused on reading comprehension strategies is a crucial part of reading instruction, since students who are not explicitly taught comprehension strategies are unlikely to either develop or use these strategies spontaneously (NICHD, 2000). In order to effectively teach comprehension strategies, teachers themselves must understand how these strategies work, and they must be accomplished at using them in their own reading.

There are three basic aspects of comprehension strategy instruction: 1) teaching and modeling, 2) providing opportunities to use and practice the strategies with feedback, and 3) providing opportunities for independent application of the strategies. The goal is for the student to develop an awareness of his or her own cognitive processes, called *metacognitive awareness*. Teachers explicitly present the strategies, guide readers in applying them, and model their use for students. They provide opportunities for students to practice using the strategies during reading and monitor student performance. Through practice and teacher feedback, students gradually internalize the strategic processes and master them so that they become a routine part of how students approach new texts that they read. Research has shown that students who learn to use cognitive strategies show greater gains in measures of reading comprehension than students who receive conventional instruction (Pressley, Johnson, Symons, McGoldrick, & Kurita, 1989; Rosenshine & Meister, 1994; Rosenshine, Meister, & Chapman, 1996). Baumann, Seifert-Kessell, and Jones (1992) summarized the cumulative result of nearly 30 years of research as supporting the efficacy of cognitive strategy training in improving students' reading comprehension. While *how* strategies are taught is important, the RAND study group (Snow, 2002) emphasized the importance of strategy instruction for its *facilitation of engagement with the text*. When a reader employs strategies, she or he must interact with the text so that there is active engagement. All of this clearly indicates the importance of making sure that students are aware of cognitive strategies for reading comprehension and are able to use them.

An important finding of the NRP was that, while strategy instruction, particularly for the seven strategies described above, does result in better student reading comprehension, teaching multiple strategies seems to be the most effective way to teach cognitive strategies (NICHD, 2000). The report on text comprehension instruction indicated that multiple strategy instruction actively involves and motivates readers who read more text as a result of instruction. Further, multiple strategy instruction seems to offer a certain flexibility that enhances a teacher's ability to engage interaction about texts. It gives students a repertoire of strategies to use in building and analyzing their understandings of text. Finally, the NRP pointed out that teaching a variety of strategies can result in increased learning, increased memory and understanding of new text material, and better reading comprehension in general.

Strategy instruction is important for all students, not just those whose reading success demonstrates that they are ready for higher level, more complex texts, but also for those who are still struggling with reading. A research synthesis by Gersten and colleagues showed that successful strategy instruction for poor comprehenders includes the teacher's explicit modeling of strategy use, increased opportunities for practice reading and using strategies with feedback from the teacher, students' demonstrating their awareness of the purpose for reading and their active engagement with the text, and the teacher's skillful adjustment to the student's level (Gersten, Fuchs, Williams, & Baker, 2001). The level of explicitness required may be greater, and the planning for teaching cognitive strategies to struggling readers may be greater, but these aspects of reading instruction are crucially important for struggling readers. In fact, teaching these students will require most clearly that teachers themselves know these metacognitive strategies, use them, and can model them well.

What Additional Research Is Needed in Reading Comprehension?

While researchers and educators alike do know that comprehension is not something that just happens when readers can decode words and read fluently, and they do know that cognitive strategy instruction has been shown to be effective, they do *not* know all that they need to know about reading comprehension. They do not fully understand how comprehension develops or all the best ways to teach comprehension to students at various ages or to different types of students, whether they are struggling to develop comprehension in reading, are newly acquiring English, or have a cultural- or background-knowledge mismatch with the subject of the text. More research needs to focus on various aspects of reading comprehension in various groups or sub-groups of students. Table 9.2 explains what we know from research and highlights some recommendations of comprehension research needs for future study. These recommendations are just a sampling of the many questions that remain to be investigated in the vast and complex area of reading comprehension.

As with any area of reading or learning, while there is always more to learn, we know a great deal that teachers can implement and are implementing in the classroom to help both typically developing

What we know from research

- Instruction in fluency leads to improved word recognition and to some gains in reading comprehension.

- Vocabulary is foundational to reading comprehension, but the role of vocabulary in comprehension instruction is complex.

- Teaching cognitive strategies can enhance student comprehension of text, and can make students attend to specific aspects of text, recall content better, and amonitor their own cognitive processes in reading.

- Teaching multiple strategies seems to be more effective in improving reading comprehension than teaching individual strategies.

What we need to know from additional research

- How do intervention programs that link orthographic, phonological, semantic, and morphological systems emphasize fluency at every step show promise for enhancing comprehension?

- What are the effects of school-based oral language activities and vocabulary activities on reading comprehension in the elementary and middle grades?

- What specific types of vocabulary instruction and texts used in vocabulary instruction actually improve reading comprehension?

- How effective are the instructional use of morphology and definitions in improving reading comprehension?

- How can technology most effectively be used to increase vocabulary and background knowledge, and what is the effect on reading comprehension?

- What are the most effective ways to teach proven strategies?

- Does instruction of comprehension strategies lead to learning skills in content areas?

(continued)

Table 9.2.   *(continued)*

What we need to know from additional research

- Is the instruction of certain strategies more appropriate for certain ages and abilities, or for readers with specific characteristics?

- Which strategies are best taught, in combination, for younger readers, poor or below average readers, or learning disabled readers?

- For poor or below average readers, how should instructional time be allocated, and would more time on comprehension instruction using currently available curricula and instructional strategies result in adequate progress?

- How can teachers best determine the knowledge, skills, and dispositions of readers in order to differentiate instruction to meet student needs?

Table 9.2.   Comprehension research needs

and struggling students make gains in reading comprehension. While researchers explore the intricacies of how the human brain functions and the complexities that make up reading comprehension, teachers will continue to teach. Using what is known as presented in this chapter and as revealed in the research literature to inform instruction is important. Keeping data on their own instructional practices and effectiveness as reflected in student work will help teachers in spite of missing research evidence in some areas. Being able to differentiate instruction based on their own monitoring of student progress is one of the best tools teachers have to ensure student success.

HOW MIGHT THIS RESEARCH ON • • • COMPREHENSION PLAY OUT IN THE CLASSROOM? • • •

Ms. Jones had a group of fifth-grade students who were generally proficient in reading and discussing fifth-grade level stories. However, when her students read their geography textbook, they seemed to just read the words and not think about whether what they were reading made sense. She decided to improve their ability to monitor their own understandings of their textbook, check whether they were accomplishing their purposes for reading in geography, and apply strategies to remedy incomplete understanding and difficulty achieving reading related tasks. She decided to use reciprocal teaching as an approach to help the students.

This instructional strategy was based on research and had been proven effective in numerous studies with various levels and types of students. The strategy involved the application of four reading comprehension activities. After reading a passage, students would provide a summary of the passage, clarify any parts that were not clear or note new vocabulary, generate a question about the passage, and make a prediction about what is coming next in the text.

Ms. Jones began by modeling how to summarize sections of text read and develop predictions. She asked students to take turns with these activities as they moved through their geography reading. She then taught them to ask questions using a cuing system to help them think about questions. She chose the system based on questions whose answers were 1) right there; 2) required using background knowledge with the information from the text, the reader, and the author; and 3) required looking across the text, sometimes checking back, and thinking beyond the text.

Ms. Jones helped students develop proficiency in generating questions while using the steps of reciprocal teaching already taught. Then she added the step of seeking clarification, modeling it before asking students to try it.

REFERENCES

Baumann, J.F., Seifert-Kessell, N., & Jones, L.A. (1992). Effect of think-aloud instruction on elementary students' comprehension monitoring abilities. *Journal of Reading Behavior, 24*(2), 143–172.

Cote, N., & Goldman, S. (2004). Building representations of informational text: Evidence from children's think-aloud protocols. In R.B. Ruddell & N.J. Unrau, *Theoretical models and processes of reading* (5th ed., pp. 660–683). Newark, DE: International Reading Association.

Gersten, R., Fuchs, L.S., Williams, J.P., & Baker, S. (2001). Teaching reading comprehension to students with learning disabilities: A review of research. *Review of Educational Research, 71*(2), 279–320.

Harris, T.L., & Hodges, R.E. (Eds.). (1995). *The literacy dictionary: The vocabulary of reading and writing.* Newark, DE: International Reading Association.

National Institute of Child Health and Human Development. (2000). *Report of the National Reading Panel. Teaching children to read: An evidence-based assessment of the scientific research literature on reading and its implications for reading instruction: Reports of the subgroups* (NIH Publication No. 00-4754). Washington, DC: U.S. Government Printing Office.

Palincsar, A.S., & Brown, A.L. (1984). Reciprocal teaching of comprehension fostering and monitoring activities. *Cognition and Instruction, 1,* 117–175.

Palincsar, A.S., Brown, A.L., & Martin, S.M. (1987). Peer interaction in reading comprehension instruction. *Educational Psychologist, 22,* 231–253.

Pressley, M., Johnson, C., Symons, S., McGoldrick, J., & Kurita, J. (1989). Strategies that improve children's memory and comprehension of text. *Elementary School Journal, 90*(1), 3–32.

Raphael, T.E. (1986). Teaching question-and-answer-relationships, revisited. *Reading Teacher, 39*(6), 516–522.

Raphael, T.E., & McKinney, J. (1983). An examination of fifth- and eighth-grade children's question answering behavior: An instructional study in metacognition. *Journal of Reading Behavior, 15*, 67–86.

Raphael, T.E., & Pearson, P.D. (1985). Increasing students' awareness of sources of information for answering comprehension questions. *American Educational Research Journal, 22*, 217–236.

Raphael, T.E., & Wonnacott, C.A. (1985). Increasing students' sensitivity to sources of information for answering comprehension questions. *Reading Research Quarterly, 20*, 282–296.

Rosenshine, B., & Meister, C. (1994). Reciprocal teaching: A review of the research. *Review of Educational Research, 64*(4), 479–530.

Rosenshine, B., Meister, C., & Chapman, S. (1996). Teaching students to generate questions: A review of the intervention studies. *Review of Educational Research, 66*(2), 181–221.

Snow, C. (Ed.). (2002). *Reading for understanding: Toward an R&D program in reading comprehension.* Washington, DC: RAND Corporation.

Tierney, R.J., & Pearson, P.D. (1994). Learning to learn from text. In R.B. Ruddell, M.R. Ruddell, & H. Singer (Eds.), *Theoretical models and processes of reading* (4th ed., pp. 496–513). Newark, DE: International Reading Association.

CHAPTER 10

Spelling

"The English spelling system is tidy, behaves itself, and has a high degree of order."

(P. Ramsden, 2001, p. 6)

KEY CONCEPTS

- Spelling instruction can help students in reading and writing.

- Spelling ability relies on the same underlying principles as decoding.

- Spelling instruction that includes basic morphology and information about word origins can also enhance vocabulary and assist students with academic language.

Mr. Fine wanted to challenge and motivate his second graders to not only learn to spell but also to learn and think about words. He provided lessons where he gave them several words and asked them how the words were alike and different. He had students come to the front of the room and draw red lines on a large chart, connecting words that were spelled the same. They drew green lines between words that could be related in meaning, such as *star* and *far*. They talked about all of the ways the words could go together and how they were different. They talked about the words, used the words in sentences that showed that they understood their meanings and how the words could be used in sentences, and wrote those sentences on the board. When students took their spelling lists home, they performed similar activities, such as listing words that were spelled like their spelling words or were related in meaning and using them in sentences. Students began to spontaneously talk about spelling patterns and the meanings of words they encountered in their reading small groups.

Literacy is clearly more than just reading; it is being able to both read and write, and spelling is part of both reading and writing. Because it relies on the same essential knowledge of the letter–sound relationships that is necessary to reading, learning to spell helps children in reading. Spelling can help us break the code, especially with large, multisyllabic words in English, and it helps people write. Yes, all word processing programs have spell checkers these days, but if writers cannot at least come close to the correct spelling of a word, the spell checker is not helpful. And there are many words that have spellings close enough that a spell checker will accept them and not help out, such as *from* and *form*. If educators want students to master literacy, then they must not only teach them to read but also to spell. And learning about spelling, especially when it involves learning about why English words are spelled as they are—the origins of words—can boost vocabulary in important ways that better enable students to navigate the areas of social studies, science, math, geography, and other subjects they encounter in the classroom. In this chapter we highlight work by several authors and discuss how their work can help teachers help the students in their classrooms. In particular, Marcia Henry and Louisa Moats have placed a major emphasis on the value of spelling instruction and have revealed the true regularity of English spelling, so we draw most heavily from those sources. Other researchers who have noted the importance of spelling in early and ongoing literacy instruction include Virginia Berninger, Steve Graham, and Karen Harris, who have focused heavily on writing but who include spelling as an important factor in writing, and we also draw from their work (among others) throughout this chapter. There are also some key resources noted at the end of the chapter that offer sample lessons, lists of words and parts of words, and other information that is helpful on a continuing basis for teachers who realize the value of teaching spelling in an integrated way as part of high-quality literacy instruction.

What Does Research on Spelling Instruction Tell Educators?

Preventing Reading Difficulties in Young Children (PRD; Snow, Burns, & Griffin, 1998) included spelling in the basics for initial reading instruction. The authors stated, "our review of the research literature makes clear…the general requirements of effective reading instruction" (p. 314). They then listed the following six areas, which should be a focus of reading instruction:

> [U]sing reading instruction to obtain meaning from print; the sublexical structure of spoken words [footnoted to include "the phonological and morphological components of words"]; the nature of the orthographic system [footnoted to mean "features of the writing system, particularly letters and their sequences in words"]; the specifics of frequent, regular spelling–sound relationships; frequent opportunities to read; and opportunities to write. (p. 314)

The clear indication from this report is that teaching students about the regularities of spelling (and exceptions to those regularities, which are fewer than one would initially guess) is an important component of reading instruction. In a follow-up publication, the named authors of that report, Snow, Griffin, and Burns (2005) indicated that knowing the spelling of a word solidifies the mental representation of that word and thereby makes it more accessible, contributing to reading fluency.

The National Reading Panel (NRP) report (National Institute of Child Health and Human Development [NICHD], 2000) did not focus on spelling specifically. They did, however, report that phonemic awareness (PA) instruction with both sounds and letters showed a moderate positive effect on later spelling outcomes in early elementary school children, and that this effect was stronger for students at mid- to high socioeconomic levels than for students from lower socioeconomic groups, and stronger for English than for other languages. PA instruction with letters was also found to be helpful for students at risk for reading difficulties, but not for children already exhibiting reading disabilities. This may have been because those students were older than the students usually targeted for PA instruction. Small-group PA instruction was more effective than individual instruction (as noted in Chapter 7 of this book, on alphabetics). Similarly, systematic phonics instruction for students in kindergarten and first grade also showed a positive influence on spelling outcomes. The NRP report indicated that students need practice reading and writing the words they have learned to decode. Although they did examine use of technology in spelling instruction, there were very few studies on this topic, and no effects were found. This does not mean that such efforts should not be pursued in the future, but does underline the need for research to document the usefulness of such programs as they are developed.

While decrying the lack of research on writing in the elementary grades, Berninger (2007) noted that elementary school spelling instruction was one of the earliest areas in which researchers evaluated instructional effectiveness (Rice, 1913). As cited by Berninger, Rice reported 15 minutes of daily spelling instruction was more effective in improving children's spelling than was an hour or more per week of drill. Berninger made an important instructional point:

> During the middle of the 20th century, educational psychologists published many studies supporting the value of distributed instruction [short lessons distributed over time] rather than massed practice [intensive instruction over a relatively short period of time]. Experimental research that tests hypotheses by gathering data [evidence] that may confirm or disconfirm a working hypothesis is important because evidence does not always support teacher philosophy or belief or the researcher's hypotheses. (p. 3)

Berninger and colleagues (Amtmann, Abbott, & Berninger, in press) also asked teachers about their instructional practices and beliefs, and learned that many teachers feel that it is not worth teaching spelling systematically, because they believe that it does not transfer to writing and that students tend to continue to make spelling errors on words previously taught, even in their independent composing. These researchers then conducted a quasi-experimental study to examine student growth in spelling, patterns of that growth over time, and whether systematic spelling instruction did transfer to reading. They found that, while it might take longer for some students, all students in their experimental treatment groups did improve. They made this strong statement:

> Following explicit instruction in spelling, students do transfer spelling knowledge into independent composing, but the transfer is not instantaneous. It takes time to consolidate learning and make the necessary progress within and across school years in the journey toward skilled writing. The widely held belief that explicit spelling instruction...does not transfer to spelling in authentic contexts has been debunked...We

have not found that explicit instruction hampers development of authentic communication—indeed it appears to enhance it." (Amtmann et al., in press, p. 17)

In another study, Berninger (2007) reported a set of spelling interventions with second graders at risk for spelling problems (in the lowest groups spelling from dictation); the interventions consisted of teaching the connections between phonemes and graphemes, connections between onset–rime in spoken and written words, connections between naming the spoken word and naming all the letters in a written word, individually or in varying combinations. Both the onset–rime and whole-word treatments were shown to be effective, in that the students were able to transfer their knowledge of the intervention words to new words, and the phoneme-to-grapheme strategy was effective in students being able to spell more words correctly in mid- and posttest than in pretest. Overall, they found that teaching multiple strategies that helped students make these connections between spoken and printed words was an effective approach, which also improved later writing abilities, such as independent composing (Hart, Berninger, & Abbott, 1997). The finding of effective early intervention in spelling leading to later composing abilities was also confirmed by Graham, Harris, and Fink-Chorezempa (2002).

While the focus of an article by Foorman and colleagues (2006) was on how teachers allocate time and the impact of their instructional practices on reading and spelling outcomes, it does reveal some important things specific to the nature of spelling instruction. For nearly half of the students (31%–50%) in the inner-city, high-poverty schools they studied, spelling achievement by the end of the year was predictable based mainly on how well they read at the beginning of the year (rather than on the teacher's instruction). It should be of concern to all that they found that

> The more time that less effective teachers spent teaching grammar, mechanics, and spelling, the lower the spelling outcomes for high ability students. Apparently, for students in these classrooms, it was not sufficient to relegate spelling instruction to workbook activities without teacher-led instruction on spelling patterns. (p. 23)

Thus, how spelling is addressed is clearly important.

Henry (2003), in *Unlocking Literacy: Effective Decoding and Spelling Instruction*, a book entirely dedicated to decoding and spelling instruction, based her focus on spelling on its clear relationship to decoding. The NRP (NICHD, 2000) indicated the effectiveness of both PA and phonics instruction as necessary to learning to read. Building on that, Henry offered teachers background and some sample lessons on instructing students, not only in PA and decoding but also in spelling, word origins, and basic morphology. Henry gave a timeline for appropriate grade levels to introduce such elements as Latin word roots and affixes and Greek combining forms, to make the entire process highly accessible as well as logical.

Further supporting the basis of Henry's very helpful guidance on spelling instruction, Moats (2005), citing Ehri (2000), indicated that

> Research has shown that learning to spell and learning to read words rely on much of the same underlying knowledge—such as the relationships between letters and sounds—and, not surprisingly, that spelling instruction can be designed to help children better understand that key knowledge, resulting in better reading. (p. 12)

Ehri and Snowling (2004) further indicated that gaining automaticity is founded on the ability to rapidly map letters and letter combinations to the sounds they represent. Educators and researchers also know that children cannot possibly memorize the entire English vocabulary as sight words, so learning the patterns inherent in English spelling is a key to spelling, to fluency, and to making gains in the academic content–area vocabulary so crucial to learning, which begins in elementary school and builds through a student's entire education.

Templeton (2003) pointed out the role of meaning in determining what might appear to be irregular spelling of words. He stated that the English spelling system is one

> On which a group of letters predictably and consistently corresponds to a particular meaning. For example, the words *senile* and *senility* are not spelled *seenile* and *suniluty*, as they might be if we tried to represent more directly the sounds in each word; instead, they retain the common spelling *senile*, thus preserving the semantic or meaning relationship shared by the base and its derivative (both words come from the Latin root sen [senilis] meaning "old"). (p. 739)

Templeton went on to provide support for using word-sorting activities for students to examine words "from multiple perspectives, noting common sound, spelling, and meaning patterns" (p. 746). Templeton also suggested that detecting and abstracting patterns in word spellings is an essential part of learning to spell and learning about spelling. He suggested that activities, such as having students correct their own spelling pretests, helps them focus on the patterns of all the words on the test, not just the ones they spelled incorrectly. Spelling instruction should not be simply having students memorize patterns; rather, as Templeton, Henry, Moats, Foorman, and many others who have studied spelling instruction have agreed, it should involve learning about words. Effective—and engaging—spelling instruction can foster higher order thinking skills rather than rely on memory and drill alone.

How Is Spelling Linked to Reading and Writing?

Decoding of words is an active but receptive process, where the child learns to recognize letters and pair them with the sounds they represent, and is thereby able to read a word. Spelling, however, is a productive process, where the student must translate the sounds heard into alphabetic symbols and then write or speak those sounds. Henry (2003) argued that decoding and spelling should be taught together, given that they are in essence two sides of the same coin.

Both reading and spelling rely on a basic working knowledge of alphabetics. Both also build and rely on the same mental representation. Being able to spell a word helps to solidify that mental representation, just as being able to write the word does; a word can only be written fluently and effortlessly if the writer can spell the word. So all three—reading, spelling, and writing—are very closely linked, and skills in one reinforce skills in the others. Students who cannot spell well are likely to write using only those words they can spell (Moats, 2005), which can be quite restrictive. This should emphasize the importance of spelling instruction for both reading and writing success.

How Can Spelling Help Students Read and Write?

Moats (2005) pointed out that spelling, if taught in the context of word origins and the structure of the English language, not only will be much more interesting to students than the traditional word lists with a Friday spelling test but will also augment student vocabulary development, because students will begin to approach new words by considering each word's sound, meaning, language of origin, and syntactic features. She described the advantages for the population at large as including the ability to look up words in phone books, dictionaries, and thesauruses, to recognize the correct words on word processing spell checkers, to write notes that actually are readable to others, and even to play parlor games. Spelling poorly can reflect poorly on a resume or job application. It is more important in individuals' daily lives than they may realize.

According to Henry, "Even those students who learn phonics for decoding and spelling short, regular words often have difficulty at a more advanced level because they have only learned rudimentary sound–symbol association rules" (Henry, 2003, p. 7). With this statement, Henry presented a continuum of instruction from phonological awareness through alphabet letter–sound correspondence, Anglo-Saxon consonants and vowels to compound words, prefixes, suffixes, and syllables, to Latin roots and Greek combining forms! She laid out a convincing set of lessons that range from kindergarten through the eighth grade and beyond, to continue to teach the regularities of English spelling based on word origins and historical influences on the English language, with the three most prevalent in orthography today being Anglo-Saxon, Latin, and Greek. Moats (2005), too, emphasized the importance and utility of teaching students about the morphology of English through word origins. This approach reveals the underlying regularities that not only facilitate student spelling but also enhance writing and significantly expand vocabulary, especially vocabulary for academic content areas, such as science, social studies, and mathematics. Henry recommended introducing Latin base words and affixes (prefixes and suffixes) as early as second grade, because that is when students begin to encounter Latinate words in content lessons, such as social studies.

It is clear that learning to spell can enhance reading ability for elementary school children. Both Henry and Moats made it clear that it can also help upper-grade students in their vocabulary and comprehension; using information about word origins and morphology can help not only with spelling but also with understanding the meaning of words. Moats pointed out that spelling is predictable for the majority of English words. More than half of English words can be spelled correctly simply based on letter–sound correspondences (Hanna, Hanna, Hodges, & Rudorf, 1966) and the regularities of English sound patterns, and more than one third would have only one error if they were spelled based on those letter–sound correspondences. Moats also pointed out that 84% of the words in English can be spelled correctly if word meaning and origin are taken into account. She offered key principles that can explain the spelling of English words, including the language of origin and some history of its use, meaning and grammatical part of speech, position of letters within a word, and so forth. The article contained various clear examples, and Moats even presented a general approach for what to teach at each grade level from kindergarten through Grade 7, beginning with phoneme awareness and letter sounds, and moving to such things as Latin-based affixes and roots in the later grades. Moats's paper is extremely helpful background for elementary and middle school teachers.

How Can the History of English
Help Teachers with Spelling Instruction?

While English is a living, dynamic language, which like all active languages is changing constantly, our written tradition has given it a certain stability. Moats wrote that 84% of the words in English have predictable spelling if certain principles are taken into account (Moats, 2005). The next section presents examples of many of those principles. The following are Moats's (2005) five principles that should be remembered in spelling English.

1. The word's language of origin and history

2. The word's meaning and part of speech

3. Speech sounds are spelled with single letters and combinations of up to four letters

4. The spelling of a given sound can vary according to its position within a word

5. The spelling of some sounds is governed by established conventions of letter sequences and patterns (Moats, 2005, pp. 42–43)[1]

In her brief history of written English, Henry (2003) explained that understanding this history can help a student understand both the consistencies and inconsistencies of our written language. She clearly explained the three primary influences on English in layers (which also mirror her recommendations for a sequence of instruction) from the early Anglo-Saxon through the Latin and Greek layers. Anglo-Saxon comprises short words of common everyday usage, while Latin gives us the base words and affixes for more academic and formal contexts, and Greek offers many of our scientific terms. A brief summary of the patterns to be found in the contributions of each of these three languages to modern-day English is presented in the following section. Hopefully these will not only convince readers of the regularity of English orthography and the tremendous value to spelling and vocabulary that result from instructing students about the origins of English, but also turn readers on to the tremendous linguistic richness of our English language.

---

[1]Numbered list paraphrased from Moats, L. (2005, Winter). How spelling supports reading: And why it is more regular and predictable than you may think. *American Educator, 12*(22), 42–43; adapted with permission.

Anglo-Saxon Influence on English

Early alphabetics instruction—letter–sound correspondences paired with PA and then phonics, as discussed in Chapter 7—enables students to learn the common, everyday words that came from the earlier part of English language history, the Anglo-Saxon influence. These include words used for animal names, family members, numbers, common objects, emotions, and common daily activities. They are short and characterized by fairly regular consonant–sound correspondences, and even some regular vowel–sound correspondences. Students learn single consonants, blends (two or three consonants whose sounds blend together, that commonly cluster in English), and digraphs (two consonants that together represent one sound; e.g., *th*). By the end of second grade, Henry (2003) recommended that students should have mastered all of the common letter–sound correspondences and their associated spelling rules. See Figure 10.1 for Henry's spelling rules for the Anglo-Saxon layer of English.

Syllable patterns are also part of the Anglo-Saxon heritage in English. Syllables are commonly recognized by most of us as the "beats" in

---

Spelling Rules for the Anglo-Saxon Layer of English

- Single consonant spellings rarely vary (e.g., *b*, *d*, *m*, *p*).
- Consonant blends (2–3 adjacent consonants in a syllable) retain their individual sounds (e.g., *bl* in *blue*, *gr* in *green*).
- Consonant digraphs (two adjacent consonants in a syllable) form only one sound (e.g., *sh* in *ship*, *ch* in *chain*).
- Single letter vowels tend to be either long or short.
  - A vowel plus syllable-final consonant is usually short (e.g., *a* in *cat*, *e* in *let*).
  - A vowel at the end of a syllable is usually long (e.g., *o* in *go*, *i* in *pilot*).
  - Silent e at the end of a word signals a long vowel (e.g., *shape*, *vote*).
  - A vowel before a doubled consonant is short (e.g., *winning*, *cutting*).
  - *Y* serves as a vowel following a consonant at the end of a word or syllable (e.g., *my*, *baby*).
  - Both *y* and *w* serve as vowels after a vowel (forming a vowel digraph, e.g., *toy*, *few*).
- Vowels change their sound when followed by *r* (e.g., *star*, *corn*, *fern*, *bird*).
- Vowel digraphs usually occur in the middle of words.
  - There are two sets of digraphs, those with a single sound (e.g., *ee*, *oa*, *oi*, *oy*) and those that have two different pronunciations (e.g., *ea* in *bread* and *bead*, *ow* in *show* and *cow*).

Figure 10.1.   Spelling rules for the Anglo-Saxon layer of English. (From Henry, M.K. [2003]. *Unlocking literacy: Effective decoding and spelling instruction* [pp. 31–36]. Baltimore: Paul H. Brookes Publishing Co., adapted by permission.)

a word. Some refer to them as the building blocks of language, as they influence the rhythm, stress, and prosody of a language, and are the key element in poetic meter. Syllables consist of a vowel and usually one or more consonants. It is commonly agreed that there are six major syllable types in English (Henry, 2003; Moats, 1995; Steere, Peck, & Kahn, 1971): 1) closed, 2) open, 3) vowel-consonant-*e*, 4) vowel digraph, 5) consonant-*le*, and 6) *r*-controlled. A *closed* syllable has a vowel with a consonant following it, so the vowel is short (as in *map, bit, cut*), while an *open* syllable ends in a vowel, so the vowel is long (as in *go, me*). Together, open and closed syllables make up about three fourths of all of the syllables in English. Henry asserted that knowing syllable structures can help a student better understand syllable division patterns.

The *morpheme* is an important concept in English, and it becomes even more important as the Latin and Greek layers are introduced. In Anglo-Saxon, however, it is important for students to learn about compound words and affixes. A morpheme is the smallest meaning-bearing unit in a language. While phonemes are the smallest unit capable of changing meaning (when we replace the *b* in *bat* with *m*, we get a new word: *mat*), the phoneme itself does not carry meaning. Morphemes do carry meaning. Thus, recognizing morphemes enhances vocabulary as well as spelling.

Anglo-Saxon base words are usually free morphemes and can be combined as compound words or can have affixes added to them. Free morphemes are those that can stand alone as words all by themselves (which becomes important when considering Latinate words that are most often bound morphemes; more on this in a little while). Combining two short words into one longer word is compounding, and usually Anglo-Saxon words that are compounded keep the meanings of both words in that combination. For instance, *dog* plus *house* becomes *doghouse*, a house where a dog lives, and *camp* plus *ground* becomes *campground*, a ground or area where one can camp.

Base words can also have affixes added to them. *Affix* is another term for prefixes (placed at the beginning of a word) and suffixes (placed at the end of a word). There are two types of affixes: inflectional and derivational. Inflectional affixes (which in English are suffixes) inflect a word. That means they can change the number (as in *dog* and *dogs*), person (from first person to third person, as in *I jump* but *she jumps*), or tense (as in *jump, jumped*). Inflectional affixes are also used to form the comparative forms of words (*big, bigger, biggest*). Derivational affixes are used to derive new words. Derivational affixes change the part of speech of a word, such as making a noun or verb into an adjective or an adverb or a verb (*hope*, which is both a noun and a verb, becomes the adjective *hopeless* or the adverb *hopelessly*) or a verb into an adjective (*jaunt* becomes *jaunty*). While some base words do not change when affixes are added, some do, and there are rules for most cases, such as doubling the final consonant (*big, bigger*), dropping the final *e* (*blame, blaming; write, writing*), or changing *y* to *i* (*copy, copies; pony, ponies*).

Latin Influence on English

Latin is the basis of all of the Romance languages: French, Spanish, Italian, Portuguese, and Romanian. The Latin layer of English includes words that generally are used in more formal situations than the everyday words of Anglo-Saxon. They are found in literature and social studies, for example. Many English daily terms have Latin-based counterparts for more formal circumstances—a favorite example of ours is "animals on the hoof" versus "animals on the table," as in *pig* and *sheep* (Anglo-Saxon) versus *pork* and *mutton* (Latin based). Latin-based words generally have short vowels, rarely have vowel digraphs, and their letter–sound correspondences tend to be regular. When vowel digraphs do appear in Latin-based words, they are usually in suffixes, such as *-ion, -ian,* and *-ial;* Henry recommended teaching these digraphs as units. There are some rules that generally hold: *-ion* is usually found after *t* or *s; -ian* is usually found after *c;* and *-ient* and *-ial* usually follow *t.* She referred to the syllable–final consonant cluster *-ct* as a signpost, indicating a Latin root (e.g., *dict, duct, tract, struct,* and *ject*) and pointed out that multisyllabic words formed from these roots (*destructive, reconstructed, extracting*) rarely give students problems in reading or spelling once the students have learned the bases.

Syllable patterns for Latin roots are usually closed or r-controlled, and the *schwa* (unstressed vowel) is commonly found in Latin-based words. Otherwise the syllable divisions are similar to Anglo-Saxon.

Morphology is where some of the real joy of Latin shows up in English (at least in the opinion of the linguist among our co-authors!). As you will recall, Anglo-Saxon words are free morphemes that can combine as compound words or can have affixes added to them. But Latin roots can only have affixes added. Latin roots are nearly always *bound morphemes,* meaning that they cannot stand alone as words on their own (as you will have noticed with the examples above: *struct* is not a word, but *destruct, construct,* and *reconstruction* all are words with a Latin root and affixes). Often the prefix or suffix will change its spelling when added to the root, but there are morpheme rules for affixing Latin roots that predict these (see Figure 10.2). Because Latin roots can have so many prefixes and suffixes added to them, they are highly productive and enable students to rapidly increase their vocabularies. These longer words may be easier to spell than shorter words and are highly decodable.

Morpheme Rules for Affixing Latin Roots

- The prefixes *-in* changes to match the pronunciation of the beginning consonant of the root: *illegal, irregular, immobile, imbalance, important*
- Roots that end in a short vowel plus consonant in a stressed syllable double the consonant when a suffix is added: *transmit + ed = transmitted*
- The suffix *-ion* has variable spellings based on pronunciation and is sometimes known as a noun suffix: *invent, invention; music, musician*
- Similarly the suffix *-al* is predicted by spelling of the root: *substantial, judicial*

Figure 10.2. Morpheme rules for affixing Latin roots. (From Henry, M.K. [2003]. *Unlocking literacy: Effective decoding and spelling instruction* [pp. 40–42]. Baltimore: Paul H. Brookes Publishing Co., adapted by permission.)

Greek Influence on English

The many words in English that are of Greek origin provide us with the vocabulary of science: *biology, geology,* and *physiology* are all words of Greek origin, as are *microscope, telescope, botanical, psychology,* and many plant and animal names (*pterodactyl, rhododendron*). Most of these are compounded, which is typical for Greek word parts that are referred to in dictionaries as "combining forms." All of the letter–sound correspondences are found in words of Greek origin, but there are also new combinations *ph, pt, ps,* and *rh,* plus the *mn* of the word *mnemonic,* the *ch* of *chlorophyll,* and the *pn* of *pneumonia* and *pneumatic.* These were reportedly introduced by Latin scribes; they make these Greek words unmistakable and create pronunciation difficulties at times even for adults. Open and closed syllables are most common in Greek-based words, but adjacent vowels in separate syllables also occur, in a syllable pattern that is unique to Greek-origin words (the/a/ter, cre/ate, cha/os, the/o/ry). The letter *y* functions as a vowel. In closed syllables it is short, and in open syllables it is long (sym/pho/ny, gym/na/si/um, but cy/clone, gy/ro/scope, and hy/per/bo/le).

Again, the morpheme patterns make Greek-origin words highly productive, so that along with Latin-based words, words of Greek origin are a powerhouse for vocabulary. By learning a relatively small number of Greek combining forms, students will be able to read and spell literally thousands of words. Henry (2003) gave the examples of a few common combining forms that hold specific meaning: *micro, scope, bio, graph, helio, meter, phono, photo, auto,* and *tele,* which open the doors to many words that students will encounter in science and technology. Similarly, she gave the example of the numeric prefixes that aid students greatly in the vocabulary of mathematics and geometry: *mono-* (1), *di-* (2), *tri-* (3), *tetra-* (4), *penta-* (5), *hexa-* (6), *hepta-* (7), *octo-* (8), *nona-* (9), *deca-* (10), and *kilo-* (1,000).

How Might Spelling Instruction Take Place?

To begin spelling instruction, Henry (2003) recommended that teachers be familiar with the common Anglo-Saxon letter–sound correspondences, characteristics of Anglo-Saxon words (as described previously), including Anglo-Saxon base words, prefixes and suffixes, important irregular words, and the common syllable patterns. Check to make sure that the children in the classroom know letter–sound correspondences and work to fill in any that are missing. A logical sequence for introducing orthographic patterns, once students have basic single letter–sound correspondences, is to introduce two-letter consonant blends, simple spelling rules (e.g., vowel-consonant-*e*), and consonant digraphs, then three-letter blends, and finally common syllable patterns, common suffixes and prefixes and their rules, compound words, and possessives and plurals (special cases of suffixes). Henry offered categories of first spelling rules, which are reproduced in Figure 10.3. These rules generally apply to Anglo-Saxon words and usually occur because of the short vowel sounds. In teaching these rules, teachers should make them concrete with real examples and have students practice by reading and recognizing them, writing them, and talking about them.

While many students start out using invented spelling, during the early grades they should transfer to standard spelling using their letter–sound correspondence knowledge together with the spelling rules that the teacher introduces, since eventually they will be expected to use conventional spelling. Learning the spelling rules can also help students by providing strategies to use when they encounter unfamiliar words. Irregular words must simply be memorized, but multiple exposures to these words will help solidify the student's mental representation of the word, as will discussing it and writing the word. This does not mean that the student should engage in simple, repetitive tasks (although a certain amount of repetition is good), but rather that the word should be used meaningfully in reading, writing, and discussion. Teachers can "stack the deck" by setting up experiences in which their students encounter target words frequently, in meaningful contexts, and provide the necessary practice and experience while building spelling, vocabulary, and background knowledge all at the same time. (Note that Henry, 2003, provided an appendix of nonphonetic rote memory word lists that may be useful.)

Irregular words need to be taught and memorized, and, of course, beginning with those that are frequently occurring in the reading materials children will encounter in the early grades makes great

---

Henry's First Spelling Rules

1. Silent *e* rule—Silent *e* on the end of a word makes the vowel long (or "say its own name"): *cube; vote; make; type; style.*

2. Consonant doubling rule—Final *f, l, s,* and *z* after a vowel in a single syllable word are usually doubled: *staff; bluff; tell; still; grass; bliss; jazz* (Note common exceptions: *pal; gal; if; clef; this; us; yes; bus; plus; quiz*).

3. Soft *c* and *g* rule—These letters have a "soft" sound when they are directly followed by *e, i,* or *y*: *cent; city; cycle; gentle; ginger; gym* (Note common exceptions: *get; give; buggy; bigger*).

4. The *-ck, -tch, -dge* rule—These are used to spell the /k/, /ch/, and /j/ sounds when they follow one short vowel at the end of a single syllable: *back; clock; duck; stick; batch; itch; stretch; Dutch; badge; ledge; bridge; fudge.*

5. Adding suffixes to Anglo-Saxon base words:

   a. Drop final *-e* rule—Drop the final *e* when adding a vowel-initial suffix: *take, taking; fine, finer; stone, stony.*

   b. Double-letter rule—Double the final consonant in single syllable words with one short vowel (closed syllable) before a vowel-initial suffix but NOT before a consonant-initial suffix: *fit, fitted, fitful; sad, sadder, sadly; red, redder, redness; ship, shipping, shipment.*

6. Plural *-s* and *-es* rule:

   a. Most nouns become plural by adding *-s*: *bat, bats; pig, pigs; girl, girls.*

   b. Nouns ending in *-s, -x, -z, -ch,* and *-sh* become plural by adding *-es*: *glass, glasses; box, boxes; waltz, waltzes; lunch, lunches; wish, wishes.*

   c. Nouns ending in *-y* change the *y* to *i* and add *-es*: *fly, flies; pony, ponies* (*Note:* An exception is when the *y* follows a vowel: *toy, toys; bay, bays*).

   d. Some special nouns (exceptions) ending in *-f* or *-fe* change the *f* to *v* and add *-es*: *shelf, shelves; leaf, leaves; knife, knives.*

   e. Nouns ending in *-o* vary between adding *-s* or *-es*, so students should be advised to check a dictionary: *piano, pianos; tomato, tomatoes.*

   f. Some plurals are irregular and must simply be learned individually: *foot, feet; mouse, mice; man, men; woman, women; goose, geese; moose, moose; pants, pants; deer, deer.*

Figure 10.3.   Henry's first spelling rules. (From Henry, M.K. [2003]. *Unlocking literacy: Effective decoding and spelling instruction* [pp. 77–79]. Baltimore: Paul H. Brookes Publishing Co., adapted by permission.)

sense. For example, the pattern *ough* has many different sounds. However, most often it is pronounced as a short *o*. So while students can be taught that this is the most frequent pronunciation of this spelling pattern, they will need to memorize the others (e.g., *rough, though, through, bough*). Henry (2003) also recommended teaching children to count, clap, or tap out syllables in the early grades, to give them a sense of the stress patterns and rhythm of English, and to get them ready to learn about syllable division. (In one of the "keys" to unlocking literacy throughout her book, Henry, 2003, p. 82, noted that "only rhy*thm* and the suffix *-ism* have pronounced syllables without a vowel.")

In her sequence and timing of instruction, Henry also recommended that in Grades 1–3 teachers instruct students on morpheme patterns, specifically Anglo-Saxon base words, and the prefixes and suffixes most commonly found with those base words. She listed the most common ones in her chapters on instruction and in appendices, but noted that, according to White, Sowell, and Yanagihara (1989) the four common prefixes *un-*, *re-*, *dis-* and *in-* (meaning not) represent more than half of the prefixed words found in Grade 3–9 textbooks. White and colleagues also reported that the suffixes *-s*, *-es*, *-ed*, and *-ing* can be found in 65% of words. These are inflectional endings that change the person, number, or tense of words, so this is not surprising, and these are ideal candidates for teaching first suffixes. As teachers introduce these, it is also a good opportunity to begin talking about grammatical concepts like noun, verb, adjective, and adverb.

Teaching prefixes and suffixes is likely to be part of the important third-grade year, which marks a transition to higher level work on morphology and writing. Concepts that might be introduced around this time include contractions, possessives (which make use of the suffix *-s*, but in a special way), antonyms (opposites) and synonyms (a nice example of Greek combining forms and academic words students will need to know that can expand their potential vocabulary in the future), and homonyms and homographs (again, using Greek combining forms). *Antonyms* are words with opposite meanings, such as *hot* and *cold*, *stop* and *go*, and children will likely enjoy giving their own examples as they demonstrate that they have grasped the concept. *Synonyms* are different words that have the same or very similar meanings, such as *wind* and *breeze* or *rain* and *precipitation*. Again, the concept lends itself well to an interactive exchange in the classroom and can be an enjoyable activity, as is likely to be the case with all of these concepts. Homonyms (or homophones) are words that sound and are (usually) spelled the same but have different meanings, such as *die* (stop living, a device for stamping, or a game piece that has dots on each side). Note, however, that some homonyms are spelled differently but sound the same (*die* and *dye*, or *through* and *threw*). Homographs, on the other hand, look the same but differ in pronunciation and meaning. Examples include *wind* (meaning a breeze) and *wind* (to power a nonelectronic clock or old-fashioned watch, or to wrap a rope around something).

In the upper elementary grades, the length and complexity of the words students will encounter and must master begins to dramatically increase. Students will need new strategies for decoding those words, and that is where the Latin and Greek layers of language can be introduced. Henry (2003) recommended introducing these Latin and Greek layers in the latter part of third grade, after reviewing the Anglo-Saxon letter–sound correspondences as a system (single consonants, blends, and digraphs; short and long vowels, *r*- and *l*-controlled vowels, and vowel digraphs). The Latin and Greek information will help students grasp many of the morphological concepts that can help them with the ever-increasing vocabulary they must know to navigate academic language. These words are more abstract, and as noted, longer and more complex, but highly regular. And as noted repeatedly, knowing the Latin base words and affixes and Greek combining forms can spur vocabulary growth dramatically.

In terms of teaching the Latin and Greek information, Henry (2003) offered several guidelines. She recommended several keys to approaching this information. For Latin, teach each root word directly, taking the frequency of these words and their spelling regularity as a guide to sequence. As students begin to learn these roots, incorporate information on etymology (word origin) and some history of the development of words. This should also involve how to find such information in the dictionary, and how to decipher that information as well as how to find synonyms in a thesaurus. Be sure to give students opportunities to use the words in discussion and to read and write them in context (phrases and sentences) as well as in word lists. Showing the matrices that can guide combining of affixes and roots and having students make morpheme webs can also be enjoyable activities that will reinforce the roots, affixes, and their meaning, and will illustrate the value of these in terms of how dramatically they can increase vocabulary and word recognition/decoding.

Moving from Latin to Greek can be a natural transition, since many of the Latin roots were borrowed from Greek. In fact, some of the Greek combining forms could be taught in combination with the Latin words and affixes, if that seems a logical fit for the lessons and if teachers feel sure it will not be confusing to their students. Greek-based English words are often related to math and science concepts, so they will prove very useful in boosting comprehension of subject matter texts. Henry (2003) recommended first teaching those letter–sound correspondences that are unique to Greek (*ph* for *f* and *ch* for *k*). She also recommended teaching 4–6 Greek combining forms per lesson and having students generate words from these. Teaching Latin and Greek information can allow for fun, creative lessons that both students and teacher enjoy, and which can be very fruitful for all areas of reading— decoding of long, complex words, vocabulary, comprehension in general, and comprehension in specific academic subject areas as well as spelling and writing!

What Additional Research is Still Needed in the Area of Teaching Spelling?

As with all areas of reading and writing, although researchers have learned a lot, more research is still needed. For example, there is always a need for research to examine the effectiveness of new instructional methods or programs and the best ways to monitor student progress. This includes not only the development of new measures researchers can use in their studies but also measures that enable teachers to quickly but accurately monitor student progress. There is also a need for tools to support teachers in differentiating instruction for individual students, such as computer programs on which students might practice concepts that seem to be more difficult for them. Additional research is also needed to examine how best to detect students with reading difficulties and how best to remediate them, probably depending on the specific nature of the difficulties they are experiencing. Table 10.1 summarizes some of what is known and areas to explore in the future.

HOW MIGHT THIS RESEARCH ON
• • • SPELLING PLAY OUT IN THE CLASSROOM? • • •

Mr. Rose wanted his sixth-grade students to develop an understanding of root words and affixes. He presented a lesson in which he wrote the word *prehendere* and told the class it was a Latin word from long ago that meant *to seize*. Then he asked students to provide words that had the root *prehend* in them. As students came up with words, they discussed their meanings, the affixes that changed their meanings, and their spelling patterns. Then students were put in triads and given a Latin root word and its meaning. Their task was to find words that came from the Latin root and their meanings. They then developed concept maps for the root words and their derivatives. Some groups added illustrations to their maps. Finally, they shared the maps with the class and discussed what they learned about words in the process.

What Other Resources Might Help in Teaching Spelling?

Moats (2005) wrote a short article that briefly but thoroughly covered the history of English orthography and provided a handy three-page

---

What we know from research

- Students who persist with spelling errors into the elementary grades are at risk for reading difficulties.

- Teaching phonemic awareness (PA) with letters had a positive influence on spelling outcomes in early-grade elementary school students, including students who are at risk but not students who already exhibited reading disabilities.

- Students benefit from knowing the origins of English words and the morphology of roots/base words and affixes.

What we need to know from additional research

- How can researchers and educators best predict the types of reading difficulty students may experience, and how best to intervene to prevent those difficulties?

- How might PA be taught more effectively to maximize transfer to spelling as well as reading, especially for students with reading difficulties?

- What are the most effective approaches to instructing students in word origins and English-language morphology?

- How can computers be used to enhance and reinforce spelling instruction and increase its positive impact on reading and writing?

- What are the best ways to provide ongoing professional development and support for teachers in teaching spelling and morphology?

Table 10.1. Spelling research needs

guide that generally lays out what to teach at which grade for spelling instruction. There are two longer but very functional resources that can help teachers more fully understand the basics of spelling in English. In her book *Unlocking Literacy*, Henry (2003) offered a slightly longer (albeit still brief) history of the development of the English language, described the regularity of English orthography, explained Latin and Greek word origins, and included several invaluable appendices listing common nonphonetic words, compound words, prefixes and suffixes, Latin roots, and Greek combining forms. The appendices alone make it worth having the book as a reference, but the clarity of explanation as well as the sample lessons in each chapter add to the usefulness of the book. In addition, a workbook by Moats (2003) contains exercises that will help teachers become more familiar with the structure of the English language. These two resources can make teaching spelling easier and even more enjoyable!

REFERENCES

Amtmann, D., Abbott, R.D., & Berninger, V. (in press). Identifying and predicting classes of responses to explicit phonological spelling instruction during independent composing. *Journal of Learning Disabilities.*

Berninger, V. (2007). Evidence-based written language instruction during early and middle childhood. In R. Morris & N. Mather (Eds.), *Evidence-based intervention for students with learning and behavioral challenges.* Mahwah, NJ: Lawrence Erlbaum Associates.

Ehri, L. (2000). Learning to read and learning to spell: Two sides of the coin. *Topics on Language Disorders, 20*(3), 19–49.

Ehri, L., & Snowling, M.J. (2004). Developmental variation in word recognition. In C.A. Stone, E.R. Silliman, B.J. Ehren, & K. Apel (Eds.), *Handbook of language and literacy: Development and disorders* (pp. 433–460). New York: Guilford Press.

Foorman, B.R., Schatschneider, C., Eakins, M.N., Fletcher, J.M., Moats, L.C., & Francis, D.J. (2006). The impact of instructional practices in Grades 1 and 2 on reading and spelling achievement in high poverty schools. *Contemporary Educational Psychology, 31,* 1–29.

Graham, S., Harris, K., & Fink-Chorezempa, B. (2002). Contributions of spelling instruction to the spelling, writing, and reading of poor spellers. *Journal of Educational Psychology, 94,* 669–686.

Hanna, P.R., Hanna, J.S., Hodges, R.E., & Rudorf, E.H., Jr. (1966). *Phoneme-grapheme correspondences as cues to spelling improvements* (USDOE Publication No. 32008.). Washington, DC: U.S. Government Printing Office.

Hart, T., Berninger, V., & Abbott, R. (1997). Comparison of teaching single or multiple orthographic-phonological connections for word recognition and spelling: Implications for instructional consultation. *School Psychology Review, 26,* 279–297.

Henry, M.K. (2003). *Unlocking literacy: Effective decoding and spelling instruction.* Baltimore: Paul H. Brookes Publishing Co.

Moats, L. (1995). *Spelling development, disability, and instruction.* Baltimore: York Press.

Moats, L. (2003). *Speech to print workbook: Language exercises for teachers.* Baltimore: Paul H. Brookes Publishing Co.

Moats, L. (2005, Winter). How spelling supports reading: And why it is more regular and predictable than you may think. *American Educator, 12,* 42–43.

National Institute of Child Health and Human Development. (2000). *Teaching children to read: An evidence-based assessment of the scientific research literature on reading and its implications for reading instruction: Reports of the subgroups* (NIH Publication No. 00-4754). Washington, DC: U.S. Government Printing Office.

Ramsden, P. (2001). Strategic management of teaching and learning. In C. Rust (Ed.), *Improving student learning strategically: Proceedings of the 2000 Improving Student Learning Conference.* Oxford, England: OCSLD.

Rice, J.M. (1913). *Scientific management in education.* New York: Hinds, Noble, & Elredge.

Snow, C.E., Burns, M.S., & Griffin, P. (Eds.). (1998). *Preventing reading difficulties in young children*. Washington, DC: National Academies Press.

Snow, C.E., Griffin, P., & Burns, M.S. (Eds.). (2005). *Knowledge to support the teaching of reading: Preparing teachers for a changing world*. San Francisco: Jossey-Bass.

Steere, A., Peck, C.Z., & Kahn, L. (1971). *Solving language difficulties*. Cambridge, MA: Educators Publishing Service.

Templeton, S. (2003). Spelling. In J. Flood, D. Lapp, J.R. Squire, & J.M. Jensen (Eds.), *Handbook of research on teaching the English language arts* (pp. 738–751). Mahwah, NJ: Lawrence Erlbaum Associates.

White, T.G., Sowell, J., & Yanagihara, A. (1989.). Teaching elementary students to use word-part clues. *The Reading Teacher, 42*, 302–308.

CHAPTER 11

Writing

KEY CONCEPTS

- Writing is closely related to reading, and the two can reinforce each other, with writing both enhancing and demonstrating reading comprehension in all content areas.

- Like reading, writing benefits from explicit instruction and the opportunity to extensively apply what is taught.

- While more research is needed, there is a fair amount of evidence that teaching strategies for writing is helpful in improving students' writing (and reading) abilities.

Bobby's first-grade classmates had written their names on lined paper and were now copying words from the board. Bobby was still working on writing his name. When he finished, Mr. Willard walked over and looked at it. He realized that Bobby was still reversing the lowercase *b*s in his name. As Bobby copied the word *dog*, he made the *d* correctly but reversed the *g*. Mr. Willard knew that this could be a sign that Bobby might have reading and writing problems. The students were halfway through the year, and most of the students were able to write the entire alphabet without errors. Mr. Willard knew that reversing some letters was not a problem in kindergarten, but halfway through first grade students should no longer be making these errors. Over the next 2 weeks, he made up special papers for Bobby with his name and alphabet letters to trace. Mr. Willard put small arrows on the letters to help Bobby remember which direction to make his circles and strokes, and once he saw that Bobby was able to trace the letters smoothly and quickly, he faded the arrows and patterns out; soon Bobby was making the letters on his own. Mr. Willard explained to Bobby's mother, in a parent conference, that being able to automatically write his letters was important for Bobby because it actually was an ability that could help him later with writing and compos-ing. Bobby's mother knew that familiarity with the letter names and the sounds they made was important for reading, but she had not realized that writing his letters was also important. She asked Mr. Willard what she could do at home for practice that would help Bobby.

The term *literacy* has often been used only to mean reading. Recently this has been changing, and the designation of literacy as reading *and* writing is increasing. Writing has become, in some instances, a hot topic, as recent meta-analyses have been published, focusing attention on the research that shows that writing, like reading, is not a natural process but an important skill for life success, which clearly develops and improves with instruction. In this chapter we highlight work by several authors currently writing about writing, including most notably Steve Graham, who has produced several meta-analyses of research on student writing and writing instruction, and Virginia Berninger, who has researched instructional interventions with student writing and spelling in elementary school. There are, of course, many others, and we cite other sources as well, discussing how the work of all of these researchers can help teachers help the students in their classrooms.

Berninger (Abbott & Berninger, 1993; Berninger, 2008) explained that writing draws upon at least three separate processes that work in unison—handwriting or keyboarding, spelling, and composition.

Thus, writing is a complex combination of motor and mental activities. It is also a complex orchestration of three major processes within composing itself: planning, translating, and revising (Hayes & Flower, 1980). Berninger and Swanson (1994; Swanson & Berninger, 1996) later broke these out into finer components for early and middle childhood writers, with planning consisting of both advance and online planning; translating consisting of generating mental ideas, putting them into language, and then translating that language into written symbols; and revising consisting of online revision and posttranslating. Further, Berninger (2008) outlined patterns of developmental change or growth in writing, arguing that these stages are reasonably predictable and have instructional implications: preschool–kindergarten emergent writing, the early elementary *conventional phase*, the upper-elementary and middle school *developing phase*, and the high school, college, and beyond *maturing phase* (p. 5), which we discuss further later in this section (see also Nagy, Berninger, Abbott, Garcia, & Carlisle, 2008; Wong & Berninger, 2005).

Berninger related writing overall to early handwriting automaticity. She stated, drawing from her own work and that of several other researchers, that the best predictor of composition length and quality of typically developing writers in elementary, middle, and high school was automatic letter writing in the early grades (Berninger, 2008). To develop that rapid automatized skill, a student must integrate and consolidate several skills, including letter recognition, working memory, and fine motor skills. Working memory, verbal reasoning, vocabulary, grammar, and discourse also contribute (Berninger, 2008). She called for explicit, systematic instruction beginning in the early elementary grades and involving both writing and spelling.

What Is the Relationship Between Reading and Writing?

There is a known correlation between reading and writing. While proficiency in one does not guarantee proficiency in the other, each skill contributes to the other. Both skills involve using knowledge of language structure, including word structure (phonics and morphology) and text structure (grammar and organization of genres). Using reading and writing together can enhance engagement and reasoning. Writing can help students gain a deeper understanding of what they have read, since summarizing what has been read requires being able to explain in an organized way the events and key facts that were part of the story. Writing about something one has read often means rereading the material, or at least reviewing it to gain or check facts or the order of events. Thus reading and writing can reinforce one another. Clearly, they should be taught in a close integration. Both are also essential to educational and later career success.

It is interesting to note, in this era of word processing, e-mail, and text messaging, that while it might seem a mechanical and potentially outdated skill, handwriting is actually important in developing some basic abilities and automaticity that can help students with their written composing as they progress through the educational process. But, as noted earlier, Berninger and colleagues have found that, in fact, automatic letter writing in the early grades predicts later composition length and quality (Berninger, in press), and that early handwriting skills are important to helping to consolidate some of the memory and motor skills necessary to literacy. Others have also noted that early intervention in handwriting can lead to improved composing (Graham, Harris, & Fink, 2000; Jones & Christensen, 1999). Graham (2006a) noted that there are a few research studies that reveal that teaching handwriting and spelling to elementary school students can improve their abilities in sentence construction, writing output, and writing quality, in addition to improving handwriting and spelling ability.

How Much Research Evidence Is There About How Best to Teach Students to Write?

While reading has overall received more research attention, research funding, and instruction, there are many who are very concerned about writing. In fact, reading and writing are skills that go hand in hand, and instruction often reflects the combination of skills. There is a body of high-quality research on writing, and there have been informative and useful meta-analyses of that research.

Graham and Perrin (2007) reported a meta-analysis of research on writing instruction for students in Grades 4–12. They drew upon five earlier meta-analyses (Bangert-Drowns, 1993; Goldring, Russell, & Cook, 2003; Graham, 2006b; Graham & Harris, 2003; Hillocks, 1986) but found that two thirds of the effect sizes identified through their search were new. This indicates that there is ongoing research addressing student writing instruction in adolescent students (including the upper elementary grades).

Berninger and her colleagues have written extensively about writing and spelling as they relate to reading disabilities. Berninger (in press), in a section reviewing the history of writing instruction, noted that writing has been neglected both in research and practice, perhaps based on a myth that children learn to read in elementary school but learn to write in the later grades (Grades 6 and higher).

Process writing is an approach in which the instructional focus is on the process of creation rather than on the end product. It is generally thought to occur in stages of planning, drafting, revising, and publishing. Berninger credited Calkins (1986), Clay (1982), Graves (1983), and the process writing movement with bringing to educators' attention the importance of primary school writing activities as written expression for social communication, going beyond penmanship and spelling. While praising the movement for bringing much-needed attention to the importance of writing as a compositional skill, Berninger noted that it is not an evidence-based practice but an approach based on philosophy and belief. She cited Applebee's (2000) statistics that more than half of teachers responding to a national survey indicated using process writing instruction, and based on this, called for experimental evaluation of its effectiveness. While Graham and Perrin (2007) do include studies on the process approach in their meta-analysis on adolescent writing instruction, they too note the dearth of studies on this approach.

The urgent need for students to have high-quality instruction in writing was underscored by research conducted by Moats, Foorman, and Taylor (2006). They examined the writing of inner-city fourth graders. These students had difficulty generating verb forms, clauses, correct word endings, punctuation, and spelling, despite their average reading scores. These difficulties interfered with their ability to juggle the cognitive demands of written composition. In comparison to students receiving poor-quality instruction, those with high-quality instruction wrote longer compositions with more correctly spelled words but still had difficulty with some of the more complex aspects of English morphology and syntax. Moats and colleagues noted that normally progressing students in fourth grade, having achieved normal reading fluency, are usually well along in the transition from transcribing the linear strings of conversational language with its unclear sentence boundaries to the more literary academic language with its greater embeddedness, more adverbial and relative clauses, passive voice, and so forth. However, they found that the ability of these fourth graders to read and comprehend standard English, despite their dialectal differences, was insufficient for them to be able to write at the fourth-grade level. For these students to master writing standard English forms, they would need not only high-quality instruction but also instruction geared to their specific language needs, possibly using a contrastive approach that highlights dialectal differences. Moats, Foorman, and Taylor concluded that "at the very least, a renewed campaign to promote explicit teaching of writing processes and the skills that support them would seem an overdue correction in federal and state reading initiatives" (p. 384).

Does the Research on Impaired Writers Help Us Understand the Writing Process?

Berninger et al. (2003, 2006) indicated that the executive functions for planning, reviewing, and revising are most likely to be impaired in dysgraphia or specific writing disability. In a meta-analysis of research on writing in students with learning disabilities, Graham and Harris (2003) outlined some key characteristics of writing in students with learning disabilities that actually may provide insight into the typical writing process and help researchers and educators recognize what might be going wrong for students who are struggling with writing.

Students with learning disabilities tend to do little or no planning when it comes to writing—they just start writing. Their works are generally very short, with few details, and they make very little effort either to evaluate what they have written or to revise their product. They do not seem to take into consideration who they are writing for (audience), what they are writing about (topical constraints), or the order in which they are presenting the information (organization). Graham and Harris (2003) offered reasons for what they call this "one-trick pony" composing: problems sustaining the writing effort, failure to gain access to the knowledge they possess, and interference from writing mechanics (since pausing to wonder how to spell a word or form a letter can pull one away from the writing process; Graham, Harris, & Fink, 2000). Students with learning disabilities also have limited knowledge of genres, problems managing the revision process, and difficulty categorizing and evaluating ideas. A particularly telling statement is made by Graham and Harris (2003), after relating an anecdote about a youngster on a television show who exhibited unwarranted overconfidence, which is also sometimes seen in students with learning disabilities: "Children who overestimate their capabilities may fail to allocate needed resources and effort, believing that this is unnecessary" (p. 327).

Graham and Harris (2003) offered two options for helping students with learning disabilities improve their writing: 1) teach them the same strategies used by skilled writers or 2) intervene to help them develop self-regulation. These authors advocated a combined approach, asserting that self-regulation alone may be insufficient. The result is self-regulated strategy development (SRSD), which was designed to teach strategies for writing, self-regulation skills, and content knowledge in an integrated fashion while building motivation (Harris & Graham, 1996, 1999).

The five characteristics of SRSD instruction include the following:

1. Explicitly teach strategies and needed content knowledge.

2. Children are active collaborators with their teachers; the model stresses interactive learning.

3. Individualized instruction, with targeted processes, skills, and knowledge, should be tailored to student needs and capabilities.

4. Criterion-based rather than time-based instruction should be employed; proceed at the student's pace, but continue until strategies and self-regulation procedures can be used efficiently and effectively.

5. Look for ongoing progression; new strategies are taught and old ones are upgraded.[4]

To accomplish their five key characteristics of SRSD instruction, Harris and Graham (1996, 1999) offered six instructional stages that they called a *metascript*. Briefly, these stages are as follows: 1) develop background knowledge; 2) discuss with the student the strategies needed and how they will contribute; 3) model aloud the strategy use, including problem definition, planning, use of the strategy itself, evaluation and correction, and self-reinforcement; 4) help the student memorize the steps for the strategy use, with mnemonics that help; 5) support the process with opportunities for practice, individually or in collaboration with other students, with any aids that help, such as reminder charts (that are then faded out as they are no longer needed); and 6) have a goal of independent performance.

What Are Some Instructional Techniques that Research Says Should Work in Teaching Students to Write?

In the elementary grades, handwriting and spelling, with spelling building on and interacting with phonemic awareness and phonics abilities, are important to beginning writing abilities. In addition, familiarity with text structure should begin in the early grades. By Grades 3 and 4, instruction begins to address higher level composition skills, and reading and writing become more integrated.

---

[4]Numbered list paraphrased from Graham, S., & Harris, K. (2003). Students with learning disabilities and the process of writing : A meta-analysis of SSRD studies. In L. Swanson, K. R Harris, & S. Graham (Eds.), *Handbook of research on learning disabilities* (p. 383). New York: Guilford Press; adapted with permission.

Berninger (in press) recommended schoolwide screenings to identify at-risk elementary school students. In a programmatic research approach, she and her team conducted experimental studies of effective treatments for at-risk second, fourth, and sixth graders in writing and spelling. As a result of this research, her team reported that at-risk second graders given explicit, integrated reading and writing instruction showed better response than those given only spelling skills instruction (Abbott, Reed, Abbott, & Berninger, 1997) and that fourth to sixth graders with dyslexia showed better response to explicit handwriting, spelling, and composition instruction than to spelling instruction, and that success in responding to spelling instruction depended on their level of reading achievement (Brooks, Vaughan, & Berninger, 1999). Subsequently, based on these findings, they launched a larger set of studies of writing instructional interventions. (These instructional interventions have been prepared as lesson plans and published in Berninger & Abbott, 2003.) In the primary grades, students were taught writing from memory to improve automatic letter writing, also shown to transfer to compositional fluency (Berninger et al., 1997; Graham, Harris, & Fink, 2000; Jones & Christensen, 1999).

As noted earlier, Graham and Perrin (2007) reported a meta-analysis of research on writing instruction for students in Grades 4–12. Their goal was to identify instructional practices that are effective in improving the quality of writing for adolescent students. Therefore, they limited their analysis to studies that were experimental or quasi-experimental, that included a reliably scored measure of student writing quality, and compared at least two groups of students receiving different instructional conditions. They required at least 4 effect sizes to conduct meta-analyses, and were able to do so for 11 instructional treatments, all but one of which resulted in positive average weighted effects sizes indicating some effectiveness for the treatment.

The one treatment for which a positive effect size was not found was the teaching of grammar; however, Graham and Perrin (2007) cautioned that this should not be interpreted as meaning that grammar should not be taught. Ten of the 11 studies that included teaching grammar used it as a control condition; seven of the effect sizes were negative, and two were negligible. Graham and Perrin called for additional research on the type of grammar instruction that might be effective, since one study by Fearn and Farnan (2005) found strong positive effects for instruction with a focus on a functional, practical application of grammar within the context of the writing activity (as opposed to simply defining and describing grammar). Bromely (1998) acknowledged that learning grammar terms and concepts provides a vocabulary for students to discuss their writing.

For the 10 instructional treatments that were found to have evidence of effectiveness, Graham and Perrin (2007) offered 10 recommendations in order of the average weighted effect size (see Table 11.1). The first instructional treatment: teaching strategies for planning, revising, and editing compositions, was shown to be the most powerful of the instructional treatments studied. Graham and Perrin also concluded that summarization instruction was effective in improving overall quality of student writing, specifically impacting the ability to write more concisely. Having adolescents work together (peer assistance) on their writing is also effective. Compared to students writing alone, all were positive, indicating that student collaborative writing activities can have a strong influence on the overall quality of student writing.

Providing clear, explicit writing goals for students is also an effective treatment. As defined by Graham and Perrin (2007), this includes identifying the purpose of the writing activity and the specific characteristics that should be found in the final product. For example, a persuasive composition should define the problem under consideration, include both sides of the argument, and offer a reasoned conclusion.

Table 11.1. Graham and Perrin's (2007) 10 recommendations for writing instruction for adolescents, ordered from largest mean weighted effect size in descending order

Recommendation	Mean weighted effect size	Grades studied
Teach strategies for planning, revising, and editing compositions.	.82	4–10
Teach strategies and procedures for text summarization.	.82	5–12
Have students work together to plan, draft, edit, and revise compositions.	.75	4–12
Give students clear, explicit writing goals.	.70	4–8
Enable the use of word processing as a primary writing tool.	.55	4–12
Teach students to write increasingly complex sentences.	.50	4–11
Provide teacher professional development when implementing the process writing approach.	.46	4–12
Design writing activities to sharpen student inquiry skills.	.32	7–12
Help students gather and organize ideas before drafting their compositions.	.32	4–9
Provide good models of the type of document that is the focus of instruction.	.25	4–12

Note: .20 = small effect size, .50 = medium, .80 = large (Lispey & Wilson, 2001).
Source: Graham and Perrin (2007).

Drawing from and confirming the analyses of previous meta-analyses on the use of word processing as compared to composing by hand, Graham and Perrin (2007) analyzed 16 effect sizes. They concluded that using word processing has a positive impact on overall student writing quality but cautioned that this also means that students must have mastery over the software required to navigate word processing programs. They do recommend that teachers make it possible for students to use word processing for their composition activities.

Teaching students to write increasingly complex sentences is also recommended. Graham and Perrin (2007) found that, as an alternative to more traditional grammar instruction, some studies examined teaching students to combine two or more basic sentences into more complex, sophisticated sentences. Graham and Perrin computed and analyzed five effect sizes for these studies and concluded that sentence-combining instruction does have a positive impact on student writing quality.

In examining studies on the process approach to writing instruction, Graham and Perrin (2007) found that professional development was associated with the moderate average weighted effect size of .32 that resulted from analyzing 21 effect sizes. As these authors pointed out, the process approach to writing instruction (termed the *natural process approach* by Hillocks, in his 1986 meta-analysis), has no universally agreed-upon definition. Since its inclusion in the National Writing Project, it has become more structured, adding more explicit instructional procedures over recent years (Nagin, 2003). The types of studies included by Graham and Perrin for analysis under their title *process writing approach* included Writers Workshop (Calkins, 1981) and the National Writing Project (Pritchard, 1987) as well as studies examining the process writing approach (Graves, 1983) and whole-language experiments or quasi-experiments that used a process approach. Graham and Perrin found that

> When teachers were involved in professional development to use the process writing approach, there was a moderate effect on the quality of students' writing. In the absence of such training, process writing instruction had a small effect on the writing of students in Grades 4–6, but did not enhance the writing of students in Grades 7–9. (p. 17)

However, they recommended caution in interpreting the findings, because often comparison conditions were not specified in the professional development studies. More clearly specified research would be helpful in this area.

Based on findings from the five effect sizes reported by Hillocks (1986), a small to moderate effect size was found by Graham and Perrin (2007). They could locate no more recent studies for instructional treatments that had students analyze data and information prior to writing. Graham and Perrin laid out components of student inquiry in their recommendation for involvement in this type of writing activity: a clearly specified goal, the analysis of concrete and immediate data using specific strategies for that analysis, and application of what was learned in composition. They again advised caution in interpretation, given that there was considerable variation in the types of interventions that were used as comparisons in the studies.

Prewriting instruction can vary tremendously. Five effect sizes were analyzed, and these included the following prewriting activities: encouragement of planning, group and individual planning, reading relevant materials, organizing with a semantic web, demonstrating planning, and then prompting planning. The impact of these studies was small but positive, indicating that having students gather and organize information, with the possible use of visual representation of ideas and information prior to beginning to write, can have a positive influence on the quality of student writing.

Finally, providing models of specific types of writing when these are the focus of instruction is recommended, based on the analysis of six effect sizes. The effect overall for these studies was small (mean weighted effect size of .25), and Graham and Perrin (2007) advised that the models provided should be analyzed, and the critical elements that students are encouraged to imitate should be clearly embodied in purposefully chosen examples.

The general overall conclusion that Graham and Perrin drew from their excellent current meta-analysis of writing instructional treatments is that explicit, systematic instruction on the processes and strategies involved in writing should be provided to adolescents in Grades 4–12 (2007). These processes should include planning, sentence construction, summarizing, and revising their written work. Providing students with clear goals and models that embody the target writing product should also positively influence adolescent writing, as can being proficient in the use of word processing and being encouraged to use it in the composing process. Graham and Perrin added this important comment:

> It is doubtful that most of the instructional procedures described above, especially the more complex ones like strategy instruction, can be widely and effectively implemented without a considerable amount of teacher preparation. If these practices are to be brought to scale, they must become an integral part of both preservice and inservice teacher education for both language arts and content area teachers. (2007, p. 28)

In calling for additional research, they noted that the studies on which they have based their 10 recommendations (presented in Table 11.1) do not include specific information on amount of instructional time, how they might integrate with other of the instructional techniques studied (since clearly several of these might be taught in combination), or how to address such issues as vocabulary, spelling, punctuation, or teacher–student conferencing on writing. Clearly there is more research to be done, but Graham and Perrin included a positive note on the improved quality of research studies done more recently, with greater reporting of details of comparisons, preimplementation training, implementation fidelity, and so forth.

Some of the most exciting and informative work done on reading and writing with struggling adolescents is the work of Donald Deshler and colleagues at The University of Kansas Center for Research on Learning. Schumaker and Deshler (2006) have recently summarized their research on learning strategies with adolescents with learning disabilities, which includes information on their Learning Strategies Curriculum and their instructional methodology for teaching strategies. Their overall findings on an eight-stage instructional methodology that focused on various specific learning strategies that address reading and writing, test taking, and task completion as well as generalization to content areas, are that the methodology can be highly effective with students with learning disabilities. There is strong evidence that the students studied were able to both master and generalize these strategies to various types of instructional tasks, and to earn higher grades in their general education tasks.

Much of the information presented by Schumaker and Deshler (2006) can help classroom teachers to more fully understand the entire writing process, including how and where their students might fail to respond to instruction. Schumaker and Deshler offered techniques that teachers might incorporate into the general instructional planning (for both reading and writing) for older students as well as use in modifying instruction for students who are not progressing well.

In this chapter we present the steps of one instructional strategy that we feel is particularly useful in teaching all students to summarize information. The written summarization strategy has been used to increase reading comprehension as well as writing ability. As Rinehart, Stahl, and Erikson (1986) succinctly outlined,

> Good summarizers (a) begin summarizing right away as they read (Taylor, 1984), (b) pay attention to the structure and know where important information is found (Taylor, 1984), (c) employ a set of rules (Brown, Campione, & Day, 1983; Winograd, 1984), (d) use judgment and effort to read skeptically, asking themselves questions as they read, (e) underline and cross out information while they read (Gajria & Salvia, 1992), and polish their products. (Rinehart, Stahl, & Erikson, 1986, p. 77)

Based on Brown, Campione, and Day's (1983) macrorules for deleting unimportant and repetitive information, locating or inventing a main idea, making lists and categorizing them, and combining ideas, Graner constructed a figure to outline the five SUM-UP steps, as reprinted in Figure 11.1.

However, these strategy steps *alone* are of little instructional value; they must be taught according to the instructional methodology outlined in Schumaker and Deshler (2006) and Graner (2007). The specific phases of the explicit instructional methodology (i.e., description of the strategy with rationales; clear and multiple models; explicit and elaborated feedback; specific instruction to generalize the strategy across tasks, settings, and circumstances; and multiple opportunities for well-designed, scaffolded instruction and practice) are where the real power lies. There are really two essential parts to effective strategy instruction: 1) a well-designed strategy in which each step guides the student to perform a critical behavior that leads to successful task completion, and 2) teaching the strategy with a sound instructional methodology

Start reading with summarizing in mind
    Read quickly for focus and content
    Know you're going to make it shorter
    Keep the rules in mind
Underline the main ideas and details
    Use the topic/main idea to details process
Make choices
    Put a star (*) next to the most important details
    Avoid repetitions
    Write category names in the margins
Use the worksheet to write the summary
    Consider one paragraph at a time
    Write the paraphrased main idea and details
    Summarize the main idea and details using a
    limited number of words
    Develop a thesis statement
Peruse your product for accuracy
    Check to see if it makes sense
    Check to see if you applied the substeps
    Check to see if you wrote the most important points
    Edit your summary

Figure 11.1. Steps of the written summarization strategy. (From Graner, P.G.S. [2007]. *The effects of strategic summarization instruction on the performance of students with and without disabilities in secondary inclusive classes.* Unpublished doctoral dissertation, University of Kansas; reprinted by permission.)

that explicitly teaches both strategy acquisition and generalization, transfer, and maintenance (Deshler, 2007, personal communication). Graner (2007) found that this approach worked well for the Written Summarization Strategy and is effective in teaching students with learning disabilities and typically developing students to write summaries in secondary inclusive classes.

There are eight stages to the instructional methodology for teaching learning strategies to students with learning disabilities, which also can be used generally in teaching strategies. These are presented by Schumaker and Deshler (2006). Stage 1, the *pretest and commitment* stage, consists of assessing the initial level of student performance and sharing this information with each student, then discussing their strengths and weaknesses and obtaining a commitment for improvement. During Stage 2, the *describe* stage, the teacher describes the new strategy as well as where, when, how, and why the student should use the strategy. Then, in Stage 3, the *model* stage, the teacher models (through think-alouds) self-instructing, problem solving, and self-monitoring behaviors, progressively including the students in the activity.

Stage 4 is the *verbal practice* stage, in which the student not only practices implementing the strategy but also labels the steps and explains them. Once this level of conscious awareness has been mastered, the student moves to Stage 5, *controlled practice and feedback*. Students practice to criterion with controlled materials, and the teacher guides the students with constructive feedback. At mastery of this stage, the student moves to Stage 6, the *controlled practice* stage, followed by Stage 7, the *advanced practice* stage; this is practice in natural environments that are similar to those of the controlled practice situations and materials.

Finally, with success, the student is ready to move on to Stage 8, *generalization*. Schumaker and Deshler (2006) recommended gaining a commitment from the student to move toward the generalization stage. This stage has four phases: *orientation, activation, adaptation,* and *maintenance*. For orientation, the teacher should point out and discuss the contexts in which the learning strategy being taught can be used. Then students should be given multiple opportunities to use (*activate*) the strategy, with a variety of materials and in a variety of settings. They may need to *adapt* the strategy to make it maximally useful in certain situations, and the teacher should prompt them and guide as necessary to help them make these adaptations. To *maintain* the skill they are beginning to master, the students should be encouraged to continue using the strategy in any settings where they need to summarize information, and the teacher should monitor their ability to fluently apply the strategy, with periodic probes to ensure that they are using the strategy with success. Graner (2007) included a sample lesson plan, an example learning sheet, and the fidelity of implementation checklist as appendices. While it is a useful and effective approach to teach students to summarize information that they read, it is important that the teacher fully understand the steps for implementation and implement it as intended, or they and their students may not experience success.

What Background Information and Planning Techniques Could Help Teachers in Working with Students?

According to Wong and Berninger (2005), there have been four paradigm shifts in how writing is viewed that have dramatically affected how writing was taught and have brought us to the present set of approaches that include a sort of hybrid of explicit instruction and process writing. First, the overall view of writing was expanded from a narrow focus on high school and college to a more developmental view that included emergent writing in preschool and developing writing in elementary school. Second, there was a shift from mainly focusing on instruction to adding attention to the writer's cognitive processes while composing. Third, the focus moved from being exclusively on the product to including the process. And fourth, writing was acknowledged as a social activity rather than a purely individual one. These shifts are viewed by Wong and Berninger as a result of the two major research approaches: *process writing* (relying on naturalistic observation) and *cognitive process* of the writer (relying on think-alouds), which have now for the most part been integrated.

Wong and Berninger (2005) pointed out that in teaching writing, teachers, like writers, must plan, translate, review, and revise. These authors laid out three sets of principles that can guide these processes and assist teachers in preparing to teach writing: instruction design principles, pedagogical principles, and evaluation and modification principles, which correspond to the planning, translations, and review and revision steps of writing.

Instruction Design Principles

The planning phase of instruction is organized developmentally, as is the review and revise phase since, as Wong and Berninger (2005) worded it, "learning to write is a long journey" (p. 2). The instruction design principles for the planning phase of instruction include the following:

1. Carefully consider timing of instructional components.

2. Teach explicitly with an interactive dialogue.

3. Design writing activities specifically to both allow for students' success and challenge them to accomplish things just beyond their current level.

4. Design activities to develop students' writing self-efficacy.

5. Teach for both near and far transfer (taught knowledge and generalization to new concepts).

6. Evaluate and provide feedback on a daily basis, to reinforce and help students improve.

7. Do not expect instant results.

8. Do not expect miracles from computers (as they cannot change poor writers into good ones without carefully planned and executed instruction).[2]

Pedagogical Principles

For the translation phase of instruction, Wong and Berninger (2005) presented 10 pedagogical principles and suggested several specific instructional approaches that teachers could utilize to implement these principles. These include work on self-regulation and self-efficacy (Principle 4) by Graham and colleagues (Graham, Schwartz, & MacArthur, 1993; Harris & Graham, 1996) and their own work (Wong, Butler, Ficzere, & Kuperis, 1997), and the Center–Activity–Rotation–System (CARS) of Flood and Lapp (2000) for classroom organization (Principle 7). For Principle 9, on self-prompting, they recommended work by Singer and Bashir (2004) and Englert and Raphael's (1988) Plan, Work, Organize, Evaluate, and Re-Work (POWER) model. Finally, for Principle 10 (strategy instruction) they used Deshler and colleagues' Strategic Instructional Model (Schumaker, Deshler, & McKnight, 2002), Writing Strategies and Paragraph Writing Strategies (Schmidt, Deshler, Schumaker, & Alley, 1989; Schumaker & Sheldon, 1985).

The pedagogical principles for the translation phase of instruction include the following:

1. Use procedural facilitators to bypass the limitations of working memory while composing.

2. Help students understand the reading–writing relationship by conferencing with students, having them write a research paper,

---

[2]Numbered list paraphrased from Wong, B., & Berninger, V. (2005). Cognitive processes of teachers in implementing composition research in elementary, middle, and high school classrooms. In B. Shulman, K. Apel, B. Ehren, E. Silliman, & A. Stone (Eds.), *Handbook of language and literacy development and disorders* (p. 606). New York: Guilford Press; adapted with permission.

helping them read and understand instructions for specific writing tasks, and increasing their audience awareness during peer conferencing.

3. Facilitate text generation through well-honed schema for paragraph structure and genre-specific text structures.

4. Motivate writing by teaching students self-regulation and self-efficacy strategies.

5. Create an optimal social environment for the composing process by giving students meaningful assignments, letting them choose topics and genres, having them read their writing aloud, having them do collaborative planning, and by modeling writing and discussing writing problems with them.

6. Adapt the physical environment, including for most schools the use of computers and word processors.

7. Organize the physical layout of the classroom to accommodate large- and small-group work as well as individual work.

8. Teach metalinguistic awareness and the difference between oral and written language styles.

9. Teach them to guide their own writing subprocesses with verbal self-prompts or questions.

10. Implement strategy instruction for low-achieving writers, which works well within a partnership between general and special education.[3]

Evaluation Modification Principles

There are three developmental stages for writing according to Wong and Berninger (2003). These include 1) emerging or beginning writing (primary grades), 2) developing writing (upper elementary and middle school/junior high school), and 3) increasingly skilled writing (high school). The developmental phase principles according to Wong and Berninger are listed next.

Beginning Writers

1. Keep a visible record of progress, such as a graph or writing portfolio of their stories, or both.

---

[3]Numbered list paraphrased from Wong, B., & Berninger, V. (2005). Cognitive processes of teachers in implementing composition research, in elementary, middle, & high school classrooms. In B. Shulman, K. Apel, B. Ehren, E. Silliman, & A. Stone (Eds.), *Handbook of language and literacy development and disorders.* New York: Guilford Press; adapted with permission.

2. For students having problems, try to distinguish whether the problem is legibility of handwriting, automaticity of letter production, or spelling.

3. Modify instruction to address problems identified and evaluate the success of these modifications.

Upper Elementary and Middle School Writers

1. Have students graph their own progress for specific goals (letters that are illegible or words misspelled, presence of topic sentences, etc.) and keep writing portfolios of their work. Review these with each student periodically.

2. Evaluate how the writing process may be breaking down for nonprogressing students (transcription, idea generation, word choice, grammar, etc.), and modify instruction to address problems.

3. Evaluate student response to modifications in instruction.

High School Writers

1. At the end of each composing session, evaluate specific target skills with the writer (clarity, appropriateness to topic, salience of themes, organization of ideas, etc.) and have students graph scores assigned according to a scale. Periodically rate student attitude, metacognition, and self-efficacy with respect to writing.

2. Note areas where students are not responding well to the program and troubleshoot with each student. Specifically address the processes of planning, reading/revising, self-monitoring, self-regulation, and executive control processes.

3. Adapt instruction to meet the problems of the student and continue to monitor progress.[4]

Other Components for Writing Instruction

Building an entire curriculum or program for writing instruction is a major undertaking, and to review all the components that Wong and Berninger (2005) drew from would be beyond the scope of a single chapter, but we hope that the previous section gave you a flavor of

---

[4]From Wong, B., & Berninger, V. (2005). Cognitive processes of teachers in implementing composition research in elementary, middle, & high school classrooms. In B. Shulman, K. Apel, B. Ehren, E. Silliman, & A. Stone (Eds.), *Handbook of language and literacy development and disorders.* New York: Guilford Press; reprinted with permission.

the types of information that can make up the component parts of a writing program.

What Additional Research Is Needed in the Area of Teaching Writing?

While we know that explicit instruction in writing is important both in its own right and to improve student reading comprehension, since it

---

What we know from research

- Students benefit from explicit instructional guidance that addresses the planning, translation, review, and revision processes in writing.

- Reading and writing are clearly related, and each has been shown to benefit from instruction addressing the other.

- Adolescent student outcomes on state assessments can be favorably influenced by learning strategy instruction for reading and writing, which if properly instructed and supported, generalizes to other areas of learning.

What we need to know from additional research

- How can teachers best develop instructional approaches, gather and use data to adapt instruction, and monitor progress at various levels of student writing?

- What are the specifics of the reading–writing–learning relationship?

- What are the optimal ways to organize instruction over a span of several years that will consistently and dramatically improve performance on the outcomes for which schools and teachers are held accountable?

- What are the long-term outcomes (including higher education, occupational, and other life experiences) of various instructional methodologies in writing, to determine which are most effective for sustained results, lasting beyond immediate or short-term outcomes?

- What constitutes a meaningful indicator of the use of strategic approaches to writing? What constitutes a meaningful indicator of both formative and summative assessments of student response to writing instruction and transfer/generalization?

- What is the effect of increased writing on the quality of student writing? (This is a common recommendation that has yet to be demonstrated as being effective.)

- What is the relationship between writing and higher order thinking skills?

Table 11.2. Writing research needs

can improve understanding of grammar, idea organization, and the structure of text in various genres, more research is needed. In fact, writing research has been a relatively neglected area. Table 11.2 lists some of the areas in which additional research on writing is needed.

HOW MIGHT THIS RESEARCH ON
• • • WRITING PLAY OUT IN THE CLASSROOM? • • •

Ms. Roma wanted her eighth-grade students to become more proficient in writing informative texts. She had noticed that they could summarize but had difficulty organizing and writing more than a page on a topic. She realized that an awareness of text structure would be one way of improving their writing. She also noted that her students needed to know how to choose relevant, important ideas to include in informative writing. She planned explicit instruction and practice for the students in detecting and analyzing text organization and the ideas that authors highlighted or omitted. She used text from web sites, textbooks, and articles to focus her instruction. She began to assign small informational writing tasks of about two pages on students' hobbies or interests. She made her criteria very clear and included the requirement of at least three sources and the use of subheadings, among other requirements. Students chose groups with similar topics in order to work together, helping each other with revisions and editing. As she noted some patterns of problems in the writing, such as paragraph construction, Ms. Roma provided short lessons to help students improve their skills in this area.

The second half of the school year, Ms. Roma and the class decided on a class project on the issue of hunger in the community and the world. The project allowed students to bring together the skills they had been developing as well as to develop and apply new skills, such as taking and summarizing notes, using the computer to develop interesting, clear publications, and conducting interviews. Student discussions helped the students think critically and creatively about the issue and bring that thinking to their writing.

What Other Resources Might Help in Planning and Implementing Writing Instruction?

All of the references at the end of this chapter are helpful in one way or another when developing writing instruction, and a few noteworthy resources are highlighted in this section. The paper by Wong and Berninger (2005), which was the source of the instructional design and pedagogical and evaluation/modification principles, is a highly readable, detailed description of how teachers can approach writing instruction. Graham and Harris (2005) have written a book which, while focused on students with learning disabilities, has many useful techniques that teachers could incorporate into their writing instruction for all students. In addition, most of the work by The University of Kansas team led by Donald Deshler at the Center for Research on Learning is highly recommended (see http://www.ku-crl.org). While these authors often address how to best instruct students with learning difficulties, they have also demonstrated that all students benefit from these approaches. Deshler and colleague's *Learning Strategies Curriculum* (Deshler and Schumaker, 2006) offers detailed information that is extremely useful not only in writing instruction but for promoting student mastery of reading and content area information as well. In addition, the Deshler University Center for Research on Learning web site provides information about conferences, with video and other media from past conferences and a conference schedule and information on training at various levels. The National Council of Teachers of English has a web site (http://www.ncte.org) that provides a variety of resources related to teaching writing. The web site for the National Writing Project (http://www.nwp.org) also offers resources and links to research on writing as well as professional development. In addition, a web site by the Noyce Foundation and the Carnegie Foundation for the Advancement of Teaching, *Every Child a Reader and Writer* (http://www.insidewritingworkshop.org/about/), provides information on professional development and classroom examples. We hope that these resources and many more identified in this book will guide teachers as they continue to advance their curricula to best meet the needs of students.

REFERENCES

Abbott, S., & Berninger, V. (1993). Structural equation modeling of relationships among developmental skills and writing skills in primary and intermediate elementary grades writers. *Journal of Educational Psychology, 85*(3), 478–508.

Abbott, S.P., Reed, E., Abbott, R.D., & Berninger, V.W. (1997). Yearlong balanced reading/writing tutorial: A design experiment used for dynamic assessment. *Learning Disability Quarterly, 20*, 249–263.

Applebee, M. (2000). Alternate models of writing development. In R. Indrisano & J. Squire (Eds.), *Perspectives on writing* (pp. 90–111). Newark, DE: International Reading Association.

Bangert-Drowns, R. (1993). The word processor as an instructional tool: A meta-analysis of word processing in writing instruction. *Review of Educational Research, 63*, 69–93.

Berninger, V. (2008). Evidence-based written language instruction during early and middle school. In R. Morris & N. Mather (Eds.), *Evidence-based intervention for students with learning and behavioral challenges*. Mahwah, NJ: Lawrence Erlbaum Associates.

Berninger, V., & Abbott, S. (2003). *PAL research-supported reading and writing lessons*. Orlando, FL: Harcourt-Brace & Co.

Berninger, V., Abbott, R., Jones, J., Wolf, B., Gould, L., Anderson-Youngstrom, M., et al. (2006). Early development of language by hand: Composing-, reading-, listening-, and speaking-connections, three letter writing modes, and fast mapping in spelling. *Developmental Neuropsychology, 29*, 61–92.

Berninger, V., Nagy, W., Carlisle, J., Thomson, J., Hoffer, D., Abbott, S., et al. (2003). Effective treatment for dyslexics in grades 4 to 6. In B. Foorman (Ed.), *Preventing and remediating reading difficulties: Bringing science to scale* (pp. 382–417). Timonium, MD: York Press.

Berninger, V., & Swanson, L. (1994). Modifying Hayes and Flower's model of skilled writing to explain beginning and developing writing. In E. Butterfield (Ed.), *Children's writing: Toward a process theory of development of skilled writing* (pp. 57–81). Stamford, CT: JAI Press.

Berninger, V., Vaughan, K., Abbott, R., Abbott, S., Rogan, K., Brooks, A., & Reed, E. (1997). Treatment of handwriting problems in beginning writing: Transfer from handwriting to composition. *Journal of Educational Psychology, 94*, 291–304.

Bromely, K. (1998). *Language arts: Exploring connections*. Needham Heights, MA: Allyn & Bacon.

Brooks, A., Vaughan, K., & Berninger, V. (1999). Tutorial interventions for writing disabilities: Comparison of transcription and text generation processes. *Learning Disabilities Quarterly, 22*, 183–191.

Brown, A., Campione, J.D., & Day, J. (1983). Macrorules for summarizing texts: The development of expertise. *Journal of Verbal Learning & Verbal Behavior, 22*, 1–14.

Calkins, L. (1981). Case study of a 9-year-old writing. In D. Graves (Ed.), *A case study observing development of primary children's composing, spelling, and motor behavior during the writing process* (pp. 239–262). Durham, NH: University of New Hampshire.

Calkins, L. (1986). *The art of teaching writing*. Portsmouth, NH: Heinemann.

Clay, M. (1982). Research update on learning and teaching writing: A developmental perspective. *Language Arts, 59*, 65–70.

Deshler, D.D., & Schumaker, J.B. (2006). *Teaching adolescents with disabilities: Accessing the general education curriculum*. New York: Corwin Press.

Englert, C.S., & Raphael, T.E. (1988). Constructing well-formed prose: Process, structure and metacognitive knowledge. *Exceptional Children, 54*, 18–25.

Fearn, L., & Farnan, N. (2005). *An investigation of the influence of teaching grammar in writing to accomplish an influence on writing*. Paper presented at the annual meeting of the American Educational Research Association, Montreal, Canada.

Flood, J., & Lapp, D. (2000). Teaching writing in urban schools: Cognitive processes, curriculum resources, and the missing links—management and grouping. In R. Indrisano, & J.R. Squire (Eds.), *Perspectives on writing* (pp. 233–250). Newark, DE: International Reading Association.

Gajria, M., & Salvia, J. (1992). The effects of summarization on text comprehension of students with learning disabilities. *Exceptional Children, 58,* 508–516.

Goldring, A., Russell, M., & Cook, A. (2003). The effects of computers on student writing: A meta-analysis of studies from 1992 to 2002. *Journal of Technology, Learning, and Assessment, 2,* 1–51.

Graham, S. (2006a). Writing. In P. Alexander & P. Winner (Eds.), *Handbook of educational psychology* (pp. 457–478). Mahwah, NJ: Lawrence Erlbaum Associates.

Graham, S. (2006b). Strategy instruction and the teaching of writing: A meta-analysis. In C. MacArthur, S. Graham, & J. Fitzgerald (Eds.), *Handbook of writing research* (pp. 187–207). New York: Guilford Press.

Graham, S., & Harris, K.R. (2003). Students with learning disabilities and the process of writing: A meta-analysis of SRSD studies. In L. Swanson, K.R. Harris, & S. Graham (Eds.), *Handbook of research on learning disabilities* (pp. 383–402). New York: Guilford Press.

Graham, S., & Harris, K. (2005). *Writing better: Effective strategies for teaching students with learning difficulties.* Baltimore: Paul H. Brookes Publishing Co.

Graham, S., Harris, K., & Fink, B. (2000). Is handwriting causally related to learning to write? Treatment of handwriting problems in beginning writers. *Journal of Educational Psychology, 92,* 620–633.

Graham, S., Harris, K., & Fink-Chorezempa, B. (2002). Contributions of spelling instruction to the spelling, writing, and reading of poor spellers. *Journal of Educational Psychology, 94,* 669–686.

Graham, S., & Perrin, D. (2007). A meta-analysis of writing instruction for adolescent students. *Journal of Educational Psychology, 99*(3), 445–476.

Graham, S., Schwartz, S., & MacArthur, C. (1993). Learning disabled and normally achieving students' knowledge of writing and the composing process, attitude toward writing, and self-efficacy for students with and without learning disabilities. *Journal of Learning Disabilities, 26,* 237–249.

Graner, P.G.S. (2007). *The effects of strategic summarization instruction on the performance of students with and without disabilities in secondary inclusive classes.* Unpublished doctoral dissertation, University of Kansas.

Graves, D. (1983). *Writing: Teachers and children at work.* Exeter, NH: Heinemann.

Harris, K., & Graham, S. (1996). *Making the writing process work: Strategies for composition and self-regulation* (2nd ed.). Cambridge, MA: Brookline Books.

Harris, K., & Graham, S. (1999). Programmatic intervention research: Illustrations from the evolution of self-regulated strategy development. *Learning Disability Quarterly, 22,* 251–262.

Hart, T., Berninger, V., & Abbott, R. (1997). Comparison of teaching single or multiple orthographic-phonological connections for word recognition and spelling: Implications for instructional consultation. *School Psychology Review, 26,* 279–297.

Hayes, J.R., & Flower, L.S. (1980). Identifying the organization of writing processes. In L.W. Gregg & E.R. Steinberg (Eds.), *Cognitive processes in writing* (pp. 3–30). Hillsdale, NJ: Lawrence Erlbaum Associates.

Hillocks, G. (1986). *Research on written composition: New directions for teaching.* Urbana, IL: National Council of Teachers of English.

Jones, D., & Christensen, D. (1999). The relationship between automaticity in handwriting and students' ability to generate written text. *Journal of Educational Psychology, 91*, 44–49.

Lispey, M., & Wilson, D. (2001). *Practical meta-analysis.* Thousand Oaks, CA: Sage.

Moats, L., Foorman, B., & Taylor, P. (2006). How quality of writing instruction impacts high-risk fourth graders' writing. *Reading and Writing, 19*, 363–391.

Nagin, C. (2003). *Because writing matters: Improving student writing in our schools.* San Francisco: Jossey-Bass.

Nagy, W., Berninger, V., Abbott, S., Garcia, N., & Carlisle, J. (2008). *Growth of phonology, orthography, and morphology and their contributions to literacy outcomes in typically developing children Grades 1 to 6.* Manuscript submitted for publication.

Pritchard, R.J. (1987). Effects on student writing of teacher training in the National Writing Project Model. *Written Communication, 4*, 51–67.

Rinehart, S.D., Stahl, S.A., & Erikson, L.G. (1986). Some effects of summarization training on reading and studying. *Reading Research Quarterly, 21*(4), 422–438.

Schmidt, J., Deshler, D.D., Schumaker, J.B., & Alley, G. (1989). Effects of generalization instruction on the written language performance of adolescents with learning disabilities in the mainstream classroom. *Reading, Writing, & Learning Disabilities, 4*, 291–309.

Schumaker, J.B., & Deshler, D.D. (2006). Teaching adolescents to be strategic learners. In D.D. Deshler & J.B. Schumaker (Eds.), *Teaching adolescents with disabilities: Accessing the general education curriculum.* New York: Corwin Press.

Schumaker, J.B., Deshler, D.D., & McKnight, P. (2002). Ensuring success in the secondary general education curriculum through the use of teaching routines. In G. Stover, M. Shinn, & H. Walker (Eds.), *Interventions for achievement and behavior problems* (pp. 791–824). Washington, DC: National Association of School Psychologists.

Schumaker, J.B., & Sheldon, J. (1985). *The sentence writing strategy: Instructor's manual.* Lawrence, KS: University of Kansas Center for Research on Learning.

Singer, B.D., & Bashir, A.S. (2004). An approach to helping students with language disorders learn to write. In L.C. Wilkinson & E.R. Silliman (Eds.), *Language-literacy learning in schools.* New York: Guilford Press.

Swanson, L., & Berninger, V. (1996). Individual differences in children's working memory and writing skills. *Journal of Experimental Child Psychology, 63*, 358–385.

Taylor, K. (1984). Teaching summarization skills. *Journal of Reading, 27*(5), 389–393.

Winograd, P.N. (1984). Strategic difficulties in summarizing text. *Reading Research Quarterly, 14*(3), 129–140.

Wong, B.Y.L. (1997). Research on genre-specific strategies for enhancing writing in adolescents with learning disabilities. *Learning Disabilities Quarterly, 20*, 140–159.

Wong, B., & Berninger, V. (2005). Cognitive processes of teachers in implementing composition research in elementary, middle, and high school classrooms. In B. Shulman, K. Apel, B. Ehren, E. Silliman, & A. Stone (Eds.), *Handbook of language and literacy development and disorders* (pp. 600–624). New York: Guilford Press.

Wong, B.Y.L., Butler, D.L., Ficzere, S.A., & Kuperis, S. (1996). Teaching adolescents with learning disabilities and low achievers to plan, write, and revise opinion essays. *Journal of Learning Disabilities, 29,* 197–212.

Wong, B.Y.L., Butler, D.L., Ficzere, S.A., & Kuperis, S. (1997). Teaching adolescents with learning disabilities and low achievers to plan, write, and revise compare and contrast essays. *Learning Disabilities Research & Practice, 12,* 2–15.

How Can Evidence-Based Research Support Classroom Teaching?

● ● ● ● ● ● ● ● ● ● ● ● ● ● ● ● ● ● ● ●

> *"If you would thoroughly know anything, teach it to others."*
>
> (Tryon Edwards, C.N. Catrevas, & Jonathan Edwards, 1842/1977)

In the first three sections of this book, we introduced readers to the book and discussed reading and reading instruction and the importance of an evidence base. We tried to indicate where that evidence comes from and offered readers the resources to access that evidence base themselves. We outlined the evidence for what we consider to be the important major components of reading instruction: vocabulary, alphabetics, fluency, comprehension, spelling, and writing. We also provided some information about what instruction on these components would look like in the classroom, integrating aspects of all of the components even when focusing on a specific single component. Part of our view of reading is that it is a tremendously complex endeavor—either to teach or to learn—and the components or aspects of reading all work together in a wonderful orchestration. Therefore, instruction in reading must also involve complex, well-integrated orchestration.

In the final section of this book, we add some other things that affect how teachers can use that evidence in the classroom. First, motivation and engagement are crucial. If students do not want to read, or find it an unpleasant activity, it is very difficult to teach them how to do it or to get them to use their skills to gain the knowledge in content areas that they need to be able to access through their reading and writing abilities. Chapter 12 addresses motivation and engagement, laying a basic theory of what motivation and engagement are. We discuss how students can be motivated and the important role that teachers play in maintaining and supporting student motivation.

It is also difficult to know exactly who is not succeeding, to what degree, and in what specific aspects of reading and writing, without assessing students. Chapter 13 addresses assessment, including why it is necessary and how it is best applied. We address the various types and purposes of assessment and how at least some of them can and should be quite helpful to teachers.

Chapter 14 is about the teacher. Here, we discuss professional development and technology. We attempt to give an overview of how teachers can stay up to date, what they will need to keep current with the changing demands that new research continuously addresses, and what sorts of support they need and will need to do this.

Finally, Chapter 15 addresses a current topic that everyone is aware of, if not being pushed to participate in: response to intervention (RTI). In this chapter, we offer a basic explanation of what RTI is, what research evidence exists to support its use, some information about the essential role of progress monitoring in RTI, and why this approach can only really succeed as a partnership between general and special education.

REFERENCE

Edwards, T., Catrevas, C.N., & Edwards, J. (1977). (Eds.). *The new dictionary of thoughts: An encyclopedia of quotations.* New York: Doubleday. (Original work published 1842)

CHAPTER 12

Motivation and Engagement

"Powerful teachers are strengths-based and student-centered. They use students' own experiences, strengths, interests, goals, and dreams as the beginning point for learning, competence, and accomplishment. Thus, they tap students' intrinsic motivation [and] their existing, innate drive for learning."

(Bonnie Bernard, 2004, p. 74)

KEY CONCEPTS

- In education, motivation is multifaceted and is a crucial part of academic success.

- Motivation plays an important role in reading development, since motivation facilitates learning.

- There are many ways to motivate students in reading, including actively involving students in the learning process, such as offering choices and opportunities in texts/reading.

- A teacher's ability to engage and motivate students is an important factor in learning and reading success.

Mrs. Sweet wanted to increase her fourth-grade students' motivation to read books on their own. She had a classroom library and took the class to the school library each week. She decided to choose a book from one of the libraries every other day and give a short book talk to rouse the interest of students in that book or others by the same author. She was modeling her own love of reading and showing the students that she knew about good books. Sometimes, she compared two books, talking about differences in the characters, the settings, and the problems to be solved. She let students write short entries in a class record of books they had chosen and read, with notes on what they thought about them.

Eventually students asked to give book talks about their favorite books. Each student kept a list of books and pages read, so they could see how much they were reading. Finally, because practice with interesting materials makes for better readers, and because confident readers are more motivated to read, she assigned 20 minutes of reading every night for homework and asked students to get parent signatures on their weekly reading records. She also allowed students who finished work ahead of time to read books they had chosen. She knew that giving time for students to practice reading and develop an interest in books and authors would increase their motivation to read.

One of the most important roles of a teacher is motivating students to learn, awakening in them the love of knowledge and empowerment they can gain as they learn to read. Motivation drives learning and the continued pursuit of knowledge and information. In reading, motivation is essential to bringing together learning to read and the desire to read and learn. Some students are intent on reading to understand; they focus on text meaning and exchange ideas and interpretations of text with peers (Guthrie & Wigfield, 2000). They like reading and enjoy opportunities to read in the classroom and in their spare time. However, this does not apply to all students. There are students who do not enjoy reading, avoid reading, and put in minimal effort in classes and subjects involving reading. In this chapter, we discuss engagement in reading and the role of motivation. In addition, we explore what teachers might do to maintain and enhance student motivation for reading within the classroom.

How Is Motivation Defined, and Are There Different Kinds of Motivation?

In education, motivation is considered a key element of success (Pintrich & Schunk, 1996). Students' desire, will, and ability to learn are all shaped by their educational experiences. Since reading skills cross all academic subjects, whether reading a math word problem or a science experiment, motivation is a part of any academic endeavor.

Psychologists often talk about two key constructs or types of motivation: intrinsic and extrinsic (Deci, 1975; Deci & Ryan, 1985; Lepper & Greene, 1978; Malone & Lepper, 1987). Intrinsic motivation refers to an individual who has the drive or will to do an activity for its own sake, out of interest and curiosity (Guthrie, Wigfield, & VonSecker, 2000). An intrinsically motivated learner will choose books and read them during free time at school or at home, seek out opportunities to engage in reading, and often lose track of time when absorbed in reading (Sweet, 1997). Those students who are high in intrinsic motivation are likely to read more frequently and report reading more than fellow students (Wigfield & Guthrie, 1997). In contrast, students who are extrinsically motivated work on tasks because they believe that participation will result in desirable outcomes, such as a reward, teacher praise, or avoidance of punishment (Pintrich & Schunk, 1996); their motivation is the desire to receive external recognition or reinforcement (Deci, Vallerand, Pelletier, & Ryan, 1991). In reading, extrinsically motivated students work hard as a means to an end (e.g., to receive good grades); their motivation is usually unrelated to the task of reading itself but to the rewards of accomplishing it (Sweet, 1997). Therefore, extrinsically motivated students are less likely to seek out opportunities to engage in reading on their own time. However, sometimes simple extrinsic motivation can lead to intrinsic motivation. For example, a teacher might have students keep lists of books they read and share their lists with peers from time to time. Students who are initially motivated to simply add to their lists might over time come to enjoy reading books.

It is not clear why some individuals choose to read and find great pleasure in reading while others do not (Sweet, 1997). As highlighted in the opening vignette of this chapter, when a child sees the importance and love of reading modeled by teachers, it helps to set a standard on the value of reading for both purpose and pleasure. Thus, by attempting to instill this value in students, teachers may contribute to motivating students for reading.

It is important that teachers' beliefs about effective strategies for motivating students are consistent with determination theory (Guthrie & Wigfield, 2000). Self-determination is a critical aspect of intrinsic motivation that focuses on three needs: autonomy, relatedness, and competence (Deci et al., 1991). Autonomy refers to self-initiating and self-regulating actions. This need is fulfilled through self-directed learning. Relatedness refers to developing satisfying social connections, a need which is addressed in collaborative classroom activities. Competence involves understanding how to reach goals and may be fulfilled in evaluation that supports progress and rewards for effort and learning (Guthrie & Wigfield, 2000). When these needs are met, students become intrinsically motivated and gain expertise (e.g., in reading). Teachers can promote self-determination, and thereby intrinsic motivation, by creating a learning environment in which students have choices in reading, are involved in collaborative reading activities, and engage in challenging reading and learning situations.

Related to intrinsic motivation is self-efficacy, where the goal is personal mastery in some area, like sports or academics. Individuals with self-efficacy believe that they have the capacity to do well. In education, students with self-efficacy believe that they have the capability to succeed. For example, in reading, students approach reading books confidently and approach challenging texts or difficult words with the expectation that they will master them (Guthrie & Humenick, 2004). It is up to teachers to provide positive feedback and to support students as they develop competence and confidence in their reading abilities. Harter (1981) emphasized the use of positive reinforcement from an early age. Bandura (1986) found that, with sufficient reinforcement, children could develop and internalize a self-reward system and internalize mastery goals. Successes produce intrinsic pleasure and perceptions of competence and control, which should strengthen self-efficacy. However, students with learning problems often believe they lack the competence to do well, and their intrinsic motivation decreases (Schunk, 1989). Self-efficacy is then diminished as children increasingly depend on others to set their goals and reinforce their efforts (Pintrich & Schunk, 1996). Strategies, such as using prior knowledge, searching for information, comprehending and interpreting text, and self-monitoring are likely to increase self-efficacy in elementary and middle school students (Guthrie & Wigfield, 2000). Teachers can coach students by modeling strategies, providing small group discussions, and offering individual feedback on progress (Guthrie & Wigfield, 2000). Therefore, teachers need to be sensitive to students' learning needs and create an environment where there are appropriate cognitive challenges and positive feedback.

Although both intrinsic and extrinsic motivation play a role in what happens in classrooms, the educational system seems to focus more heavily on providing extrinsic motivation (Ryan, Cornell, & Deci, 1985) by using reward systems, such as grades and test scores, as reinforcement. Research with students of various age groups and differing types of rewards and target activities has shown that engaging in an intrinsically interesting activity to obtain an extrinsic reward can undermine intrinsic motivation (Lepper & Greene, 1978; Lepper, Greene, & Nisbett, 1973; Pintrich & Schunk, 1996; Sweet, 1997). According to self-determination theory, receiving extrinsic rewards for completing tasks makes people feel that the reason for participation was obtaining a reward rather than the intrinsic worth of the task. This undermines autonomy, thereby weakening intrinsic motivation (Sweet, 1997).

How Does Engagement Relate to Motivation in Reading?

Engagement is a term generally associated with motivation. Reading for enjoyment, or for its own sake, is essential to *engaged reading* (Oldfather & Dahl, 1994; Turner, 1995). Often, learners are described as engaged based on their on-task behavior (Berliner & Biddle, 1995; Tobin, 1984). There are variations in how engaged reading is defined, but a key point of agreement is that engaged reading involves desires and intentions of the reader. Engaged readers are those who read not only because they can but also because they want to and are motivated to read (Guthrie & Wigfield, 2000). Guthrie, McGough, Bennett, and Rice (1996) described engaged readers as motivated to read for a variety of personal goals, strategic in using various approaches to comprehend, knowledgeable in their construction of understanding of text, and socially interactive, working with peers in their literacy activities. Thus, they described engaged reading as strategic and conceptual as well as motivational and intentional.

Cognitively, engaged readers make deliberate choices within a context and select strategies for comprehending text content (Guthrie & Wigfield, 2000). For example, engaged readers seek conceptual understanding by asking questions about the text, constructing meanings using multiple perspectives, and incorporating comprehension strategies with an intrinsic desire to learn (Guthrie & Wigfield, 2000). This can be a positive process that enhances both motivation and learning. Strategic reading results in conceptual understanding (Beck, McKeown, Worthy, Sandora, & Kucan, 1996) and advanced knowledge acquisition (Alexander, Jetton, & Kulikowich, 1996). The new knowledge in turn results in the reader engaging in more extended inquiry, including broader topic areas of reading, such as literature, history, or science (Guthrie & Wigfield, 2000), and thus seems to promote a higher level of engagement. In addition, in many classrooms, readers are interacting with peers (cooperative learning) to socially construct meanings, and this type of activity also increases student engagement (Almasi, 1995).

Guthrie and Wigfield (2000) emphasized that the cognitive and social dimensions of engaged reading are distinguishable from the motivational dimension but engagement cannot occur without all three components. This clearly indicates the relation of motivation and engagement, as illustrated in Guthrie and Wigfield's definition of engagement, which integrates cognition, social interaction, and motivation: "Engaged readers in the classroom or elsewhere coordinate their strategies and knowledge (cognition) within a community of literacy (social) in order to fulfill their personal goals, desires, and intentions (motivation)" (Guthrie & Wigfield, 2000, p. 404).

How Are Motivation and Reading Development Connected?

Motivation and reading are linked long before a child enters the classroom. Early exposure to books and promoting reading at home have been shown to be beneficial for giving students a head start in the classroom (Edwards, 2007; Snow, Burns, & Griffin, 1998). Teachers can continue to support motivation for reading by adjusting their teaching to meet students' specific learning needs, thereby maximizing student success. A teacher's goal is for students to learn; when students are engaged, they are more likely to learn, to gain the skills they need for reading, and to move toward the ultimate goal of reading, comprehension.

It cannot be assumed that poor readers are all unmotivated. In fact, many children who struggle with reading do want to be able to read (*Hearing on Education Research and Evaluation and Student Achievement: Quality Counts*, 2000). Motivation in reading is the bridge that links the concepts of reading, learning to read, and the joy of reading for meaning. In order to reach that point where reading becomes effortless and automatic, several skills must be mastered, as is discussed in Section II of this book. However, the desire to read and understand is extremely important in promoting the learning process. Reading ability also influences motivation to continue reading and using academic skills. Therefore, a great deal of motivational research has focused on the cognitive aspects of learning, including learning to read. Reading ability and motivation are logically linked, because if children are unable to read, they will become frustrated and view reading as a difficult, laborious activity that they do not want to pursue. On the other hand, if children read with ease and understanding, they do not perceive reading as a task but rather a skill, used for understanding and enjoyment. Thus, motivation is a major factor influencing reading and life success.

Promoting intrinsic motivation at the same time reading skills are being developed is a crucial part of instruction. Once students have developed the necessary reading skills, from phonemic awareness to comprehension instruction, they should want to read and continue to develop their skills based on interest, curiosity, and the fact that they find reading enjoyable (Wigfield & Guthrie, 1997). An intrinsically motivated reader will choose books and read them during free time at school or at home.

How Can Research on Motivation and Engagement Inform Instructional Planning?

One of the fundamental keys to instructional planning and developing or effectively using curricula is creating lessons that are not only cognitively challenging but that also promote learning using topics and ideas that optimize or promote engagement. The outcomes of teaching reading, such as text comprehension ability and knowledge acquisition from text, depend on engagement to be sustained. So, the question becomes how to develop lessons that both cover the instructional information students need and promote motivation and engagement at the same time. Guthrie and Humenick (2004) discussed classroom practices that simultaneously influence reading motivation and achievement.

The Power of Student Choice

One influence is the power of choice. Offering choices to students in what they read is one way for teachers to empower students. When teachers create opportunities for choice, students can feel some control over their own learning process. Students can be offered various types of choices, such as selecting authors or genres that appeal to them, deciding whether to read alone or with a partner, and even choosing where to do their reading within the classroom (Guthrie & Humenick, 2004; Guthrie & Wigfield, 2000). Guthrie and Humenick (2004) cited research indicating that both elementary and secondary schools that provide choices in reading activities increase students' interest and time spent in reading.

Promoting Student Interest

Another classroom practice that influences reading motivation is providing interesting texts for instruction. Adult readers gravitate towards books or magazines about certain topics that interest them and scan the newspaper until they find articles that they think they will enjoy reading. Interesting texts have been shown to increase motivation for reading and to facilitate comprehension (Wade, Buxton, & Kelly, 1999).

Students have been shown to continue reading enjoyable texts in their free time, which in turn promotes intrinsic motivation (Guthrie & Humenick, 2004).

Sometimes students are not aware of their interests, at least as they relate to what they read. Teachers can help students develop or identify their interests in reading by giving book talks and reading aloud from different books. Talking to students about their interests and having students share favorite books with each other helps students become aware of their reading interests, a critical step in making their own choices of what to read.

It is logical that students are likely to pay more attention to texts and topics that interest them. The question that teachers are then faced with is what students find interesting and what makes a text interesting to those students. In general, *interesting* can be defined as both entertaining and informative. Guthrie and Humenick (2004) referred to interest as "qualities of a text that help students learn from a text" (p. 345) and highlighted the importance of background knowledge. Students are more interested in familiar topics; while they are often open to new topics, they gravitate to topics or texts that they are initially familiar with. Thus it may fall to the teacher to introduce new topics that may interest students, thereby setting up the possibility that they will choose books on those topics in the future. In addition, connecting interesting texts to real-world interactions provides connections between the academic curriculum and the personal experience of the learner (Guthrie & Wigfield, 2000). Real-world interactions, such as role playing or hands-on activities, can be enjoyable and can help the reader connect the text and personal experiences.

Social Collaboration to Increase Motivation

Teachers who develop instruction that includes social collaboration among students are often promoting motivation. Social collaboration in academic study, including reading, can increase intrinsic motivation, whereas individual activities are often less motivating (Sweet, Guthrie, & Ng, 1998). It is important for students to learn to work together to build on reading strategies (e.g., cooperative learning). Students' intrinsic motivation can increase when they read together, share information, and present information to each other (Guthrie & Humenick, 2004). Collaboration can include both working in small groups and working together in the class as a whole. Sharing information and learning from others emphasizes the collaboration in a classroom and is one of the most important ways that teachers not only set the tone for learning but provide students with the support structure to work with their peers in a collaborative environment.

When Does Motivation for Reading Begin?

Motivation is established very early in life. Motivation does not simply begin when formalized education begins. Long before children start elementary school, they are exposed to literacy and language and are developing skills that will define their academic journey. For instance, Snow et al. (1998) stated that "early childhood educators represent an important resource in promoting literacy through the acquisition of rich language and emergent literacy skills" (p. 332). Preschool teachers are involved with students at an impressionable time, promoting positive attitudes and motivation in early reading development through their interactions and support.

In addition, it is important to note that the first "teacher" a child has is involved long before a child enters a classroom. The role of the caregiver or parent and the home environment should not be underestimated. The home environment is the first place where children may be exposed to print and the idea and activity of reading. Parents and caregivers within the home environment contribute to the preparation of children for reading and writing instruction (Lesemen & deJong, 2001). The presence of newspapers, magazines, and children's books in the home provides children with the opportunity to become familiar with literacy and print (Lesemen & deJong, 2001). This can foster positive attitudes towards eventual literacy learning in school (Lesemen & deJong, 1998).

As a child progresses to school, the home environment may continue to play an important role as parents and caregivers reinforce the skills being learned in school (Edwards, 2007). Therefore, it is important for teachers to involve parents in the child's educational process. For example, teachers can provide information to parents about home activities that support their children's reading achievement. These include parents showing children that they value reading by reading to them, letting them see that they enjoy and use reading to get information, providing things for children to read (even if it includes the comics in the newspaper), taking their children to the library, talking to their children, giving them explanations of events and actions, and listening to their children talk about their reading and their activities (Edwards, 2007; Snow et al., 1998).

How Does Motivation Change over Time?

While teachers work with their students to develop a love for learning and reading, essentially moving them towards being intrinsically motivated to read, there is some research that indicates that reading motivation shifts over time, with decreases in intrinsic motivation occurring in early to middle elementary school years and then again as students move into middle or junior high school (Gottfried, 1985; Guthrie & Wigfield, 2000). Children's extrinsic motivation tends to increase, with more of a focus on performance goals, such as grades and standardized tests. This may be due in part to the changes from a responsive, more self-contained classroom in the earlier academic years to an environment in which students often have fewer opportunities for self-directed learning in later grades, where the focus shifts to grades and performance (Oldfather & Dahl, 1994).

Some researchers believe that this change occurs because children are more aware of their capabilities or perhaps their lack of capabilities as they get older, and that this shift in awareness can affect their desire to read as well as the perception of what kind of readers they are. For example, if Sarah, a fourth grader, who has struggled with fluency in reading in the third grade, continues to have difficulty, she will realize as she gets older that she is different from her peers. She is likely to become more cognizant of her reading difficulty, perhaps as she watches other students read together effortlessly or discuss stories they have read. As Sarah becomes more aware that she has a hard time reading, she will not look forward to reading, whether it is aloud or silently. Therefore, it is up to teachers to identify when students are having difficulties with reading, offer strategies and appropriate feedback, and reinforce the love for learning. Teachers are instrumental in providing clear and consistent guidelines, feedback, and involvement opportunities to promote interest (Pintrich & Schunk, 1996) and a lifelong positive relationship with reading.

How Does Assessment Relate to Motivation?

One of the most difficult parts of instructional planning is determining the best way to assess student proficiency in an area. Assessment activities can range from objective and standardized (e.g., standardized tests) to student centered and personalized (e.g., portfolios). Some standardized measures are necessary to monitor group proficiency and to comply with specific school, district, and state standards as well as to provide a context in which to view a student as compared to his or her peers receiving the same instruction within the same educational environment. However, some assessment methods commonly seen in an academic environment have been shown to decrease interest and intrinsic motivation (Deci & Ryan, 1987). Individualized assessments more readily support student motivation but can be more difficult to administer and report (Guthrie & Wigfield, 2000).

The goal of assessment is for teachers to evaluate and encourage student effort and progress and to use this information to plan for instruction. Some standardized measures are necessary to accomplish this. At the same time, less formal assessments can help to empower students to take ownership of the knowledge being gained and to enjoy reading and writing. Thus, student-centered assessment provides students with feedback on their progress and increases their sense of self-efficacy (Schunk & Zimmerman, 1997), and the cycle of increased intrinsic motivation, which increases learning, which enhances intrinsic motivation, is set in motion. However, it is unrealistic for classrooms to have student-centered assessments only; a combination of methods is necessary in order to be able to monitor student progress toward standards, know how the class as a whole is achieving, and provide feedback for both student and teacher that can serve to warn of potential problems and provide a basis for differentiated instruction. (See also Chapter 13, in which we discuss assessment as it relates more broadly to reading.)

Throughout this chapter, we have focused on what motivation and engagement mean and how motivation influences the reading development and learning process. In addition, we have discussed instructional techniques that focus on engaging students. However, none of these components are relevant without the most important piece of the puzzle: the teacher. A knowledgeable, informed, and flexible teacher is crucial. Ultimately, the optimal environment is one in which students prosper with appropriate instruction and guidance from teachers.

What Are the Teacher Characteristics and Roles that Best Help to Motivate Students?

There are several factors that characterize highly qualified and informed teachers. The International Reading Association (IRA) position statement describes excellent classroom reading teachers. Important features for classroom reading teachers include extensive teacher knowledge, the ability to manage a classroom so that students are engaged, and the use of strong motivation strategies to encourage independent learning (IRA, 2000). Guthrie and Wigfield (2000) described social support, encouragement, and involvement from the teacher as characteristics of highly qualified teachers. This is based on research that has demonstrated that teachers can have strong effects on children's motivation to read (Guthrie & Wigfield, 2000; IRA, 2000; Skinner & Belmont, 1993). For example, social support in the classroom is closely connected to students' intrinsic motivation for reading and writing (Guthrie & Wigfield, 2000). When students have a caring teacher, one that instills a sense of belonging, they are likely to be motivated in their academic subjects (Wentzel, 1997). Praise, rewards, and encouragement represent what Guthrie and Wigfield (2000) identified as the most pervasive strategies for encouraging effort and attention in students, because students who feel recognized and accepted in the classroom social structure are more motivated to read, write, and express themselves directly (Oldfather & Dahl, 1994). Effective teachers give informative compliments that make learners feel a sense of accomplishment and pride in the work they complete (Guthrie & Wigfield, 2000). Of course, praise should be given not only because a goal has been successfully reached but also for effort; while we all want children to succeed in learning and to eventually be able to complete tasks, simply trying to complete a task or develop a skill is important to motivation and can be a stepping stone to eventual success. A teacher who shows knowledge of and interest in students as individuals (e.g., remarking on the books or topics a students chooses) provides social support through that type of interaction.

Teacher involvement is integral to the learning process. The teacher's knowledge of individual learners, ability to recognize student progress, and skill at fostering student participation are essential aspects of teacher involvement (Guthrie & Wigfield, 2000). Synonyms of the word *involvement* include *participation, engagement,* and *commitment.* These words seem to define the very reasons teachers choose their profession. Guthrie and Wigfield (2000) described the involved teacher as focused on student learning, caring about personal interests, and promoting realistic but positive goals. Such behavior in turn influences students' engagement in the classroom. For instance, Skinner and Belmont (1993) found that when students perceived teachers to be interested in their progress and supportive of their learning process, they were engaged in the classroom (e.g., participating in class discussions and actively learning). This influence was reciprocal: Student engagement affected teacher involvement as much as teacher involvement influenced student engagement. This nicely illustrates that motivation can have an impact on everyone involved in the learning and engagement process.

If one word must be chosen to describe the teacher's contribution to the learning and motivation cycle besides instruction, we believe it is *support*. The teacher not only provides the appropriate and challenging tools for learning but also is an encouraging presence as the student develops the skills necessary for successful knowledge building, and the teacher helps the student move from learning to read to reading to learn. The teacher can also offer support to parents and caregivers in their role in promoting literacy development. In each of these steps, the teacher is supporting the students, not simply instructing them but acting as a positive guide for each step of the learning process. Therefore, the role of the teacher is central to the development and sustainability of motivation, especially in reading development.

HOW MIGHT THIS RESEARCH ON
• • • MOTIVATION PLAY OUT IN THE CLASSROOM? • • •

Mr. James wanted to have his fifth-grade students learn how to do a research project in social studies. Knowing that collaborative activities tend to increase motivation, he had them work in groups to read different articles on things that have changed over time, including cars, radios, food in the United States, and the sport of football. Each group reported on the most interesting idea in the article they read. Then, as a class, they discussed the fact that the author of such an article needed to do research to gather information and then decide what information to use and how to use it. Mr. James encouraged the students to think of questions they might ask the authors about how they had gone about writing the article; they also discussed possible answers the author might give them. Mr. James also invited a reporter from the local paper to visit the class and tell students about developing articles. Then Mr. James told his students they would be working in groups to do a research project on something that has changed over time, how it has changed, and why. He gave them several topics from which to choose, knowing that choice also improves motivation. He had already picked the topics based on books he knew were in the school library, web sites he had already checked out, and some resources he had brought from the public library.

Over the next 2 weeks, Mr. James gave short lessons on how to take notes, how to organize information for a report, and how to present information in interesting ways. He also taught students to skim for a general understanding of an article or a web site and to search quickly for details. He provided opportunities for students to practice all of these skills and gave the students feedback. He knew that if his students had the skills necessary to do the project, they would regard themselves as effective learners and be more motivated to do the work well. After the students completed the group projects, they went on to complete individual projects. The confidence they had gained from the lessons and group projects, along with choice and interest in the second set of topics, helped maintain their motivation to engage in the reading, writing, and thinking required in the individual project.

REFERENCES

Alexander, P.A., Jetton, T.L., & Kulikowich, J.M. (1996). Interrelationship of knowledge, interest, and recall: Assessing a model of domain learning. *Journal of Educational Psychology* , *87*, 559–575.

Almasi, J.F. (1995). The nature of fourth-graders' sociocognitive conflicts in peer-led and teacher-led discussions of literature. *Reading Research Quarterly, 30*, 314–351.

Bandura, A. (1986). *Social foundations of thought and action: A social cognitive theory*. Upper Saddle River, NJ: Prentice-Hall.

Beck, I.L., McKeown, M.G., Worthy, J., Sandora, C.A., & Kucan, L. (1996). Questioning the author: A yearlong classroom implementation to engage students with text. *Elementary School Journal, 96*, 385–414.

Berliner, D.C., & Biddle, B.J. (1995). *The manufactured crisis: Myths, fraud, and the attack on American public schools*. Reading, MA: Addison Wesley.

Bernard, B. (2004). *Resiliency: What we have learned*. San Francisco, CA: West ED.

Deci, E.L. (1975). *Intrinsic motivation*. New York: Plenum Press.

Deci, E.L. (1980). *The psychology of self-determination*. Lexington, MA: Lexington Books.

Deci, E.L., & Ryan, R.M. (1985). *Intrinsic motivation and self-determination in human behavior*. New York: Kluwer Academic/Plenum.

Deci, E.L., & Ryan, R.M. (1987). The support of autonomy and the control of behavior. *Journal of Personality and Social Psychology, 53*, 1024–1037.

Deci, E.L., Vallerand, R.J., Pelletier, L.G., & Ryan, R.M. (1991). Motivation and education: The self-determination perspective. *Educational Psychologist, 26*, 325–346.

Edwards, P.A. (2007). Home literacy environments: What we know and what we need to know. In M. Pressley, A.K. Billman, K.H. Perry, K.E. Reffitt, & J.M. Reynolds (Eds.), *Shaping literacy achievement research we have, research we need* (pp. 42–76). New York: Guilford Press.

Glass, D.C., & Singer, J.E. (1972). *Urban stress: Experiments on noise and social stressors*. San Diego: Academic Press.

Gottfried, A.E. (1985). Academic intrinsic motivation in elementary and junior high school. *Journal of Educational Psychology, 77*, 525–538.

Guthrie, J.T., & Humenick, N.M. (2004). Motivating students to read: Evidence for classroom practices that increase reading motivation and achievement. In P. McCardle and V. Chhabra (Eds.), *The voice of evidence in reading research* (pp. 329–354). Baltimore: Paul H. Brookes Publishing Co.

Guthrie, J.T., McGough, K., Bennett, L., & Rice, M.E. (1996). Concept-oriented reading instruction: An integrated curriculum to develop motivation and strategies for reading. In L. Baker, P. Afflerbach, & D. Reinking (Eds.), *Developing engaged readers in school and home communities* (pp. 165–190). Mahwah, NJ: Lawrence Erlbaum Associates.

Guthrie, J.T., & Wigfield, A. (2000). Engagement and motivation in reading. In M.L. Kamil, P.B. Mosenthal, P.D. Pearson, & R. Barr (Eds.), *Handbook of reading research* (Vol. III, pp. 403–422). Mahwah, NJ: Lawrence Erlbaum Associates.

Guthrie, J.T., Wigfield, A., & VonSecker, C. (2000). Effects of integrated instruction on motivation and strategy use in reading. *Journal of Educational Psychology, 92*(2), 331–341.

Harter, S. (1981). A new self-report scale of intrinsic versus extrinsic motivation in the classroom: Motivational and informational components. *Developmental Psychology, 17,* 300–312.

Hearing on education research and evaluation and student achievement: Quality counts: Hearing before the Committee on Education and the Workforce, House of Representatives, 106th Cong. (2000) (testimony of G. Reid Lyon).

International Reading Association. (2000). *Excellent reading teachers: A position statement of the International Reading Association.* Newark, DE: Author.

Lepper, M.R., & Greene, D. (1978). *The hidden costs of reward: New perspectives on the psychology of human motivation.* Hillsdale, NJ: Lawrence Erlbaum Associates.

Lepper, M.R., Greene, D., & Nisbett, R.E. (1973). Undermining children's intrinsic interest with extrinsic reward: A test of the "overjustification" hypothesis. *Journal of Personality and Social Psychology, 28,* 129–137.

Lesemen, P.P.M., & deJong, P.F. (1998). Home literacy: Opportunity, instruction, cooperation, and social-emotional quality predicting early reading achievement. *Reading Research Quarterly, 33*(3), 294–318.

Lesemen, P.P.M., & deJong, P.F. (2001). How important is home literacy for acquiring literacy in school? In L.T. Verhoeven & C.E. Snow (Eds.), *Literacy and motivation: Reading engagement in individuals and groups* (pp. 72–94). Mahwah, NJ: Lawrence Erlbaum Associates.

Malone, T., & Lepper, M. (1987). Making learning fun: Taxonomy of intrinsic motivation for learning. In R.E. Snow & M.J. Farr (Eds.), *Aptitude, learning, and instruction: Cognitive and affective process analyses* (Vol. 3, pp. 223–253). Hillsdale, NJ: Lawrence Erlbaum Associates.

Oldfather, P., & Dahl, K.L . (1994). Toward a social constructivist reconceptualization of intrinsic motivation for literacy learning. *Journal of Reading Behavior, 26*(2), 139.

Pintrich, P.R., & Schunk, D.H. (1996). *Motivation in education: Theory, research, and applications.* Columbus, OH: Charles E. Merrill.

Ryan, R.M., Cornell, J.P., & Deci, E.L. (1985). A motivational analysis of self-determination and self-regulation. In C. Ames and R.E. Ames (Eds.), *Research on motivation in education: Volume 2, the classroom milieu* (pp. 13–51). Orlando, FL: Academic Press.

Schunk, D.H. (1989). Self-efficacy and cognitive achievement: Implications for students with learning problems. *Journal of Learning Disabilities, 22,* 14–22.

Schunk, D.H., & Zimmerman, B.J. (1997). Developing self-efficacious readers and writers: The role of social and self-regulatory processes. In J.T. Guthrie & A. Wigfield (Eds.), *Reading engagement: Motivating readers through integrated instruction* (pp. 34–50). Newark, DE: International Reading Association.

Skinner, E.A., & Belmont, M.J. (1993). Motivation in the classroom: Reciprocal effects of teacher behavior and student engagement across the school year. *Journal of Educational Psychology, 85,* 571–581.

Snow, C., Burns, S., & Griffin, P. (Eds.). (1998). *Preventing reading difficulties in young children*. Washington, DC: National Academies Press.

Sweet, A.P. (1997). Teacher perceptions of student motivation and their relation to literacy learning. In J.T. Guthrie & A. Wigfield (Eds.), *Reading engagement: Motivating readers through integrated instruction* (pp. 86–101). Newark, DE: International Reading Association.

Sweet, A.P., Guthrie, J.T., & Ng, M.M. (1998). Teacher perceptions and student reading motivation. *Journal of Educational Psychology, 90*(2), 210–223.

Tobin, K. (1984). Student task involvement in activity oriented science. *Journal of Research in Science Teaching, 21*, 469–482.

Turner, J.C. (1995). The influence of classroom contexts on your children's motivation for literacy. *Reading Research Quarterly, 30*, 410–441.

Wade, S.E., Buxton, W.M., & Kelly, M. (1999). Using think-alouds to examine reader-text interest. *Reading Research Quarterly, 34*(2), 194–216.

Wentzel, K.R. (1997). Student motivation in middle school: The role of perceived pedagogical caring. *Journal of Educational Psychology, 89*(3), 411–419.

White, R.W. (1959). Motivation considered: The concept of competence. *Psychological Review, 66*, 297–333.

Wigfield, A., & Guthrie, J.T. (1997). Relations of children's motivation for reading to the amount and breadth of their reading. *Journal of Educational Psychology, 89*, 420–432.

CHAPTER 13

The Value and Uses of Assessment

KEY CONCEPTS

- Reading assessment serves many purposes, including accountability, informing the public and parents, providing evidence of progress, and diagnosing student needs.

- It is essential that assessment tools (e.g., tests, projects, portfolios, interviews, and checklists) be used for the purposes for which they were designed and that assessment data be valid in terms of both content and consequences of its use.

- Effective teachers use assessment data from a variety of sources to plan and determine the effectiveness of instruction and to measure and monitor student progress.

John Jones and other teachers at the elementary school received data from a state assessment indicating that their students were generally weak in recognizing organization in nonfiction. They decided to make that issue a major goal for instruction across the school. They also wanted to track the effectiveness of some of the new instructional approaches. The teachers discussed how to adapt and improve them. In addition, the teachers wanted to help students monitor their own growth in this area. They knew that ongoing assessment would help them in all of these efforts. They made a list of organizational structures and strategies for helping students detect them. As they taught each type of structure and strategies for showing text structures, such as graphic organizers, they met each week to share data on how their students were doing and discuss ways to improve instruction and learning.

Assessment is an often misunderstood and maligned activity that can actually be very helpful. There are many different types of and purposes for assessment. Here we attempt to sort through these many choices and offer some useful guidance. Two major reports based on research recommend that teacher certification requirements and professional development topics include knowledge of ongoing, in-class assessment as well as how to use data from large-scale, district and state assessments (Snow, Burns, & Griffin, 1998; Snow, Griffin, & Burns, 2005).

What Is Assessment, and What Are the Purposes of Assessment?

The purpose of all educational assessment is student learning and its documentation. Assessment can be employed for a variety of purposes that ultimately serve learning:

- Providing diagnostic information about what students can do and what they need to learn in order to inform decisions about instruction (classroom assessments and commercial assessments)

- Determining the effectiveness of an instructional approach and whether a proven instructional method is then effective in improving student learning for individual students (classroom assessments and commercial assessments)

- Informing educational stakeholders: accountability information for making decisions (state assessments), status information for the public (National Assessment of Educational Progress [NAEP], state assessments), and achievement information for parents (classroom and state assessments)

These purposes can overlap so that a classroom assessment of the effectiveness of specific instruction can provide achievement information to parents and guidance for decision making for teachers.

Education stakeholders look at assessments at different levels for making decisions about instructional policy and practice. State assessments provide information to policy makers, administrators, and teachers to support decisions about those aspects of instruction that fall within their purview. Because they are designed for different purposes, there are limitations to the uses of specific types of assessments. For example, a large-scale state assessment is not designed to be used to diagnose the individual needs of students but to indicate broad areas in which schools and teachers are doing well or need to improve instruction. A diagnostic battery of tests is designed to give very detailed information about the strengths and instructional needs of individual students, but it is not an efficient way of gathering information on achievement at the school or district levels. Teacher-developed tests can provide excellent data on student progress and where instruction needs to be rethought and revised but lack the psychometric characteristics required for formal diagnosis. In addition, these classroom assessments cannot provide large-scale information about student achievement. Table 13.1 summarizes the most common characteristics and uses of various assessments. While it is not comprehensive, it indicates the multiple aspects of assessments.

Because different types of assessment address different levels and specific purposes, a variety of assessments are currently necessary to provide the various types of data needed for decision making at the different levels of the education system. In the future, it may be possible to design single assessments that meet many different purposes, but at present several different types of assessments are necessary to gain the information needed to coordinate resources, policies, and instruction to most effectively support student learning.

What Are Some Basic Terms and Principles Related to Assessment?

When educators write or talk about assessment, there are some important concepts that they often include. These concepts include *validity, reliability, formative assessments,* and *summative assessments.* For those who may not be very familiar with these concepts, we would like to review them in the following sections.

Table 13.1. Aspects of assessment

	Large-scale assessment	Commercial diagnostic assessment	Publisher-generated classroom assessment	Researcher-developed individual or classroom assessment	Teacher-generated classroom assessment	Student self-assessment
Characteristics	Administered to large groups of students	Administered to individual students or small groups	Usually, but not always, geared to a basal reading program	Developed to measure specific constructs in learning	Developed by classroom teachers. Includes observations, notes, tests, classwork, and interviews	Developed by teachers or teachers and students
Uses	Indicates achievement of students, schools, districts, states, and nations	Diagnoses areas that are weak and need instructional intervention	Diagnoses areas that are weak and need instructional intervention with relation to the contents of the reading program, or provides summative information on performance	Developed to gauge effectiveness of instruction, student progress, or to assess current levels of ability in specific task types	Tracks and communicates student progress to students and parents, diagnoses specific needs related to specific instructional goals, reflects on and discusses instructional effectiveness with colleagues, and enables students to track their own progress	Monitors students' own progress and often motivates students to take charge of their learning
Limitations	Does not provide individual diagnostic information	Does not give a big picture of overall achievement	May not be related to classroom or state educational goals	Not standardized and often requires specialized training to administer initially	Does not have the reliability of commercial assessments and cannot provide comparative data beyond the classroom	Does not have the reliability of commercial assessments and cannot provide comparative data beyond the classroom
Examples	Scholastic Aptitude Tests (SAT), state assessments		Tests that accompany basal reading materials		Observations, checklists, projects, portfolios, tests, retellings, miscue analysis, oral reading fluency checks	Portfolios, charts of books, pages, or hours read

Validity

Validity refers to whether the test assesses what it says it assesses. One type of validity is *construct validity,* which in reading refers to whether the test assesses reading. For example, some tests might focus on an aspect of reading, such as the ability to recognize isolated words, but not address the full range of reading skills, including comprehension. Such a test is valid for drawing inferences about word recognition but not about reading and understanding connected text. By the same principle, listening to a story and answering questions about it is not a test of reading comprehension but a test of listening comprehension. There is another type of validity called *consequential validity,* which refers to whether the assessment is used for the appropriate purposes. A large-scale assessment can provide data on student performance that gives a general level of individual achievement, but is not really valid for drawing diagnostic conclusions about the specific needs of individual students.

Reliability

Reliability refers to whether a student would get the same score on an assessment if it was given to that student repeatedly. The number of items on a specific skill influences reliability. If we gave a student three questions on recognizing the main idea on a test and gave that student the same questions a day later, the student might respond differently on one or two of the questions and get a very different score simply by changing one or two answers. If we give the student 10 items on main idea, it is not likely that the student will give different answers on enough of the items on a second testing to dramatically change the score. Thus, the number of items on an aspect of reading influences the reliability of the scores or the inferences drawn. A reading test with 30 items on a variety of reading skills can give a relatively reliable picture of a student's reading achievement, but since only a few of the items focus on any one skill, information on the student's ability to use a specific skill is not very reliable. Here there is a connection to validity. When inferences are drawn about specific reading needs based on data from a test designed to measure general reading achievement, it violates the consequential validity of the test.

Formative Assessments

Formative assessments are used to provide information to teachers, students, and parents about progress and what additional learning and instruction are necessary. Listening to a student read aloud and taking notes on the student's performance in order to decide what instructional activities to plan for that student is an example of formative assessment.

Summative Assessments

Summative assessments are used as final checks on learning. Large-scale assessments used for accountability are summative assessments. End-of-unit tests are often summative assessments.

What Does Research Indicate About Assessment?

Although there is a lot of research on how to measure various abilities and thought processes, much of this is technical information about measurement in general. There are not large bodies of research on reading assessment, as is the case with information about specific factors in beginning reading. However, there are some single studies that provide important evidence to guide the development and use of assessments. A study by Black and William (1998) indicated that constructive comments on student tasks were more likely to improve students' performance than just general praise or grades. Another study indicated that highlighting general, innate traits, such as smartness or quietness actually lessens students' resilience (Dweck, 1999) and thus can have a negative impact on how well they perform on assessments. Having students ask and discuss their own questions can provide useful information about students' comprehension (Comeyras, 1995), and this self-assessment can be helpful to student learning. Assessment strategies that provide opportunities for socialization and self-regulation actually support students' ability to learn and their literacy achievement. In summarizing theory and research in assessment, Johnson and Costello (2005) suggested that assessment influences and is influenced by theories of literacy and learning, culture, and politics. Assessment is always affected by the beliefs and goals of those designing the measure, and the measure in turn affects curriculum, instruction, and learning. This is the case whether assessment is being designed by state level officials for accountability, by researchers for a study, or by a teacher in the classroom. For example, an assessment designed by a teacher to sort students for grading purposes is different from an assessment designed by a teacher who wants all students to learn and is looking for ways to provide additional instruction to those who continue to struggle.

What Are Some of the Types of Assessment Tasks, and How Do They Vary from One Type of Assessment to Another?

One way that assessments differ is in the format of the items and responses. Large-scale assessments mainly use multiple-choice items. This is due, for the most part, to a need to score these assessments in a cost-effective and timely manner. The problem with such items is that they require students to recognize a correct answer, which is very different from constructing it. A multiple-choice item can ask a student to *identify* a main idea or good summary; it cannot call for a student to *state* a main idea or write a summary. These are different skills. It is difficult, but not impossible, to develop multiple-choice items that tap higher order thinking skills. It is impossible to use such items to determine students' abilities to develop their own complex, creative responses to what they read.

Some large-scale assessments of reading, such as the National Assessment of Educational Progress (NAEP), use a substantial number of open-ended items where students must construct their own answers. These items can make assessments more likely to gather data about the abilities of students to *construct* rather than *recognize* meaning from what they read. However, even open-ended items have limitations, due to the requirement of providing sufficient information in the question and directions to guide students in providing responses that fit the parameters of the scoring guides. Open-ended items have other drawbacks, too. They are time consuming for students to complete and more costly to score than multiple-choice items.

Performance assessment tasks ask the students to do something with their reading. They are designed to capture authentic reading behaviors, activities that readers would carry out using reading in and out of the classroom. Using several information sources to write a description of life in the middle ages would be a performance assessment task. Another reading task that attempts to capture more authentic reading is to have students read a story that actually appears in a children's magazine and respond to questions that reflect what readers might discuss about the story. The research on the use of these types of assessments in large-scale accountability contexts is sparse and not conclusive (Valencia & Wixson, 2000). In classrooms, they can be excellent tools for engaging students, providing opportunities for self-assessment and collaboration, and challenging students' thinking.

Observations that are used in classrooms may include several types of tasks. Teachers take notes on student behavior or use a checklist to record information about students' reading achievement and needs. For example, a teacher might take notes on students working in pairs on making words with letter tiles that fit a specific pattern, such as *vowel–consonant–silent e*. A teacher might take notes on a student's reading aloud for fluency or retelling of a story to demonstrate comprehension. These types of classroom assessment tasks provide information on individual students' instructional needs as well as their achievement. Even with this type of less formal assessment, it helps to have a standard against which to judge student performance; this might be simply whether this student has mastered the tasks that were taught, how well he or she performs compared to a rubric or scoring guide, or the number of words read correctly in a minute of reading for fluency.

Classroom assessments like those described above are also known as *curriculum-embedded assessments,* since they are administered as part of the instructional program, as compared to tests that are not connected to what is happening in the classroom, such as commercial tests and large-scale assessments. Classroom or curriculum-embedded assessments allow teachers to continuously monitor student progress toward learning goals, making adjustments in instructional activities to reflect conclusions about learning based on the classroom data. The data from such assessments can be charted over time to demonstrate progress to students, parents, and teachers themselves. For example, students' oral reading speed and expression can be charted over time to show progress. The monitoring can be done as part of everyday classwork on fluency.

Another important aspect of assessment is *alignment*. Alignment refers to the degree to which the skills and contexts for applying those skills match across instructional activities, classroom assessments, standards and curriculum, and large-scale assessments used for accountability. For example, if a classroom instructional task asks students to clap for each syllable they hear in a word, the classroom assessment asks students to write a number for the syllables they hear, and the large-scale assessment asks students to look at a word and write the number of syllables, then the three tasks are not aligned. This does not mean that they are not valid. The instructional task of clapping is engaging and great practice. However, teachers should also help students learn the other two types of syllable identification tasks, if students are going to be asked to do them on an assessment. In addition, being able to recognize syllables and demonstrate that ability in multiple ways is valuable in student learning. Thus, teaching students these tasks need not be considered simply "teaching to the test," as it is adding to the student's skills and helping him or her learn more generally what syllables are.

Another example, frequently encountered in classroom and instructional materials, is that students are asked during instruction to give a main idea for an article or a lesson for a story. This is usually an oral response accompanied by teacher support and immediate feedback. Students need to be taught how to select the best statement of a main idea from a list of distracters on a multiple choice test. Sometimes students are confused by tasks like this, since none of the distracters fits the main idea they would have articulated. These students need to receive explicit instruction on how to make a good choice for the answer. However, in order to use the detection of main ideas in analyzing and responding to texts and to gather information for classroom projects, students need to be able to articulate rather than choose a main idea statement.

It might seem only common sense that these tasks should match, but it is easy to lose sight of this when in the midst of planning instruction, assessing progress, and dealing with all of the other tasks of running a classroom. On the other hand, the goal of promoting true, substantive reading achievement would not be achievable if all classroom tasks were in the format used on large-scale assessments. In addition, it is often the case that large-scale assessments do not align with curriculum standards. For example, an assessment might ask students to recognize a character's traits from a list of possibilities, while the standards say students should be able to describe a character in their own words. In considering alignment, it is essential not to lose sight of the goal of having students develop rich, highly proficient literacy that goes well beyond what is tested on large-scale assessment. It is also important to ensure depth of learning such that students can produce information when asked, or spontaneously, beyond the classroom, in many different ways, rather than only responding to assessments in a certain format.

What Does Accountability Mean to Teachers?

Accountability should mean that each person who makes decisions about schools and classrooms, including policies, financial resources, standards, curricula, and materials, should be held responsible for the success of school systems in helping all students learn to read. In reality, accountability mainly focuses on the performance of schools, teachers, and students. This means that accountability drives much of the testing, including classroom testing. It also drives instruction, since it is widely recognized that what gets assessed is what gets taught.

The emphasis on assessment for accountability purposes has grown from the mid 1980s to 2007, with the strongest push in this direction coming as a result of the demands of the No Child Left Behind (NCLB) Act of 2001 (PL 107-110). The law requires states to test every student in every grade from Grades 3 to 8. The results are reported as percentages of students reaching a certain score that places them in a specific category or level, similar to the National Center for Educational Statistics (NCES; 2000) levels of below basic, basic, proficient, and advanced. The NCLB Act requires levels of achievement to be reported for subgroups within the school, such as students who are English language learners or students from minority racial and cultural backgrounds. If students or specific subgroups of students in a school do not make adequate progress toward reading proficiency each year, for 3 years in a row, then sanctions are applied. It is not surprising that schools and teachers would be almost consumed with the need for their students to do well on these assessments.

One of the positive results of the reporting requirements of the NCLB Act (PL 107-110) is that teachers and schools are beginning to expect all students to be successful and are modifying instruction to accelerate the progress of students who have fallen behind to ensure that those students can achieve proficiency. Teachers and schools cannot ignore the groups of students who have fallen through the cracks in the system in the past.

The state tests used for accountability consist mainly of multiple-choice items that focus on discrete skills. Consequently, classroom instruction frequently focuses on the same skills, especially in schools where a large percentage of the student population is at risk of not progressing adequately due to their backgrounds of poverty, culture, or language.

However, research indicates that students who are taught to use higher order thinking skills, such as synthesis, analysis, and abstraction in the classroom do better on large-scale achievement tests than students who are not taught those skills (Taylor, Pressley, & Pearson, 2002). Often it is difficult for teachers to teach the skills needed to pass the state assessments and still address higher order skills. To design instruction that will help students develop and use higher order thinking skills requires sound knowledge of those skills and the strategies for teaching them. In addition, teachers must believe that if they spend their instructional time on higher order thinking skills and problem solving, students will do well on tests of basic skills.

What Are the Characteristics of Good Classroom Assessment?

In spite of all of the time spent preparing for and taking state assessments, good classroom assessments are essential. What are the characteristics of useful classroom assessment? A good classroom assessment should meet four basic criteria:

- Assessment should be aligned with standards and curriculum laid out by the state and district.

- Assessment should reflect what has actually been taught or, in the case of diagnostic or pre-assessments, what will be taught.

- Assessment should provide data that can actually inform teachers' decision making, not just provide numbers to support grades.

- Assessment should indicate progress to teachers, students, and parents. This means that the criteria for success or learning are clear to students.

Teachers can be tempted—even required—to use commercial tests that come with reading programs. However, those tests cover what the program has covered, what has been taught thoroughly (as compared to what was introduced in class but not carried through to mastery), and what is important in learning to read. Teachers need to decide whether tests that come with reading programs are truly useful for assessing student achievement and the effectiveness of instruction. Following the lesson plans in a commercial program does not ensure that students have sufficient opportunities to understand and practice using the skills and concepts associated with reading. This is especially true for students with different or limited background knowledge, who may lack the everyday concepts taken for granted in the reading materials, or who have insufficient English language skills to be able to learn from the materials when used as prescribed. Teachers need to develop their own additional ways of checking to make sure students are progressing.

In addition to traditional paper and pencil activities, teachers can use observation notes to keep track of students' progress. An obvious area where observation and notes are needed is in oral reading; teachers should note students' progress and needs related to fluency in terms of rate, expression, and patterns of frequent errors. There are formal but simple observation procedures for fluency that can be used (e.g., counting the number of words produced and the number of errors made per unit time), but they are not complete measures of fluency, especially by Grade 2, unless they also account for expression. Teachers can also observe when students choose to read on their own and what they like to read about. They can observe what skills need to be taught so that students can participate in real discussions with peers about what they read. Checklists are another classroom assessment tool. These are helpful in following how students participate in discussions, what and how they write or draw in response to reading, what letters and sounds they can identify, and whether they have mastered certain knowledge and skills, such as the ability to hear the number of syllables in a word.

Teachers can combine assessment methods in a strategy, such as retelling of stories. Both checklists and observations can help teachers track progress in this skill and note what needs further instruction. Retellings can be scored by using a checklist of components (Bembridge, 1994; Johns, Lenski, & Elish-Piper, 1999)

What Types of Assessment Are Needed to Address What Is Beyond the Scope of the Classroom Teacher?

There are times when assessment is beyond what can reasonably be expected of individual teachers in classrooms. For individual assessments of students that are time consuming, require special training, and are used diagnostically, trained specialists, such as the school psychologist, educational testing specialist, or speech-language pathologist should be called upon. While this varies by district and school, there are some general principles that teachers need to be familiar with in gaining the information they need to fully understand their students and to appropriately serve and advocate for them.

There is a difference between screening assessments, that use broad measures to determine whether students are at risk or have general difficulties with reading, and diagnostic assessments, that indicate specific strengths and needs of students. Sometimes a classroom teacher can administer a broad screening, such as an informal reading inventory. This can eliminate doing in-depth diagnostic testing of each student and indicate groups of students who need remedial instruction in specific skill areas as compared to those who are ready to move on. However, it cannot provide enough information to plan instruction to meet the specific needs of individual students who are struggling. Thorough diagnostic assessment for students having major problems learning to read usually consists of several tests that require special training to administer and interpret. These might include tests of auditory and visual processing as well as tests of language and the components of reading.

Teachers do not need to wait for diagnosis to begin to intensify their focus on instruction for students at risk. Their own observations and samples of student work can provide informal diagnostic information for initial instructional planning. Classroom teachers can give extra support and adaptations to assignments for students who are clearly struggling with reading. As more formal diagnostic information is available, teachers can revise and strengthen their instructional plans for particular students, working in consultation with specialists who administer and interpret those formal diagnostic assessments. (Ongoing assessment for progress monitoring is also important; for additional information on progress monitoring, see Chapter 15 on response to intervention.)

Can Students Assess Themselves?

When students are given the opportunity to keep track of their own progress, it can provide motivation and encouragement. It can also help students understand the criteria for good work (Klenowski, 1995). When teachers effectively involve students in self-assessment, it is important to make expectations and goals clear, so that students know what they should be trying to accomplish.

How Can Teachers Make Assessments and Their Instruction Coherent?

It is a huge challenge for teachers to balance and align the assessments they use in the classroom and their instructional practice and materials with the standards embodied in large-scale assessments. One approach to accomplishing this is backmapping instructional goals, classroom content and skills to be taught, and classroom assessments to large-scale assessments used for accountability (Tomlinson & McTighe, 2006). *Backmapping*, or backward design, is a process that involves starting with education outcomes and mapping backward to determine what skills or what levels must be taught and learned for students to reach those outcomes. However, once the content of instruction has been backmapped, there remains a need to determine the most promising instructional strategies to enable students to learn the content and skills. In addition, it is necessary to design instruction to address multiple learning goals in order to teach all that is required for student success. For example, a reading text that has been read and discussed to promote and expand comprehension strategy development might also be used for some brief word study activities, such as looking for examples of phonics generalizations and exceptions to generalizations. Students need a variety of experiences in order to consolidate what they have learned, and students who have these experiences are more likely to do well on assessments.

What Additional Research Is Still Needed in the Area of Assessment?

The area of reading assessment does not have nearly as much research to inform it as one would expect, given its growing role in accountability as well as its traditional role as an essential element of a reading program. New assessments are constantly being developed, and researchers are working to gather information that will enable test and curriculum developers to better align materials and assessment tools. Nonetheless, as with all other areas of literacy, more research is needed. See Table 13.2 for examples of additional assessment research needs.

HOW MIGHT THIS RESEARCH ON
• • • ASSESSMENT PLAY OUT IN THE CLASSROOM? • • •

Mr. Smith had a second-grade class of students reading on levels K–4. He needed to plan instruction that would provide for individual differences in needs and strengths among his students while making sure they made progress. He used the state standards and the descriptions of expectations on the state assessment along with the scope and sequence of his basal series and some additional goals not mentioned in those sources as his overall set of goals. Then he considered the records that were sent to him from the students' previous teachers. Some of the students were new to the school and the district, and there were no folders for them. Mr. Smith used the placement tests that come with the basal program with all of the students to get an indication of what materials to use with groups of students. Records from the previous year offered information, but Mr. Smith knew that with different materials, teachers, and programs, students perform differently, and consequently he used the records as only one aspect of his information gathering. He also knew that growth or

---

What we know from research

- Teachers in effective schools use a variety of assessments (Paris, Paris, & Carpenter, 2002).

- Promoting student self-assessment helps improve student motivation, sense of self-efficacy, and learning.

What we need to know from additional research

- How can researchers and educators design valid, reliable assessments for students with disabilities and learning difficulties?

- How can researchers and educators design valid, reliable assessments for English language learners?

- What are the most efficient yet valid and reliable ways of gathering large-scale assessment data on students' reading achievement?

- What skills do teachers need to become more effective in developing and using classroom assessments?

Table 13.2. Assessment research needs

loss can occur over the summer, so he needed up-to-date information on each student. He developed charts of where students were and what they needed to accomplish to be on course in relation to the state performance standards. He also assessed other areas not tested by the state but critical to literacy, such as motivation, critical thinking, and organizational skills and concepts essential for reading in content areas. Mr. Smith used student interviews, records of self-selected reading, and samples of students' response to open-ended questions to keep track of student progress in these areas.

REFERENCES

Bembridge, T. (1994). A multilayered assessment package. In S.W.Valencia, E.H. Hiebert, & P.P. Afflerbach (Eds.), *Authentic reading assessment: Practices and possibilities* (pp. 167–184). Newark, NJ: International Reading Association.

Black, P., & William, D. (1998). Assessment and classroom learning. *Assessment in Education: Principles, Policy, and Practice, 5*(1), 7–74.

Comeyras, M. (1995). What can we learn from students' questions? *Theory into Practice, 34,* 101–106.

Dweck, C.S. (1999). *Self-theories: Their role in motivation, personality, and development.* Philadelphia: Psychological Press.

Johns, J.L., Lenski, S.D., & Elish-Piper, L. (1999). *Early literacy assessments and teaching strategies.* Dubuque, IA: Kendall/Hunt Publishing Company.

Johnston, P., & Costello, P. (2005). Theory and research into practice: Principles for literacy assessment. *Reading Research Quarterly, 40*(2), 256–267.

Klenowski, V. (1995). Student self-evaluation process in student-centered teaching and learning contexts of Australia and England. *Assessment in Education, 2,* 145–163.

National Center for Education Statistics. (2000). *National Assessment of Educational Progress.* Retrieved September 22, 2007, from http://nces.ed.gov/nationsreportcard

No Child Left Behind Act of 2001, PL 107-110, 15 Stat. 1425, 20 U.S.C. §§ 6301 *et seq.*

Paris, S.G., Paris, A.H., & Carpenter, R.D. (2002). Effective practices for assessing young readers. In B.M. Taylor & P.D. Pearson (Eds.), *Teaching reading: Effective schools, accomplished teachers* (pp. 141–160). Mahwah, NJ: Lawrence Erlbaum Associates.

Snow, C.E., Burns, M.S., & Griffin, P. (Eds.). (1998). *Preventing reading difficulties in young children.* Washington, DC: National Academies Press.

Snow, C.M., Griffin, P., & Burns, M.S. (2005). *Knowledge to support the teaching of reading.* San Francisco: Jossey-Bass.

Taylor, B.M., Pressley, M., & Pearson, P.D. (2002). Research-supported characteristics of teachers and schools that promote reading achievement. In B.M. Taylor & P.D. Pearson (Eds.), *Teaching reading: Effective schools, accomplished teachers* (pp. 361–373). Mahwah, NJ: Lawrence Erlbaum Associates.

Tomlinson, C.A., & McTighe, J. (2006). *Integrating differentiated instruction and understanding by design.* Alexandria, VA: Association for Supervision and Curriculum Development.

Valencia, S.W., & Wixson, K.K. (2000). Policy-oriented research on literacy standards and assessment. In M.L. Kamil, P.B. Mosenthal, P.D. Pearson, & R. Barr (Eds.), *Handbook of reading research: Vol. III* (pp. 909–935). Mahwah, NJ: Lawrence Erlbaum Associates.

CHAPTER 14

Teachers
The Most Important Factor in Student Success

KEY CONCEPTS

- Teachers need an array of skills and knowledge to successfully teach students to read well, and they need to continue to develop their professional capacity throughout their careers.

- There is a link between student achievement and teachers' knowledge of content and pedagogy.

- Effective professional development involves reflection, discussion, support, collaboration, and continuous reference to the classroom and student work.

Jane Adams, a fourth-grade teacher, was concerned. Several students
in her class were having problems with reading their science textbook,
and she really did not know what to do to help them. They were capable
readers when reading basal stories and had good word recognition
and fluency. What caused them difficulty was finding and using information in text to respond to science tasks that called for synthesis of ideas,
inferences, and critical thinking. These were areas in which she felt
her own teacher training and professional development were weak. She
knew that she needed to know more in order to help her students.

Teaching reading is a challenging task. Today's teachers need to consider the wide literacy demands of the 21st century. These literacy
demands include the ability to locate and sift through information
from a variety of sources, to judge the usefulness and truthfulness of
information, to relate information from disparate source and topic
areas, and to communicate their findings, hypotheses, conclusions, and
critical responses. These considerations influence their learning goals,
instructional planning, and classroom contexts.

To address this daunting task, teachers use a combination of
pedagogical knowledge and skills, content knowledge, observational
skills, organizational and management skills, and social and cultural
awareness to plan, teach, and assess the effectiveness of their instruction and of student learning. While they come to their classrooms
equipped with a set of capabilities in these areas, all teachers need
to continue to grow in the understanding of teaching and learning.
Things change from the time educators leave their initial training
programs, and no training program can cover everything that every
teacher needs to know. In many professions, individuals need to
constantly learn and update their knowledge with the latest
research. Teachers should be provided continuous opportunities to
developtheir knowledge and skills throughout their career (Snow,
Griffin, & Burns, 2005). While there is not a large body of research
directly related to teacher education and professional development
in reading, existing research has indicated some important things
about the processes of reading and learning to read that teachers need
to know. There is also some research indicating approaches to
professional development that help teachers continue to grow
professionally.

The previous chapters in this book concerning how to teach reading components laid out that body of evidence and its implications.
They mapped much of the *what* of teacher learning. This chapter will
focus mainly on the *how* of teacher education, although it is difficult to

completely separate the two. How to best support and sustain the continuous growth of teachers is an essential question to consider if education is to continue improving. Since educators tend to teach the way they were taught, the contexts and activities of teacher education, both preservice and inservice, affect a teacher's beliefs and style as well as practice.

What Does Research Say About Teacher Education?

There are studies that indicate that the teacher is the critical factor in a student's success in learning to read (National Institute of Child Health and Human Development [NICHD], 2000). The teacher accounts for more of the variance in student achievement than materials or programs (Bond & Dykstra, 1967; Chall & Feldman, 1967). This supports the importance of effective teacher education and professional development.

As was the case with reading assessment, teacher education, both preservice and inservice, does not have a large body of research to inform practice. However, there is some information. The National Reading Panel (NRP) reviewed studies that focused on teacher education and reading instruction and found only a small number of experimental studies that dealt with preservice and inservice teacher education (NICHD, 2000). Generally, results showed that inservice professional development produced higher student achievement. The NRP was not able to draw many specific conclusions but highlighted the importance of professional development and indicated that more research is needed in several key areas of teacher education, both preservice and inservice.

In the following sections, we discuss key areas for teachers that affect teachers' effectiveness in the classroom and therefore their impact on student learning: teacher knowledge and student achievement, quality professional development, use of technology to assist teachers in their own continuing education, literacy coaches, and assessment/evaluation. All of these areas are important to help teachers stay abreast of new information that is continuously being produced; to help them solve implementation problems that invariably arise in real life situations that may not have been anticipated or discussed in workshops, teacher education courses, or professional development seminars; and to help them in the ongoing challenge of meeting individual student needs while keeping the entire class of students moving forward.

Teacher Knowledge and Student Achievement

One thing is clear from teacher education research: There is an important link between student achievement and teachers' knowledge. This includes both their pedagogical knowledge (what they know about teaching and learning) and their content knowledge. Studies have shown that the number of courses on instruction teachers had taken and their participation in professional development related to instruction accounted for student achievement almost as much as students' background factors (Ferguson & Womack, 1993; Wenglinski, 2000).

A strong knowledge background supports effective teaching. Research has shown that students whose teachers themselves have strong content knowledge and have learned to adapt instruction to accommodate students from different cultures achieve more than students whose teachers do not possess that knowledge (Wenglinski, 2000).

Having a peer support group helps teachers increase their effectiveness and their understanding of the teaching and learning of reading. First, in order to be able to talk about and explain things to a peer, professionals must have that information coherently organized in their own minds. Second, fellow teachers may have some insights or suggestions that can help their peers. Third, just articulating questions and listening to peers can help educators solve problems and deepen their understanding of reading, learning to read, students, and teaching. Research on professional development "has stressed the importance of teachers learning and changing together over an extended period of time as they reflect on practice and implement new teaching strategies" (Taylor, Pearson, Peterson, & Rodriquez, 2005, p. 44). Research by Lieberman (1995) indicated the importance of teachers working as a collaborative community of learners sharing challenges, knowledge, and insights. Snow, Burns, and Griffin (1998), in their review of research, concluded that ongoing collaborative approaches to professional development were linked to changes in teachers' knowledge and practice. Snow et al. (2005) made a case for *usable knowledge* as the core of professional development. Usable knowledge is not simply knowledge about what to do on a particular day. It also includes knowledge that increases understanding of content and pedagogy. It includes vocabulary that helps teachers communicate with each other about their goals, strategies, and classroom data. An essential goal of professional development for teachers is the continuous growth of this shared language for communicating with each other as they deepen their understanding of both the content and pedagogy of reading instruction.

Quality Professional Development

In an analysis of 140 studies of professional development, Anders, Hoffman, and Duffy (2000) identified a set of features that characterized quality professional development:

- Intensive/extensive commitments of support and effort are necessary for success.

- Monitoring, coaching, and/or clinical support should be provided in the context of classroom practice.

- Reflection is a critical tool for assisting teachers in examining their practice systematically.

- Deliberation, dialogue, and negotiation through discussions are important in promoting change and adaptation in teaching.

- Voluntary participation and choice affect the success of professional development.

- Collaboration among teachers, outside educators, and school-based mentors seems to be a common factor in effective professional development (Anders et al., 2000).

The authors go on to point out that there is a conflict between knowing that sometimes ineffective teaching is the result of technical problems that can be easily remedied by training and recognizing that teachers must be thoughtful, flexible, and responsive in addressing students' problems and planning effective instruction. For example, teachers who do not have sufficient strategies to effectively develop students' phonemic awareness can easily be taught some approaches that will work for most students. But what about the students for whom the strategies do not seem to work? Teachers need to know what to do, and the solutions can vary from student to student. There is a deeper knowledge of the nature of reading, reading instruction, and learners that is developed over time and influences how instruction is planned and delivered, how the contexts of instruction are organized, what goals are set for learning, and how students are perceived and treated. In addition, teachers hold beliefs about teaching, learning, and students that direct instructional decisions and may need to be modified for teachers to be as effective as possible. All of these factors affect how teachers plan and adapt instruction, respond to students, use classroom data, and generally orchestrate all the aspects of teaching reading.

Studies of effective schoolwide reading programs indicate some characteristics of professional development that improve student achievement. Study groups in which teachers learn about new strategies, gather data on the effective use of strategies, analyze student work, and share reflections on their teaching promote teachers' understanding of what they need to do, what students need, and how to plan instruction to meet both the needs of students and literacy goals. Research indicates that, in schools that are successful in improving student achievement, teachers participate in communities focused on professional learning, informed by analyses of classroom data and shared examination of practice (Fullan, 1999; Killon, 2002; Taylor et al., 2005).

Professional development should be focused on the specific needs of teachers so that they can teach the students they have rather than some idealized student. As educators teach in a standard, evidence-based way, there will still be some students who do not progress as fast as the other students or at all. This is where progress monitoring helps educators see how individual students are doing. This is also where response to intervention (RTI) approaches can be helpful (see Chapter 15). Whether a school is using RTI or some other model, progress monitoring is something all teachers need to know. It also is something that a peer group can help with, as can a reading coach or other professional support person in the school.

Professional development that offers ongoing boosters or refreshers or provides ongoing support in the school to help with problem solving is a better model than professional development that simply trains teachers in new techniques or approaches for a few days during the summer. Usually these techniques are not reinforced when they actually try it out in the classroom. Any new technique or approach is likely to raise practical questions and issues that may not occur to teachers when they are learning it in a workshop. Just as professionals would never be given a new computer software program without a help line or technical support number, ongoing support and resources should be an essential part of any teacher professional development program (Anders et al., 2000).

Valli and Hawley (2002) concluded that the professional development programs that were most valuable for student learning were those that were school based, ongoing, and tied to the implementation of new or adapted strategies in the classroom. They also suggested that effective professional development should include the discussion of student work, outcome measures, and information on teachers' classroom instructional practice. Introducing actual problem solving during professional development workshops or training makes a clearer link to what actually happens in the classroom.

Use of Technology to Assist Teachers in Their Continuing Education

Technology can also offer help in teacher professional growth and development. Online videos can support teachers in gaining "expertise, confidence, and the ability to implement literacy instructional practices" (Teale, Labbo, Kinzer, & Leu, 2002, p. 656). Video-based hypermedia programs can help preservice teachers gain insight into the cultural differences of students and how to build inclusive classrooms. They can also be used to promote teachers' reconsidering their own assumptions about teaching and learning (Bolig, 2004). One example of a hypermedia video program for teacher education is Reading Classroom Explorer (RCE; Bolig, 2004). Seeing what a behavior or teaching technique actually looks like in live implementation can often be more informative than reading about it or having someone discuss it, and video offers a chance to review the same information more than once to consider different aspects of it. For instance, the first time a tape is viewed, the viewer may focus on the teacher's behavior, the next time the students' responses, and then as questions arise the tape can be viewed again. Or a teacher may try out the technique that is demonstrated and it may not go as smoothly as expected; reviewing the tape may be helpful in figuring out why difficulties occurred. This is just one way that video technology can be a major asset to professional development. In schools where teachers' lounges have online access, teachers can participate in online training in small groups and discuss what they observe, or teachers can use some of their planning time to independently engage in professional development.

Teacher online communities also hold promise for providing the support needed in professional development. These networks are an emerging and promising area for teacher professional development (Bransford, Brown, & Cocking, 1999). Teacher online communities also help teachers learn and use the technology that is part of their students' everyday lives.

Literacy Coaches

One promising practice in supporting teachers in their professional growth is the use of literacy coaches (Sturtevant, n.d.). These are (or should be) master teachers with expertise in reading who can provide ongoing professional development and classroom support for teachers. They can help plan and coordinate teachers' meetings where teachers learn about new strategies, reflect on and discuss the implementation and adaptation of those strategies, share students' work and videos of their teaching, and work together to plan, implement, and improve a school's reading program. While there is little research on coaching right now (Neufeld & Roper, n.d.), there is beginning research available on this practice that indicates its potential (Schares, Desai, Williams, & Pinnell, n.d.).

Assessment/Evaluation

Assessment as a learning tool, also referred to as teacher inquiry or teacher action research, appears to support teachers' improving their knowledge and practice. It entails teachers gathering data on student learning through classroom assessments and systematically analyzing the data to determine what is working and what needs adjustment, or how instruction influences learning. Research by Gove and Kennedy-Calloway (1992) and Hancock, Turbill, and Cambourne (1994) indicated that this approach influenced teachers' practice and understanding of reading instruction. Snow et al. (1998) also found that teachers' collaborating over time with researchers can have positive results, including more lasting changes than one-time sessions of collaboration.

Portfolios can be a tool for teachers. Portfolios can be used as a focus for conversations with other teachers about students work (Anders et al., 2000). Teachers can share portfolios of student work with each other, confirming what the student work demonstrates or gaining further insight into the work and how it is connected to instruction. They can discuss and refine criteria for students' work and thus come to a better understanding of what they need to teach. As teachers examine portfolios collaboratively, they think more deeply about their practice and their students. The background sections and explanation material in some basal reading series can be useful to teachers in gaining a better understanding of the reading theory that underlies the components and tasks in the program. In addition to informing decisions about what components of the program to use, the manual's background information can sometimes indicate by its omissions the aspects of reading that might need more emphasis provided by the teacher. For example, some programs lack sufficient attention to truly higher order, critical thinking, and teachers using those programs need to plan instructional strategies to fill that gap.

What If There Is Little or No Research Evidence on Instructional Strategies to Meet Certain Student Needs?

There are always some areas of reading that have not been the focus of much research; however, there are several ways to find information and systematically develop interventions and instructional strategies. One way to begin is by looking at literature and research on what good readers do in general and how readers construct meaning and use text cues. There is a large body of research about the processes of reading. Much of this has been cited in earlier chapters, but there is always more being published in journals and in newer books. Periodically checking to find out if there are studies on teacher effectiveness and understanding the reading process is an excellent way to address areas where teachers want to know more.

Research is published in many journals, but there are two types of journals (with some overlap among them in what they address): research journals and more practice-oriented journals. Increasingly, researchers are writing for both types of journals, since they know how important it is to get reliable information into the hands of those who will be able to use that information to help students. Teacher educators creating professional development programs and fellow teachers who have worked with new techniques and approaches also write for these journals. Check practitioner journals, such as *The Reading Teacher* or *Education Leadership*, for descriptions of strategies and research studies. The strategies described are frequently based on researched strategies but have been adapted for specific applications, such as using a story map to organize information about a historical event. In addition, further details of the research can sometimes be found by looking at the resources cited in journals that focus on practice.

When trying out new strategies, even if they are well supported by research, it is always important for teachers to gather data on student performance in order to determine whether the strategies are working for their particular students or whether adaptations should be made or other strategies tried. In addition, strategies may appear to be working but with unwanted consequences. For example, if a teacher overemphasizes speed in promoting reading fluency, some students may not only fail to develop sufficient comprehension skills but may not even realize that comprehension, not just speed or accuracy, is the goal of reading. In such cases, the teacher needs to examine both comprehension data and fluency data to determine how to balance and adapt instruction and practice.

Professional organizations are a means of teachers taking charge of their own professional development. The International Reading Association (http://www.reading.org) is a source of publications and holds a major conference featuring both research and promising practices every year. It has state affiliates that hold their own conferences and meetings. These conferences provide wonderful opportunities to share ideas with and learn from other teachers and researchers. The Association for Supervision and Curriculum Development (http://www.ascd.org) is another association that produces useful resources for teachers and for professional development. The National Council of Teachers of English (http://www.ncte.org) also provides resources related to teaching reading and holds two conferences each year. Finally, while they focus mainly on students with reading difficulties, associations, such as the International Dyslexia Association, the

Learning Disabilities Association, and the National Center for Learning Disabilities, provide a great deal of information about both reading instruction and reading remediation.

What Additional Research Is Needed to Enable Teachers to Be Highly Effective?

A great deal of research is still needed about how to provide better education to teachers. Reading is a complex activity, students are complex individuals, and learning is a complex process, so teaching educators to address all of these issues is a challenge about which far too little information is available. Table 14.1 presents some of those research needs.

HOW MIGHT RESEARCH ON PROFESSIONAL
• • • DEVELOPMENT ACTUALLY PLAY OUT IN THE CLASSROOM? • • •

Jane asked the other fourth-grade teachers if they had students with problems similar to those in her class. When they acknowledged that

---

What we know from research

- Teacher education and professional development can improve student reading achievement (National Institute of Child Health and Human Development [NICHD], 2000).

- Teacher professional development must concentrate on encouraging teachers to become strategic decision makers (NICHD, 2000).

What we need to know from additional research

- What are the ways that preservice and inservice teacher education can be designed and delivered in order to best support teacher effectiveness (NICHD, 2000)?

- How can we assess the effectiveness of teacher education (NICHD, 2000)?

- What knowledge (about reading, assessment, motivation, human development, language, social processes, and culture) do teachers need to be effective?

- What are the best ways to provide both preservice and inservice teacher education?

- What motivates teachers to continually improve their practice?

Table 14.1.   Teacher effectiveness research needs

they did, she asked them to meet one morning before school to discuss what they had observed as the students struggled with content reading and what they might do to help these students. As a result of the initial discussion, they agreed to each look for an article that might give them ideas for interventions and to meet the next week to share what they found. At subsequent meetings, they discussed some of the strategies they had tried and their students' responses. They began to develop a repertoire of new teaching strategies to help students in content area texts. Later in the year, they were able to report their progress to their principal and convince him to release them to attend a state reading conference featuring several workshops on content reading.

What Other Resources Might Help in Planning and Advocating for Effective Professional Development?

There are some sources, in addition to what was indicated previously, for educators to use to inform themselves about reading instructional practice research. Some of the sites also provide information on effective professional development. Reading Rockets (http://www.reading rockets.org) and Reading Is Fundamental (http://www.rif.org) offer resources for both teachers and parents. The National Council of Teachers of English (http://www.ncte.org) provides information on research, practice, and advocacy for teachers. The Association for Supervision and Curriculum Development (http://www.ascd.org) has resources and research briefs on many aspects of education, including reading. The International Dyslexia Association, the Learning Disabilities Association, and the National Center for Learning Disabilities also offer web sites that have information that can be especially helpful with struggling readers. One example of a hypermedia video program for teacher education is Reading Classroom Explorer (http://www.eliteracy.org) (Bolig, 2004). Another Internet-based professional development program is Every Child a Reader and Writer (http://www.inside writing workshop.org).

REFERENCES

Anders, P.L., Hoffman, J.V., & Duffy, G.G. (2000). Teaching teachers to teach reading: Paradigm shifts, persistent problems, and challenges. In M.L. Kamil, P.B. Mosenthal, P.D. Pearson, & R. Barr (Eds.), *Handbook of reading research: Volume III* (pp. 719–742). Mahwah, NJ: Lawrence Erlbaum Associates.

Bolig, E.C. (2004). Preparing novices for teaching literacy in diverse classrooms: Using written, video, and hypermedia cases to prepare literacy teachers. In C.M. Fairbanks, J. Worthy, B. Maloch, J.V. Hoffman, & D. Schallert (Eds.), *53rd yearbook of the National Reading Conference* (pp. 130–145). Oak Creek, WI: National Reading Conference.

Bond, G.L., & Dykstra, R. (1967). The cooperative research program in first-grade reading instruction. *Reading Research Quarterly, 2,* 10–41.

Bransford, J.D., Brown, A.L., & Cocking, R.R. (Eds.). (1999). *How people learn: Brain, mind, experience, and school.* Washington, DC: National Academies Press.

Chall, J.S., & Feldman, S. (1967). First-grade reading: An analysis of the interaction of professed methods, teacher implementation, and child background. *Reading Teacher, 19,* 569–575.

Ferguson, P., & Womack, T.S. (1993). The impact of subject matter and education coursework on teaching performance. *Journal of Teaching Education, 44*(1), 55–63.

Fullan, M. (1999). *Change force: The sequel.* Philadelphia: Falmer.

Gove, M.F., & Kennedy-Calloway, C. (1992). Action research: Empowering students to work with at-risk students. *Journal of Reading, 35,* 526–534.

Hancock, J., Turbill, J., & Cambourne, B. (1994). Assessment and evaluation of literacy learning. In S.W. Valencia, E.H. Hiebert, & P.P. Afflerbach (Eds.), *Authentic reading assessment: Practices and possibilities* (pp. 46–62). Newark, DE: International Reading Association.

Killon, J. (2002). *What works in elementary schools: Results-based staff development.* Oxford, OH: National Staff Development Council.

Lieberman, A. (1995). *The work of restructuring the schools: Building from the ground up.* New York: Teachers College Press.

National Institute of Child Health and Human Development. (2000). *Teaching children to read: An evidence-based assessment of the scientific research literature on reading and its implications for reading instruction: Reports of the subgroups* (NIH Publication No. 00–475). Washington, DC: U.S. Government Printing Office.

Neufeld, B., & Roper, D. (n.d.). *Coaching: A strategy for developing instructional capacity: Promises and practicalities.* Providence, RI: Annenberg Institute for School Reform. Retrieved September 22, 2007, from http://www.annenberginstitute.org/images/Coaching.pdf

Schares, P.L., Desai, L., Williams, E.J., & Pinnell, G.S. (n.d.). *Literacy collaborative: A multiyear analysis.* Retrieved September 22, 2007, from http://www.literacycollaborative.org/docs/2003MultiYearAnalysis.pdf

Snow, C.E., Burns, M.S., & Griffin, P. (Eds.). (1998). *Preventing reading difficulties in young children.* Washington, DC: National Academies Press.

Snow, C.E., Griffin, P., & Burns, M.S. (2005). *Knowledge to support the teaching of reading.* San Francisco: Jossey-Bass.

Sturtevant, E.G. (n.d.). *The literacy coach: A key to improving teaching & learning in secondary schools.* Washington, DC: Alliance for Excellent Education. Retrieved September 22, 2007, from http://www.all4ed.org/publications/LiteracyCoach.pdf.

Taylor, B.M., Pearson, P.D., Peterson, D.S., & Rodriquez, M.C. (2005). The CIERA school change framework: An evidence-based approach to professional development and school reading improvement. *Reading Research Quarterly, 40*(1), 40–69.

Teale, W., Labbo, L., Kinzer, C., & Leu, D. (2002). The CTELL project: New ways technology can help educate tomorrow's reading teachers. *Reading Teacher, 55*, 654–659.

Valli, L., & Hawley, W.D. (2002). Designing and implementing school-based professional development. In W.D. Hawley (Ed.), *The keys to effective schools: Educational reform as continuous improvement* (pp. 86–96). Thousand Oaks, CA: Corwin.

Wenglinski, H. (2000). *How teaching matters: Bringing the classroom back into discussions of teacher quality.* Princeton, NJ: Educational Testing Service.

CHAPTER 15

Response to Intervention

A New Partnership Between General and Special Education

KEY CONCEPTS

- Response to intervention (RTI) is a combined general education–special education tiered approach that requires high-quality instruction, ongoing monitoring of student progress, and instruction tailored to student needs.

- RTI is now an acceptable alternative approach to identifying students with learning disabilities.

- The implementation of RTI will require a working partnership between general and special education.

A recent buzzword, but a not-so-recent approach to classroom education, RTI, or a tiered approach to education instruction, seems to have hit the big time. With the reauthorization of the Individuals with Disabilities Education Act of 2004 (IDEA 2004; PL 108-446), RTI has been legislated as an acceptable option for the identification of students with learning disabilities. But it begins in the regular classroom.

Before that legislation, students with learning disabilities were identified for special education services based on a discrepancy between their academic achievement and their IQ. With IDEA 2004 (PL 108-446), that discrepancy is no longer the only way to identify students for special education services based on a learning disability. This decision was influenced by evidence that the IQ–discrepancy model is ineffective in identifying all students with learning disabilities (Lyon et al., 2001). However, exactly how RTI can be used, both as a new approach to differentiated instruction and for identification of learning disabilities, is still an open question, so there are a variety of implementations of RTI across the nation. And of course some schools are sticking with the good old tried (but not so true) IQ–achievement discrepancy approach for identification. The discrepancy approach consists of basing eligibility for special education services for learning disabilities on students' demonstrating achievement that is significantly lower than their IQ scores (hence discrepant); it may take as long as 2 years for students to demonstrate sufficiently low achievement to reveal such a discrepancy, and this approach inherently assumes that students with lower IQs cannot also have learning disabilities. This has been characterized as the "wait to fail" approach to identification for special education services. While the specific problems with the IQ–achievement discrepancy definition of learning disabilities are beyond the scope of this volume, information available from several sources clearly lays out the problems. The report of the President's Commission on Excellence in Special Education (2002) summarized that information nicely, and a chapter by McCardle, Keller-Allen, and Shuy (in press) also reviewed this information and applied it to English language learners (ELLs), advocating an RTI approach. Fletcher, Lyon, Fuchs, and Barnes (2006) clearly presented research on this issue in a more technical but very thorough treatment. The issue of RTI versus the IQ–achievement discrepancy approach presents a research opportunity, since the two approaches could be compared if enough other factors between schools and districts were comparable.

In this chapter, we will explore what RTI looks like in some cases where it has already been in use for some time, and what is happening in the community to help teachers, schools, and districts that are opting to give it a try. Researchers in education do not know *all* they need to know about how best to implement RTI and how best to use it to identify students with learning disabilities, but they do know a lot, and major research funding agencies, most notably the National Institute of Child Health and Human Development (NICHD) and the Institute of Education Sciences (Department of Education), support research to address these issues.

What Is Response to Intervention?

RTI is a tiered approach to education. We specifically are interested in it as an approach to teaching children to read. While RTI may seem like a new term to many, multitiered interventions have been around for years and are being implemented in many places already (Denton, Foorman, & Mathes, 2003; Foorman & Nixon, 2005). RTI is a framework within which to deliver high-quality instruction and to identify, through students' responses or failures to respond to at least two tiers of increasingly intensive, focused instruction, those children with learning disabilities who truly need special education services.

For some time, the number of children not succeeding in learning to read has far exceeded the proportions who could reasonably be expected to have learning disabilities, so that a new approach to identification and prevention of reading failure was needed. The National Reading Panel (NRP) report (NICHD, 2000) was an important step in that direction, in that it provided an evidence base on what methods of reading instruction had been shown to be effective, and the No Child Left Behind (NCLB) Act of 2001 (PL 107-110) legislated that this evidence base be used to guide instruction. RTI is a framework within which to use evidence-based instruction in increasingly intensive tiers to prevent reading failure in those who simply need more tailored, explicit instruction and more focused attention to reading in order to succeed. Tier 1 is high-quality, explicit classroom instruction. Tier 2, for those students falling behind despite high-quality instruction in the classroom, is the same basic instruction but more intensive (i.e., delivered in small groups, with perhaps more time dedicated to reading instruction). Tier 3 (some approaches may have more than three tiers, although three is a typical model) is then targeted to those who actually need intervention (special education). There is not much evidence on how well RTI will work, but there is enough evidence to date that high-quality instruction can reduce the number of children requiring special education (Al Otaiba & Fuchs, 2002; Torgesen, 2004; Torgesen et al., 1999) to warrant confidence in this process and to at least allow it as an alternative to something we know is not effective in successfully identifying all children with learning disabilities.

How Did All of This Attention to Response to Intervention Get Started?

The President's Commission on Excellence in Special Education (2002) called for evidence-based practice in special education with a strong emphasis on the process of identifying students and determining their eligibility for special services. The Commission criticized the "wait to fail" model of identifying students with disabilities, so called because it resulted in waiting until a student's achievement was far enough behind to create a discrepancy with expected achievement based on IQ. Among the Commission's recommendations was the use of RTI models for the identification and assessment process and for progress monitoring. Based on the information presented in that report, legislators made significant changes in IDEA 2004 (PL 108-446). The most important one was to allow the use of RTI as an alternative to the IQ–achievement discrepancy approach for identification of learning disabilities. IDEA 2004 is a major reauthorization and revision of IDEA, which is the primary federal program that authorizes state and local aid for special education and related services for children with disabilities. This reauthorization allows the optional use of RTI rather than the IQ–achievement discrepancy formula for the identification of students with learning disabilities.

Why Is Response to Intervention Important?

RTI is important because it offers a way to monitor and thus achieve the progress that everyone wants in educating all children. The NCLB Act of 2001 (PL 107-110) demands accountability and high levels of student learning. If educators are to succeed in reducing the proportion of students who fail to learn to read successfully, and thus enable those students to have choices and viable options for future education and employment, they need ways to implement effective practices on a large scale. Foorman, Kalinowski, and Sexton (2007) presented a clear and cogent argument that integrating and coordinating general education and special education within the context of standards-based reform can help reduce the achievement gap caused by poverty. They described how this can be done by imposing standards-based reform linked to an RTI-style implementation plan that provides layers of instructional interventions, with the intensity and duration of each tier or layer determined by the assessment of student progress. RTI, if properly implemented, can accomplish all of this. And there are already cases where it is working. Researchers already know quite a bit about what it can do and how to do it.

What Is Already Known About Response to Intervention?

Based on the greater latitude permitted by IDEA 2004 (PL 108-446) in identifying students for special education, many schools are implementing or considering implementing an RTI approach. Some schools have been using a tiered approach for a few years already. To gather information to assist schools in considering implementation of RTI, the International Dyslexia Association (IDA) convened a meeting in December of 2004. This jointly sponsored meeting was attended by representatives of 33 interested organizations. Co-sponsors were IDA, NICHD, the Office of Special Education and Rehabilitation Services, the American Speech-Language-Hearing Association (ASHA), the Council for Exceptional Children/Division of Learning Disabilities, the National Center for Learning Disabilities, and the National Research Center on Learning Disabilities. Participants reviewed models of implementation for RTI, information on implementing tiered models of instruction, what would constitute adequate teacher preparation, and information on scaling innovative practices. At this meeting, participants heard from researchers who had been studying RTI and educators who had been implementing it or were gearing up to do so. The goal of that meeting was to share information so that organizations and associations could help their constituencies understand RTI and, if they chose to, implement it in their own districts and schools. The resulting document (IDA, 2006) laid out steps in planning, implementation, and evaluation of RTI in schools and classrooms. The keys to understanding and succeeding in implementing RTI are that it begins in the general education classroom but must involve an ongoing partnership among general and special education teachers and specialists, and that it requires the entire school to support it.

What Are the Two Main Models of Response to Intervention?

There are two main models or approaches to RTI implementation (Chhabra, 2006): the problem-solving model and the standard protocol model. The problem-solving model usually has four stages: problem identification, problem analysis, intervention design, and evaluation.

Tilly (2003) presented these stages as questions that the school team has to keep in mind and answer. Tilly's questions were

1. What is the problem?

2. Why is it happening?

3. What is going to be done about it?

4. What has the team been doing that has been working?

In the first phase, *problem identification,* the consultant and teacher work together to identify the most significant issue, typically a child who is difficult to teach. In the second phase, the problem is analyzed to try to determine what is causing or sustaining the problem, and an intervention or educational plan is designed (this encompasses Questions 2 and 3). In the third phase, teachers and other specialists implement the intervention. Finally, the effectiveness of the plan and its implementation are evaluated.

The problem-solving model as described by Tilly (2003) seeks to systematize practice in a data-based way; thus it requires more stringent measurement and discipline in practice than did the historical special education model. Student engagement and enthusiasm are not sufficient markers of success. Real achievement is the goal. In this model, problems are objectively defined, observed, and measured directly in the natural environment, and analyzed based on available empirical information in the research and clinical professional literature on problem etiology. Hypotheses are developed that relate observed performance to the assumed causes of the problem, and interventions are developed and piloted. Student progress is monitored for responsiveness and the intervention is adjusted as needed. Tilly pointed out that problem-solving systems are designed to be self-correcting, rather than relying on a priori assumptions about what ought to work; instead the assumption is that educators will not know if an intervention works with a particular student until they try it, so that the monitoring of student progress is absolutely crucial. On this, all approaches to RTI agree: careful monitoring of student progress is an essential element. Adjustments to interventions are made based on student performance.

The other model for RTI implementation is the standard treatment protocol. This model or framework involves a well-defined treatment procedure designed to be used for all at-risk students, employing, as its name would imply, a protocol that is standard across all teachers and classes. Teachers can be trained specifically how to implement it and can gain high reliability. Doug Fuchs (Fuchs, 2004; Fuchs & Fuchs, 2006) advocated the standard protocol, which appears to be able to be more uniformly implemented on a large scale (see the information on scaling up implementation in the section that follows) than the problem-solving model, which by its nature is more tailored to beginning with individual cases. It is important to realize that "standard protocol" does not mean one that is found in a book somewhere, but rather one that an entire school or district selects as a standard approach so that all teachers can be trained in its implementation; in this way RTI can be implemented on a large scale.

Barbara Foorman and colleagues have worked with schools in Texas on scaling up tiered interventions, in which they have demonstrated that assessment-driven instruction is key (Foorman, Santi, & Berger, 2007). They also showed that teacher professional development, including information on how to use assessment data in instructional planning and implementation, and systemic support from principals and district administrators are crucial. Foorman, Santi, et al. (2007) also emphasized the importance of systemic buy-in; school leadership must support the approach, devote resources to it, and allow for scheduling flexibility for the approach to work. (See additional details in this chapter where we address the question of how some schools have implemented RTI.)

One thing that is clear about both models is that they can only work if classroom teachers and special educators work together. That is why this chapter is subtitled "A New Partnership Between General and Special Education." Successful RTI implementation will have to be not only a partnership between general education and special education; it will have to be a team effort. That is clearly demonstrated in the work of Foorman, Santi, et al. (2007). Of course, both models offer advantages and challenges. The choice of model will depend on school policies, resources, and current staff and their existing training and willingness to be trained in a new approach. In either model, as we have mentioned, monitoring student progress carefully and responding to it through instruction is essential. The standard protocol may prove more feasible for schools and districts, as it offers greater opportunities for uniformity and consistency of implementation. In any implementation of RTI, teacher fidelity of implementation of the chosen model is crucial. In a sense, then, the *response* in RTI is not only how students respond to instruction but also how teachers respond to students' responses! To accomplish this, it will be important for classroom general education teachers to work collaboratively with coaches, reading specialists, and special educators. It is important that teams work to ensure the greatest flexibility in differentiating instruction without losing the key elements that make an instructional approach or technique effective. (See the section on resources for additional information on implementation.)

What Is Progress Monitoring?

Progress monitoring has been around for a long time. The primary means of monitoring student progress in the classroom has been *curriculum-based measurement* (CBM), which has a substantial history of research supporting its use. Specifically, there is evidence that it makes a significant difference in how teachers view students and set learning goals for them, in how teachers differentiate instruction, and in how students progress and ultimately perform on standardized tests (Fuchs, Deno, & Mirkin, 1984; Fuchs & Fuchs, 2007; Fuchs, Fuchs, & Hamlet, 1989). While not exclusive to RTI, CBM does play a central role in the implementation of RTI, since assignment to the different tiers of instruction or intervention, differentiation of instruction to ensure student learning, and decision making about returning successful students to lower tiers and then tracking their progress in the lower tier, all depend on a careful, systematic observation and analysis of the student's response.

How Does Progress Monitoring Work in Response to Intervention?

Progress monitoring enables teachers to maximize instructional effectiveness because it gives them a scientific approach, using information gathering, data analysis, theorizing, and then testing their theories through more information gathering. An entire issue of *Perspectives on Language and Literacy* (IDA, 2007) is dedicated to progress monitoring. We recommend this issue as a handy reference since it has several case illustrations, suggestions for measures, and sources for web-based graphing programs, some free and some not. (Since that information is very complete, we will simply offer a brief summary here.) In addition, Jenkins, Hudson, and Lee (2007) offered steps in using progress monitoring to improve reading instruction for students with reading disabilities, the cycle of data collection using CBM, and sources of reading passages and commercial scoring. The use of standardized administration and scoring is important because it enables the teacher to make valid comparisons between a student's own earlier and later performance as well as compared to benchmarks for children of the same age and grade. Information on scoring and charting student progress on CBM passage reading fluency is provided in detail, along with examples (Jenkins et al., 2007). Mahdavi and Haager (2007) offered examples of what can be learned about individual students through progress monitoring, with case examples and graphs to illustrate how to link this information to interventions.

Hasbrouck (2007) provided information on benchmarking and how to interpret benchmark scores as well as a chart with percentiles by grade for the CBM passage reading fluency 1-minute measure. Both Hasbrouck (2007) and Jenkins et al. (2007) offered resources for reading about CBM benchmarking; these are combined in the following section.

CURRICULUM-BASED MEASUREMENT RESOURCES

Aimsweb **Progress Monitoring and Assessment System**

- Web site: http://edformation.com/
- E-mail: info@edformation.com

Dynamic Indicators of Basic Early Literacy Skills

- Web site: http://dibels.uoregon.edu
- E-mail: support@dibels.uoregon.edu

Easy CBM System

- Web site: http://easycbm.com
- E-mail: accounts@easycbm.com

Edcheckup

- Web site: http://www.edcheckup.com
- E-mail: info@edcheckup.com

National Center on Student Progress Monitoring

- Web site: http://www.studentprogress.org

Read Naturally Reading Fluency Benchmark Assessor and Reading Fluency Progress Monitor

- Web site: http://www.readnaturally.com

Peabody CBM

- E-mail: flora.murray@vanderbilt.edu

How Might a School Implement Response to Intervention?

How a school or district might actually implement RTI is best described through real-life examples. We will offer two real-life examples: one that describes a standard protocol type approach and one that describes a problem-solving approach.

• • • A REAL-LIFE SCENARIO OF RESPONSE
TO INTERVENTION STANDARD PROTOCOL SCALE-UP • • •

Barbara R. Foorman described her team's scale-up of a standard protocol approach that she and her colleagues in Texas conducted, which involved a tiered instruction model of assessment-driven instruction (Chhabra, 2006; Foorman, 2004; Foorman, Kalinowski, et al., 2007; Foorman, Santi, et al., 2007). They used a reciprocal relation to effectively maximize both what could be learned and the buy-in and communication among teachers and researchers (Foorman, Santi, et al., 2007). Assessment-driven instruction requires substantial professional development and is not something that classroom teachers have had in their preservice education. In this project, since not all schools were using the same reading program, schoolwide professional development was provided on the reading program that the school was using. The school then worked on implementing their chosen program with fidelity within a multilayered approach. Thus, a critical point was that each school had an intervention plan that was integrated into their core reading program. They also had additional time allocated for reading instruction: in Texas, 90 minutes is typical, but some schools offered extra periods of reading instruction. In addition, there are various grouping arrangements during the school day and in after-school, before-school, and home programs. A critical part of implementation is continuous monitoring of progress. In this case, the schools had 8-week assessments.

Students were screened to determine which ones received more intensive small-group instruction. Student performance was monitored in these small groups by the classroom teacher or occasionally by a specialist. In addition to the particular curriculum selected by the school, there were systemic issues that had to be addressed. For example, in these schools there was very strong leadership in a positive climate, along with strong accountability, ongoing professional development based on demonstrably effective strategies, and consistency across the school in the particular approach to reading that teachers were delivering. The continuous monitoring of student achievement and the increased amount of time available for reading instruction were essential—90 minutes was just a beginning. Involvement of parents and the schools' administrators were also an integral part of these schools' success.

In discussing other issues that contributed to school success, Foorman highlighted what she termed *structural support:* that these schools had a process for mentoring new teachers. For example, one district in Texas hired retired teachers who were really good reading teachers to mentor the new teachers. Those mentors provided co-teaching, used paired teaching, worked on classroom management problems, and offered advice on technical issues about language problems, second-language issues, or special learning needs. In addition to mentoring, the successful schools offered adequate professional development on site and focused on new practices, with general agreement at all levels of leadership. Another important element was ongoing teacher engagement: involving more advanced teachers in helping with the assessment plan and bringing in information about research, mentoring the less experienced teachers, taking a part in planning the professional development, and helping with management. A teacher cannot do small-group instruction without good classroom management skills; Foorman's team observed that while teachers were attending to small groups, the students not in those small groups were not always engaged in meaningful activities.

Key to RTI is the issue of scaling up assessment-driven instruction. Teachers must be able to use ongoing assessment data to understand, interpret, and translate research to classroom instruction. Foorman used the example of the early reading assessment administered in Texas, whose screen was used by districts to obtain additional funding for early intervention. The teachers appreciated receiving information on their students but had no training on how to use it to inform instruction. Foorman's team worked on helping teachers make sense of assessment results; this type of information is an essential element of professional development for RTI.

In another project led by Foorman, mentors worked with teachers to actually translate this information to instruction. Teachers had a checklist for lesson planning, so once a student was identified for additional work in some area, the teacher was assisted in developing a plan, and mentored in implementing that plan and working through implementation problems. Foorman commented that systemic issues can slow down the spread of RTI, and that the critical issue in implementation on a large scale is professional development that focuses on assessment-driven instruction.

A REAL-LIFE SCENARIO OF
• • • RESPONSE TO INTERVENTION PROBLEM SOLVING • • •

David Tilly, a school psychologist by training, is an assessment services coordinator for the Heartland Area Education Agency in Johnston, Iowa, with responsibility for over 90 public and private schools. Tilly described the Iowa statewide RTI implementation that began in the 1989–1990 school year, with a four-level model that has evolved into the relatively familiar three-tier model (IDA, 2006; Tilly, 2003, 2004). Like many school districts, the Heartland Area Education Agency spent the 1970s engaged in "child find" activities and the 1980s refining that process and writing IEPs. The agency had developed an efficient system, but they realized that there were still many children not becoming successful readers. In their search to find ways to improve the system, they held a series of statewide meetings. They involved parents, teachers, administrators, area education agencies, policy makers, legislators, and anyone else they could interest in the issues. They asked these thousands of people what they thought was working with the system, what needed to be changed, and what barriers existed to making the needed changes. The agency received help from Iowa State Department of Education and began building the Renewed Service Delivery System. They began their approach to RTI through special education.

Tilly and his group systematically piloted several "rule replacements," telling schools they would help them meet federal laws and regulations in new and different ways (Grimes & Tilly, 1996). To do this, they obtained guidance from the U.S. Department of Education Office of Special Education Programs (OSEP) as to the legalities of the proposals that were developed within the state, and they found that they had far more flexibility than they had formerly realized. They put together a set of principles to guide RTI: data-based decision making, professional development, improved instruction, and accountability. They approached the state legislature and Iowa State Department of Education with their ideas, and by 1995, they had rewritten and passed new state rules for special education. These rules now define systematic problem solving, which for their state is systematically data-based instruction (Iowa State Department of Education, 2000). This approach promotes assessment interventions tailored to individual needs, and the assessment system, originally developed for special education, is no longer limited to that population. The approach is now used to determine interventions that will work for all students, at the individual, small-group, and large-group levels. The focus has moved from diagnosing the disability to diagnosing the learning-enabled student—that is, evaluating the conditions under which the student's learning will be enabled.

In looking back over the process Iowa went through, Tilly (2003) presented four big ideas for implementing RTI in practice on a large scale, which increase the likelihood that RTI will be effective. First, it is important for everyone or nearly everyone in the system to understand *why* service delivery is changing; knowing *what* is changing is not enough. Second, resource deployment structures must be changed. Third, the scientific method must be imported into applied practice, and fourth, scientifically validated practices must be used to the extent available.

The first idea, having everyone know *why* change is needed, is critical in schools. Psychologists and educational testers have spent many years helping general educators identify students with disabilities and refer them for assessment and services. From the general education teacher's standpoint, that referral system was working just fine, since students were getting services. Under the new system, the classroom teacher's role is no longer referring out for services, but helping to find instructional interventions that will work for the student, and then being part of a team that decides who will deliver that intervention. If classroom teachers do not understand why the system is changing, efforts to enlist their participation are unlikely to succeed. Fletcher, Coulter, Reschly, and Vaughn (2004) noted that decision making in schools often is not based on research. While Tilly's team used research in those *why* conversations, they also cited logical, common-sense reasons why the changes were needed. They appealed to people's intuitions, reasoning that those working in schools know what is working, what is not, and what the problems are. Tilly asserted that implementing RTI is as much about thinking differently about what we do as it is about doing things differently. The objective is improved instruction for all. It is finding those things that enable student learning. It is a real mind shift, and it is not so subtle. So "Big Idea One" is that everybody has to understand why change is happening.

"Big Idea Two" is to fundamentally reengineer the resource deployment system. In this, Tilly cited Maynard Reynolds at the University of Minnesota, who has described the evolution of how schools deploy resources. Over time, schools have evolved a system in which various groups have identified groups of students who needed different interventions, lobbied for these programs, and succeeded in getting a new law or bill to establish a new program (Reynolds, 1988). As a result, there are many different independent programs for specific groups: talented, migrant, Title 1, at risk, special education, and so forth. Each program makes perfect sense independently, but each contributes to a system that is disjointed and competing for resources. The result, Tilly pointed out, is redundancy, lack of coordination across programs, grouping of students and resource allocation based on instructionally irrelevant student characteristics, nonsensical rules about who can get what services, and extreme complexity in administration. Thus, Tilly called for a move toward smart system structures, such as the three-level RTI model (Tilly, 2003). In any curriculum area, it is nearly guaranteed that there will be some students who do well despite poor instruction, some who need something different, and a few who need something that is very intense.

"Big Idea Three" is to import the scientific method into practice. That is, teachers must actually implement instruction based on systematically gathered data. According to Tilly, problem solving can be very simple, whether done on an individual or large- or small-group level. Using the four steps of finding the problem, analyzing the cause, developing an intervention, and evaluating the response is a cycle of continuous improvement that allows the system to be self-correcting. Tilly pointed to that as one of the greatest advantages of RTI. When instruction is implemented as designed, the data obtained from student performance gives feedback on whether that instruction is working or not.

"Big Idea Four" is using research-validated practices to the extent possible. Tilly asserted that RTI is not about revolution but about evolution. We know what educators have been doing in the past 3 decades, and we know to some extent what parts worked and what did not. We can learn from that. Research has been happening during all of those years and is still happening. Just as researchers build on prior studies to improve their research designs to design and evaluate better instructional approaches and interventions, educators should be continuously improving their practices by incorporating newly validated practices.

Since the late 1990s, the Iowa schools have had a problem-solving RTI model in place and evolving. Tilly reported that they had few schools in need of improvement for NCLB and have had significant decreases in special education incidence rates. But the people there are not finished—they embrace the opportunities that lie ahead, with the broad base of experimentation and implementation that can take place across the country with RTI. Tilly saw a single variable that distinguishes between those who have tried implementation and succeeded and those who did not—leadership. A leader is a person you would follow to a place you would not go yourself. Here, he said, we all have the opportunity to be leaders.

How Will Response to Intervention Affect the Roles that Teachers, Special Educators, and Others Play in Identifying Students with Special Education Needs?

The International Reading Association realized that RTI would mean some major changes for many professionals, including classroom teachers, reading specialists, school psychologists, and others who play important roles in delivering instruction to all students and in identifying and qualifying students for special services. They convened a working group of representatives from professional associations and concerned organizations. In an unprecedented collaboration, this group developed a compendium of role definitions for their constituencies, using a template so that the same types of information would be provided to all. That set of role definition documents is contained in *New Roles in Response to Intervention: Creating Success for Schools and Children* (International Reading Association, 2006). If those individuals whose roles are addressed in this set of documents can work together within schools as collegially and productively as their representatives did in developing these documents, children will surely benefit!

In addition to teachers having a fundamental knowledge about RTI and what it offers students, it is important for educators to know that parents are becoming more involved in understanding and advocating for their children when RTI is considered. There are resources available to parents (e.g., Cortiella, 2006) that explain the RTI process and what parents need to know. Teachers can assist by empowering parents with information about the influence of RTI and major components that may help their child.

HOW MIGHT THIS RESEARCH ON RESPONSE TO
• • • INTERVENTION PLAY OUT IN THE CLASSROOM? • • •

At the beginning of the year, Mr. Johnson's third-grade class was excited about reading, because he had taken them to the school library and let them each choose a book to read from a section specially designated for beginning third graders. He let them select partners and read their books together. While they were doing this, he went to each pair of students and had them read aloud for him, for 1 minute, from a passage he had printed on a sheet of paper. He used this CBM for reading as a screening tool, and he compared the students' scores to a word-count-per-minute chart (Hasbrouck, 2007). He noticed that for the fall semester of third grade, students should read 71 words per minute correctly to place at the 50th percentile. Four of his students were reading at 40 words per minute or less, and he knew that this placed them at risk in reading. He knew that they would probably need greater intensity of reading instruction than the rest of the class. That night, using one of the web-based programs the school reading coach had showed them how to use, he constructed graphs for these four students. He made an aim line on the graph, which showed the progress they should make in the next several weeks. They received the same reading lessons as the entire class, but Mr. Johnson also did extra work with these four students in a group. When they were making sufficient progress to catch up to the class, he would cut back on the small-group work, but he knew he would need to monitor their progress every week or two, to be sure that they were continuing to make progress. If they fell behind, he would begin the more intense instruction again. If any of them did not progress or was making very slow progress, he would speak with the school reading specialist about individual tutoring for that student. He was confident that, with their new RTI model, his students would succeed in reading. It might take more intensive instruction for some of them, but with the system of monitoring their progress, he knew that each student could be targeted for the help he or she needed to become a successful reader.

What Kind of Research Is Still Needed on Response to Intervention?

A great deal more research is needed about how well RTI works. We need research on how effective RTI is as a new approach to education as well as how well it works for identifying students with learning disabilities. One group of researchers reviewed research addressing use of RTI with students with reading difficulties in the early grades and found 42 studies meeting their criteria (Vaughn, Wanzek, Woodruff, & Linan-Thompson, 2007). Based on their analysis and synthesis of those studies, they reported that "it is clear that before RTI can be used effectively as an identification approach, agreement on what constitutes response and nonresponse to intervention is needed" (p. 14). There is no consistent agreement as to what constitutes nonresponse, at what point of this nonresponsiveness students should be referred for special education, or what constitutes adequate responsiveness once intervention is provided. In addition, research on effective instructional programs and effective interventions will contribute significantly to the success of RTI, since it is a framework within which to provide increasingly intensive and differentiated instruction.

What Are Some Resources that Can Help Teachers Understand and Implement Response to Intervention?

Given RTI's status as a "hot topic" that many school districts are implementing or planning to implement, many publications to assist teachers and education administrators are appearing. Researchers are writing very practical articles and chapters. As mentioned earlier, an entire issue of the IDA journal, *Perspectives on Language and Literacy* (2007), is dedicated to progress monitoring. There are two major books that provide clear information and practical advice from leading researchers who have studied tiered models of reading intervention at various ages. The first, *Evidence-Based Reading Practices for Response to Intervention* (Haager, Klingner, & Vaughn, 2007), has five major sections: background and overview of the three-tier model, primary, secondary, and tertiary intervention, and implementation. Each section contains multiple chapters, some of which include illustrative case studies, and all of which should be helpful to schools planning or actively implementing RTI. *RTI: A Practitioner's Guide to Implementing Response to Intervention* (Mellard & Johnson, 2008) is, as titled, a guide for implementation. In addition to chapters on the three tiers (general education, intervention, and special education), it contains chapters on what RTI is, policy, schoolwide screening, progress monitoring, and fidelity of implementation. Some of the chapters include charts, checklists, and decision rules that should prove very helpful to anyone implementing RTI. These two resources complement one another in the information that they provide, and teachers and education administrators as well as specialized service providers will likely find both resources useful.

The U.S. Department of Education funds regional comprehensive centers with specialized missions to provide technical assistance to state and local education agencies. The Northwest Regional Comprehensive Center's mission focuses on RTI. The center's web site (http://www.nwrel.org/nwrcc/rti/) provides information on implementation research as well as examples of schools implementing RTI, and should also prove to be a useful resource. Also funded by the U.S. Department of Education, the Center on Instruction (http://centeroninstruction.org/index.cfm) has helpful information on RTI. In addition, many professional and advocacy associations have helpful information on RTI on their web sites.

The National Center for Learning Disabilities established an RTI Action Network to provide information and a means of networking and communication on RTI (Information can be found at http://www.ncld.org/content/view/1002/389/). Many other associations also provide information on RTI, which can be found usually with a simple search on their web sites.

REFERENCES

Al Otaiba, S., & Fuchs, D. (2002). Characteristics of children who are unresponsive to early literacy intervention: A review of the literature. *Remedial and Special Education, 23,* 300–316.

Chhabra, V. (2006). Building capacity to deliver multitiered reading intervention in public schools and the role of response to intervention (RTI). Executive summary from the meeting of the International Dyslexia Association, the National Institute of Child Health and Human Development, and the U.S. Department of Education Office of Special Education and Rehabilitative Services [Special issue]. *Perspectives on Language and Literacy, 32*(5).

Cortiella, C. (2006). A parent's guide to response to intervention [Special issue]. *Perspectives on Language and Literacy, 32*(5).

Denton, C., Foorman, B., & Mathes, P. (2003). Schools that "beat the odds": Implications for reading instruction. *Remedial and Special Education, 24,* 258–261.

Fletcher, J.M., Coulter, W.A., Reschly, D.J., & Vaughn, S. (2004). Alternative approaches to the definition and identification of learning disabilities: Some questions and answers. *Annals of Dyslexia, 54*(2), 304–331.

Fletcher, J.M., Lyon, G.R., Fuchs, L.S., & Barnes, M.A. (2006). *Learning disabilities: From identification to intervention.* New York: Guilford Press.

Foorman, B. (2004, December). *Building capacity to deliver multi-tiered reading intervention in public schools and the role of response to intervention (RTI).* Paper presented at the meeting of the International Dyslexia Association, the National Institute of Child Health and Human Development, and the U.S. Department of Education Office of Special Education and Rehabilitative Services, Seattle.

Foorman, B.R., Kalinowski, S.J., & Sexton, W.L. (2007). Standards-based educational reform is one important step toward reducing the achievement gap. In A. Gamoran (Ed.), *Standards-based reform and the poverty gap: Lessons from No Child Left Behind* (pp. 17–42). Washington, DC: Brookings Institution.

Foorman, B.R., & Moats, L.C. (2004). Conditions for sustaining research-based practices in early reading instruction. *Remedial and Special Education, 25,* 51–60.

Foorman, B.R., & Nixon, S. (2005, Fall). Curriculum integration in a multitiered instructional approach. *Perspectives on Language and Literacy, 26,* 8.

Foorman, B.R., Santi, K., & Berger, L. (2007). Scaling assessment-driven instruction using the Internet and handheld computers. In B. Schneider (Ed.), *Scale up in practice* (pp. 69–89). Lanham, MD: Rowan & Littlefield Publishers, Inc.

Fuchs, D. (2004, December). *Building capacity to deliver multi-tiered reading intervention in public schools and the role of response to intervention (RTI).* Paper presented at the meeting of the International Dyslexia Association, the National Institute of Child Health and Human Development, and the U.S. Department of Education Office of Special Education and Rehabilitative Services, Seattle.

Fuchs, D., & Fuchs, L. (2006, March). Introduction to response to intervention: What, why, and how valid is it? *Reading Research Quarterly, 41*(1). Retrieved January 10, 2008, from http://www.reading.org/Library/Retrieve.cfm?D=10.1598/RRQ.41.1.4&F=RRQ-41-1-Fuchs.html

Fuchs, L.S., Deno, S.L., & Mirkin, P.K. (1984). The effects of frequent curriculum-based measurement and evaluation on pedagogy, student achievement, and student awareness of learning. *American Educational Research Journal, 21,* 339–460.

Fuchs, L.S., & Fuchs, D. (2007). Progress monitoring within a multitiered prevention system. *Perspectives on Language and Literacy, 33*(2), 43–47.

Fuchs, L.S., Fuchs, D., & Hamlet, C.L. (1989). Effects of instrumental use of curriculum-based measurement to enhance instructional programs. *Remedial and Special Education, 10*(2), 43–52.

Grimes, J., & Tilly, W.D. (1996). Policy and process: Means to lasting educational change. *School Psychology Review, 25,* 465–476.

Haager, D., Klingner, J., & Vaughn, S. (2007). *Evidence-based reading practices for response to intervention.* Baltimore: Paul H. Brookes Publishing Co.

Hasbrouck, J. (2007). Using oral reading fluency as a benchmark assessment. *Perspectives on Language and Literacy, 33*(2), 19–21.

Individuals with Disabilities Education Improvement Act of 2004, PL 108-446, 20 U.S.C. §§ 1400 *et seq.*

International Dyslexia Association. (Ed.). (2006). Response to intervention [Special issue]. *Perspectives on Language and Literacy, 32*(5).

International Dyslexia Association. (Ed.). (2007). Progress monitoring [Special issue]. *Perspectives on Language and Literacy, 33*(2).

International Reading Association. (2006). *New roles in response to intervention: Creating success for schools and children.* Newark, DE: Author. Retrieved January 9, 2008, from http://www.reading.org/downloads/resources/rti_role_definitions.pdf

Iowa Department of Education. (2000). *Iowa administrative rules.* Des Moines, IA: Author.

Jenkins, J.R., Hudson, R.F., & Lee, S.H. (2007). Using CBM-reading assessments to monitor reading progress. *Perspectives on Language and Literacy, 33*(2), 11–16.

Lyon, G.R., Fletcher, J.M., Shaywitz, S.E., Shaywitz, B.A., Torgesen, J.K., Wood, F.B., et al. (2001). Rethinking learning disabilities. In C.E. Finn, Jr., A.J. Rotherham, & C.R. Hokanson, Jr. (Eds.), *Rethinking special education for a new century* (pp. 259–287). Washington, DC: Thomas B. Fordham Foundation and the Progressive Policy Institute.

Mahdavi, J.N., & Haager, D. (2007). Linking progress monitoring results to interventions. *Perspectives on Language and Literacy, 33*(2), 25–29.

McCardle, P., Keller-Allen, C., & Shuy, T. (in press). Learning disability identification: How does it apply to English language learners? In E. Grigorenko (Ed.), (title in press). New York: Springer.

Mellard, D. & Johnson, E. (2008). *RTI: A practitioner's guide to implementing response to intervention.* Corwin Press.

National Institute of Child Health and Human Development. (2000). *Report of the National Reading Panel. Teaching children to read: An evidence-based assessment of the scientific research literature on reading and its implications for reading instruction: Reports of the subgroups* (NIH Publication No. 00–4754). Washington, DC: U.S. Government Printing Office.

No Child Left Behind Act of 2001, PL 107-110, 115 Stat. 1452, 20 U.S.C. §§ 6301 *et. seq.*

President's Commission on Excellence in Special Education. (2002). *A new era: Revitalizing special education for children and their families.* Washington, DC: U.S. Department of Education, Office of Special Education and Rehabilitative Services.

Reynolds, M.C. (1988). A reaction to the JLD special series on the regular education initiative. *Journal of Learning Disabilities, 21*(6), 352–356.

Tilly, D. (2003, December). How many tiers are needed for successful prevention and early intervention? Heartland Area Education Agency's Evaluation from four to three tiers. In R. Bradley (Project Officer), *Responsiveness-to-intervention.* Symposium conducted at the meeting of the National Research Center on Learning Disabilities, Kansas City, MO. Retrieved January 10, 2008, from http://www.nrcld.org/symposium2003/tilly/tilly2.html

Tilly, D. (2004, December). *Building capacity to deliver multitiered reading intervention in public schools and the role of response to intervention (RTI).* Paper presented at the meeting of the International Dyslexia Association, the National Institute of Child Health and Human Development, and the U.S. Department of Education Office of Special Education and Rehabilitative Services, Seattle.

Torgesen, J.K. (2004). Lessons learned from research on interventions for students who experience difficulty learning to read. In P. McCardle and V. Chhabra (Eds.), *The voice of evidence in reading research* (pp. 355–382). Baltimore: Paul H. Brookes Publishing Co.

Torgesen, J.K., Wagner, R., Rashotte, C., Rose, E., Lindamood, P., Conway, T., & Garvan, C. (1999). Preventing reading failure in young children with phonological processing disabilities: Group and individual responses to instruction. *Journal of Educational Psychology, 91,* 579–593.

Vaughn, S., Wanzek, J., Woodruff, A.L., & Linan-Thompson, S. (2007). Prevention and early identification of students with reading disabilities. In D. Haager, J. Klingner, & S. Vaughn (Eds.), *Evidence-based reading practices for response to intervention* (pp. 11–28). Baltimore: Paul H. Brookes Publishing Co.

Index

Page numbers followed by *f* and *t* indicate figures and tables, respectively.